The Desert

MW01407983

Communities, Arts, Science, and Education in the Negev

Edited by
A. Paul Hare and Gideon M. Kressel

University Press of America,® Inc.
Lanham · Boulder · New York · Toronto · Plymouth, UK

4501 Forbes Boulevard
Suite 200
Lanham, Maryland 20706
UPA Acquisitions Department (301) 459-3366

Estover Road
Plymouth PL6 7PY
United Kingdom

Printed in the United States of America
British Library Cataloging in Publication Information Available

Library of Congress Control Number: 2009933245
ISBN-13: 978-0-7618-4840-0 (paperback : alk. paper)
ISBN-10: 0-7618-4840-1 (paperback : alk. paper)
eISBN-13: 978-0-7618-4841-7
eISBN-10: 0-7618-4841-X

Cover photographs by Wolfgang Motzafi-Haller

™ The paper used in this publication meets the minimum requirements of American National Standard for Information Sciences—Permanence of Paper for Printed Library Materials, ANSI Z39.48-1992

Contents

Preface vii

1 The Desert Experience 1
A. Paul Hare and Gideon M. Kressel

PART I COMMUNITIES IN THE DESERT 7

2 A Call for Desert Communities and Science 9
David Ben-Gurion

3 The First Days at Kibbutz Revivim 13
Yonat and Alexander Sened

4 The Pioneer at Kibbutz Sde Boqer 19
John Krivine

PART II WHAT IS A DESERT? 25

5 Midbar, Shmama, and Garbage Can 27
Michael Feige

6 The Conquest of the Desert and the Settlement Ethos 33
Yael Zerubavel

7 The Perception of the Four Winds 45
Gideon M. Kressel

Part III INSPIRATION 53

8 Religion and the Desert 55
Yigal Granot

9 The Arts 59

Photographs 59
Arie Bar Lev

Angels in the Desert 64
A visit with Binah Kahana by Gretel Rieber
Translated from the German by Wolfgang Motzafi-Haller

Theater 67
Ofra Faiman

Literature 71
Chaim Noll

Sculpture 76
Ezra Orion

Sculpture 77
Dalia Meiri

Poetry 81
Elaine Solowey

Poetry 84
Arie Issar

Bedouin Poetry 86
Translated by Alexander Borg

10 Linguistic and Ethnographic Observations on the Color Categories of the Negev Bedouin 91
Alexander Borg

Part IV RESEARCH 117

11 Founding of the Institute for Desert Research 119
Amos Richmond

12 Desert Research 139

Solar Power Plants 139
David Faiman

Solar Surgery 143
Daniel Feuermann

Fossil Water 147
Arie S. Issar

Microalgae 151
Zvi Cohen

Runoff Agriculture 155
Pedro Berliner

Fish 157
Samuel Appelbaum

Desert Architecture 160
David Pearlmutter

Apology for Architecture, or The Planner's Craft 163
Isaac Meir

Part V EDUCATION AND SCHOLARSHIP 171

13 Environmental High School 173
Sol Brand

14 Field School 177
Eran Doron

15 Ben-Gurion Research and Heritage Institutes 181
Allon Gal

References 189

Name Index 203

Subject Index 207

About the Contributors 209

Preface

Permission to reprint articles or selections from books has been granted for: the "Introduction" by David Ben-Gurion in *Masters in the Desert: 6000 Years in the Negev* by Yaakov Morris, 1961:11-16 (copyright© 1961 by Yaakov Morris. Used by permission of G.P. Putnam's Sons, a division of Penguin Group (USA) Inc.); an article on "The Pioneer," by John Krivine in Lives in the Negev Desert, The Jacob Blaustein Institute for Desert Research, Ben-Gurion University, 1991; for reprinting an Enghlish translation of Chapter 1 in Earth Without Shadow by Jonath and Alexander Sened, Jerusalem, Ariel, 1951; for the reprinting, with some additions, of the paper by Alexander Borg on "Linguistic and Ethnographic Observations on the Color Categories of the Negev Bedouin," published in The Language of Color in the Mediterranean, Stockholm Oriental Studies 16, Acta Universsitatis Stockholmensis, 1999. The publishers of the photographs and descriptions of the work of Ezra Orion and Dalia Meiri have given permission to reprint their material.

For Chapter 6 by Yael Zerubavel we have permission from the Central Zionist Archives in Jerusalem to reprint the JNF Poster from 1953 and the Logo of the 1953 state-sponsored exhibit showing a worker's hand holding up a flower. We also have permission to reprint the cartoon by the late Dosh (Kariel Gardosh) the famous Israeli cartoonist from his daughter, Daniella Santo. Kariel Gardosh (1921-2000) of Hungarian origin was the creator of the national symbol "Srulik." For almost 50 years Dosh was the leading political cartoonist of his newspaper Ma'ariv and of Israeli journalism. We also have permission from Ma'ariv in the 1953 September 22 issue, on page 4.

The cover photograph is by Wolfgang Motzafi-Haller. We also wish to thank Wolfgang Motzafi-Haller for translating the article about Binah Kahana from German.

Thank you to all of the contributors who dictated their ideas about the influence of the desert on their work or submitted articles on aspects of the desert experience.

A. Paul Hare and Gideon M. Kressel

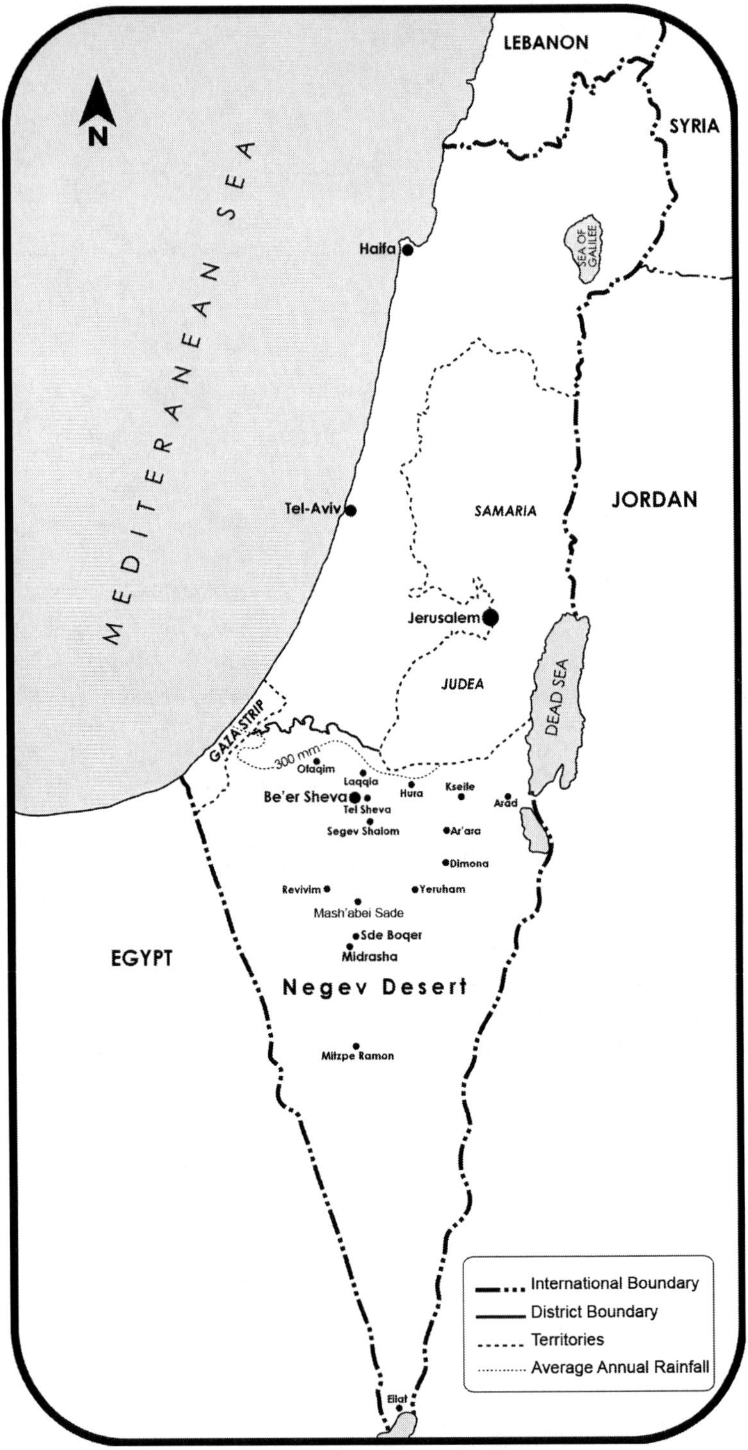

N
MEDITERANEAN SEA
LEBANON
SYRIA
SEA OF GALILEE
Haifa
JORDAN
SAMARIA
Tel-Aviv
Jerusalem
JUDEA
DEAD SEA
GAZA STRIP
300 mm
Ofaqim
Laqqia
Be'er Sheva
Tel Sheva
Hura
Kseife
Arad
Segev Shalom
Ar'ara
Dimona
Revivim
Yeruham
Mash'abei Sade
Sde Boqer
Midrasha
EGYPT
Negev Desert
Mitzpe Ramon
Eilat
International Boundary
District Boundary
Territories
Average Annual Rainfall

Chapter 1

The Desert Experience

A. Paul Hare and Gideon M. Kressel

An earlier working title for this book was *The Zin Desert in Israel: A Source of Inspiration*. We had noted that the experiences of people living in the high deserts of the Middle East over many years had provided inspiration for three major world religions, Judaism, Christianity, and Islam. So there must be something rather special about the area. At first we chose to focus on the experiences and the effects on their horizons of people who lived in one community, the '*Midrasha*' or 'College.' The community was named for the Teachers College there that Ben-Gurion had hoped would become the University of the Negev and did become the site of several research and educational institutions, of which the Blaustein Institute for Desert Research is the largest.

However this focus was later expanded to include descriptions of some of the nearby communities, which Ben-Gurion had called for to develop the Negev and the scientific activities of the scientists who settled in the community, also part of Ben-Gurion's plan to find ways to make the Negev and deserts in other parts of the world more habitable and productive. The middle section of the book includes papers on different definitions of the desert and the experiences of artists, poets, dramatists, and sculptors about the ways in which the desert inspired their work, plus a chapter on the vocabulary of color terms used by Bedouin to describe aspects of their herds and their environment.

We initially thought of reprinting a description of the main concepts used in the dramaturgical perspective with some notes on their application to the present work at the end of the volume. However this seemed to be an example of "the tail trying to wag the dog." So we now refer the reader to previous publications that include this material and only cite the some of the applications in this chapter.

For some variations of the concepts included in the dramaturgical perspective and their application, see: Hare (1985), *Social interaction as drama: Applications from conflict resolution*; Hare and Blumberg (1988), *Dramaturgical analysis of social interaction*; Hare (2001), Dramaturgical analysis; Hare and Kressel (2001), *Israel as center stage: A setting for social and religious enactments*; and especially Hare, Golan, and Osher (2006), *The stage is our world: An English speaking musical theater group in Israel* for some thoughts about the effect of being on stage on the actors.

Dramaturgical analysis

In brief, *Dramaturgical analysis* of *social interaction* assumes that *social acts* are 'staged,' consciously or unconsciously, and thus embody all the elements found in enactments in the theater. Plays on the theater stage highlight all the elements of ordinary social life to present to an audience a new perspective on some aspect of social interaction. Thus, concepts used in theater production can be turned back again for the analysis of the social behavior that they are designed to reflect (Brissett and Edgley, 1990; Hare and Blumberg, 1988).

Dramaturgical analysis has been used in several ways. One way, used more by sociologists of the symbolic interaction tradition, is to view everyday social interaction as if the participants were performing roles, consciously monitoring their performance to create *impressions*, with Goffman's *The Presentation of Self in Everyday Life* (1959) as an outstanding and often-quoted example. A second way, introduced by the philosopher-linguist Burke (1968), is based on the analysis of the 'act' in terms of the agent, scene, agency (means), and purpose. Sets of concepts are linked in 'ratios,' such as the 'scene-act ratio,' where the scene (the situation) has implicit in it the attitudes and behaviors that will become explicit through action.

The *meaning of the event* binds all the participants together. The overall meaning has been termed the 'definition of the situation,' the 'frame,' and the 'illusion.' Sarbin emphasizes meaning in his list of the principal characteristics of the dramaturgical perspective (Allen and Scheibe, 1982: 20-21): "Individuals construct and reconstruct meanings to make sense of their observations."

Another approach, used primarily by anthropologists, follows Turner (1974) to describe the function of 'social dramas' that are enacted by members of a society to bring about conflict resolution, to signify a rite of passage, or to memorialize some important event in the history of the society.

The aspect of dramaturgical analysis that we will use here is based more on Burke's concepts, especially his idea that any situation has implicit in it the attitudes and behaviors that will become explicit through action. Before each of the contributors from the Midrasha spoke or wrote about some part of his or her experience for this volume, we asked "What part has living in the desert year-round played in what you do here, be it art, education, or science?"

Life in other deserts

The typical book written about desert life is by an anthropologist describing the nomadic people who lived there in the past (Morris, 1961) or in the present (Abu-Rabia, 1994). Or the book is written to document some military campaign that took place in the desert (Jarvis, 1936, 1938; Lawrence, 1927; Mountfort, 1965). More recent books deal with the ecology of the desert (Hillel, 1982) or with possibilities for development (Gradus, 1985). The book that comes closest to the present analysis of the implications of the desert for people is by Krutch (1954) entitled *The Voice of the Desert: A Naturalist's Interpretation.*

Krutch, who lived in a cabin in the desert near Tucson Arizona in the United States, notes that the desert is an "unfavorable environment" (1954, p. 22) and that "we grow strong against the pressure of a difficulty..." (p. 24). Plants and animals have learned to fit the environment and all humans are capable of drawing conclusions from observable facts (p. 209). Krutch continues with the observation that "...nothing, not even the sea, has seemed to affect men more profoundly than the desert, or seemed to incline them so powerfully toward great thoughts, perhaps because the desert itself seems to brood and encourage brooding. To the Hebrew the desert spoke of God, and one of the most powerful of all religions was born. To the Arabs it spoke of the stars, and astronomy came into being" (p. 220).

For Krutch "...the desert is conservative, not radical... The heroism it encourages is the heroism of endurance, not that of conquest." Adaptability of plants and animals, problems of erosion and overexploitation are plainer and more acute. The desert "brings man up against his limitations, turns him upon himself and suggests values which more indulgent regions minimize." Sometimes it inclines to contemplation men who have never contemplated before. And of all answers to the question "What is a desert good for?" "Contemplation" is perhaps the best (p. 221).

Krutch compares the "beautiful" with the "sublime." Something can be beautiful... even when it escapes being merely pretty, is easy and reassuring. The sublime... is touched with something which inspires awe. It is large and powerful; it carries with it the suggestion that it might overpower us if it would. "Here if anywhere the most familiar realities recede and others come into the foreground of the mind" (pp. 221-222). "To have experienced it is to be prepared to see other landscapes with new eyes and to participate with a fresh understanding in the life of other natural communities" (p. 223).

The desert as a source of inspiration

In our application of dramaturgical analysis to help understand the desert experience we assume that social behavior is response to situation. What is there about desert that has led so many people to experience an "altered state of consciousness" during which they had a vision that inspired a religion, or a social structure, or art, or science? As several of the authors in this collection have noted, living in the desert can also be an ordeal. It is a stark environment that requires an effort to survive. The settlers provide a glimpse of the hardships, the poets sense this starkness, and the scientists hope to make the environment more livable. We now note some of the applications of our dramaturgical perspective to each of the accounts contained in this volume.

Part I: Communities in the Desert

Chapter 2. In his introduction to *Masters of the desert: 6000 years in the Negev* by Morris (1961), David Ben-Gurion calls for Israelis to give new meaning to the desert, by developing new communities for immigrants and providing science to explore comfortable ways of housing and new ways of making a living through hydrology, agriculture, industry, and mining. The lessons that are learned in the Negev can then be applied to the many arid parts of the world.

Chapter 3. Yonat and Alexander Sened, in the first chapter of a book written in Hebrew, *Earth without shadow* (1951), translated by Gideon Kressel, describe the first few days of hazardous travel to the south in the Negev, by two of the founding members, where they established Kibbutz Revivim.

Chapter 4. John Krivine (1991) interviews Rafi Bachrach who describes his experience as a founding member of Kibbutz Sde-Boqer in 1952, where David Ben-Gurion came to live, seeing the kibbutz as an example of the type of community he had hoped for.

Part II: What is the Desert?

Chapter 5. Michael Feige sees the actions of people coming to live and work in the desert of Zin as responses to a situation defined either as a frontier or wasteland.

Chapter 6. Yael Zerubavel discusses the perception of the desert as a Zionist frontier and posits that the settlement ethos of the pre-state and early state period constructs the Jewish settlement as a continuing process of a struggle between the *Yishuv* and the desert.

Chapter 7. Gideon M. Kressel notes that the four directions of the compass had different meanings. For the ancients, East meant birth and West meant death. Right (South) was associated with purity and left (North) with defilement. These conceptions changed over the years, especially following the holocene and, as of late, a reverse trend southward following the discovery of oil in the Middle East.

Part III: Inspiration

Chapter 8. Yigal Granot, on religion and the desert (translated from Hebrew by Gideon Kressel), records the changing connections between the symbolism and practice of religion and the desert over many millennia.

Chapter 9. A collection of accounts describing the ways in which different artists experience the desert. Arie Bar Lev captures in photographs views of the landscape and flora and fauna near the Midrasha. Binah Kahana (Rieber, 2004) explains how she tries to capture the experience of living in the desert in her painting. Ofra Faiman records the way that living in the desert has influenced the production of plays in the high school. Chaim Noll summarizes the way the desert has been depicted in literature and poetry over the years. As examples of desert-inspired sculpture, Ezra Orion (2000) designed sculpture in the desert to represent his feelings. Dalia Meiri sees environmental sculpture as a dialog between the landscape and herself. Some examples of different meanings that the desert can have are given in the poetry of Elaine Soloway (with three poems about the desert, especially during a sand storm) and Arie Issar (in a selection of three of his poems from many). Alexander Borg has translated Bedouin poetry that is inspired by transportation and women, two essentials for desert life.

Chapter 10. Alexander Borg, in a version of an account first published in a collection on *The language of color in the Mediterranean* (Borg, 1999), describes the influence of the desert and its herds of sheep, goats, and camels on the concepts of color used by Bedouin.

Part IV: Research

Chapter 11. Amos Richmond, the founder of the Blaustein Institute for Desert Research, records the events during the first five years after he was given the task of attracting scientists to do their research in an isolated desert community.

Chapter 12. A collection of short accounts of the ways that living in the desert has made a difference in science and education. As an example of the research at the Blaustein Institute for Desert Research, David Faiman proposed solar power plants as a source of electricity. Daniel Feuermann, and a team of scientists, demonstrated how sunlight could be used for laser surgery. Arie Issar, recording his walk into the desert, describes the importance of water and of the presence of fossil aquifers under the desert. Zvi Cohen uses the advantages of the desert, with its high solar irradiance, to grow microalgae. Pedro Berliner notes how his walk across part of the desert to his office in the morning suggested the importance of controlling evaporation as an influence in the use of runoff agriculture. Samuel

Appelbaum accepts that desert water is brackish, so he grows fish. In the development of forms of architecture suitable for desert conditions, David Pearlmutter demonstrates how the design of houses and collections of buildings can respond to the environment, and Isaac Meir records that living in the desert has influenced his conception of heating and cooling houses.

Part V: Education and Scholarship

Chapter 13. Sol Brand describes the desert-inspired teaching program at the Environmental High School.

Chapter 14. Eran Doron provides a glimpse of the work of the Field School created to inculcate respect for the rhythm of life adapted by desert people's flora and fauna. Translated by G.M. Kressel.

Chapter 15. Allon Gal records and analyzes the origin, functions, and activities of the Ben-Gurion Research Institute, based on an archive where documents pertaining to Israel's history is at the disposal of scholars.

PART I

COMMUNITIES IN THE DESERT

Part I introduces the main theme of the book with a reprint of Prime Minister David Ben-Gurion's call for the establishment of communities in the Negev and for scientists to find new ways to make life there more habitable. Accounts from kibbutzim near the Midrasha relate some of the hardships.

Chapter 2

A Call for Desert Communities and Science*

David Ben-Gurion

The appearance of *Masters of the Desert* by Yaakov Morris at this juncture of Israel's development is very timely. Within these 5,000 square miles of sand, eroded soil and mountain are vested Israel's major hopes of advancement in the absorption of further large numbers of the Jewish people still in dispersion, and in the attainment of the country's full economic independence. The transformation of the Negev into a center of agriculture, industry, mining, commerce, learning and research, and as a bridge of trade and political ties between the continents of Africa, Asia and Europe, is the central pioneer task of this generation of Israelis and of world Jewry, as was the draining of the swamps of Jezreel and Jordan over fifty years ago.

The reclamation of the Negev desert, however, has more than local interest, vital as that interest may be, to the State of Israel itself. Here, man is faced with a fateful and momentous challenge of nature. To conquer the wastelands, all his will and devotion, labor and energy, time-tested as well as newly invented techniques of science, will have to be employed. The experience so far gained in this battle against aridity, in the search for new sources of water and power, and new techniques of human settlement, not to mention the experiences which will undoubtedly be acquired in the future, give to the Negev a universal value. The Negev, in short, is in many respects a small and modest pilot plant in mankind's over-all battle against the desert regions anywhere.

* Published as the introduction to Morris (1961), pp. 11-16.

The universality of the drama inherent in this struggle for reclamation of the Negev wastelands is sharply emphasized by the region's geopolitical position. It is at the crossroads between Europe and two vast continents wherein scores of newly independent nations have embarked upon a struggle to transform their own landscapes, many of them jungle and wasteland, into centers of fertility and of modern societies.

It is therefore natural that to many of these young nations the experience of our Negev pioneers and, in fact, of the builders of all parts of modern Israel, represents a source of encouragement and knowledge from which universal benefit may be drawn. These pioneer experiences are not merely linked to the technique of science, of hydrology, agriculture, industry, and mining. They also represent discoveries of interest and importance in man's relation to man himself, in forms of society which embody the elements of individual freedom, mutual help and purposeful planning. These human values of equality are of no less concern than the material achievements of the modern world. Israel, which had the good fortune of receiving generous aid from more developed countries, as the U.S., is in turn privileged in having the opportunity of being able to extend the fruits of her experience to others.

Although the Negev is small in area compared to vaster regions of wasteland and desert in the world, its history of civilization is among the wealthiest of mankind.

For some 900 years, covering the period of the Judaean kingdom, the Maccabean dynasty, the Nabateans and the Byzantines, it was the scene of continuous civilization and widespread settlement. Even before this period, is the record of settlement by the Hebrew patriarchs and earlier the civilization of Chalcolithic man, the ruins of which were first uncovered by the archaeologist, Jean Perrot.

The contemporary civilization advancing into the Negev embodies many of the characteristics of those which have appeared in the past. It is based as they were upon a combination of agriculture, industry, mining and international trade, the settlement of large units of population, the combination of settlement and defense. The heritage of the past is here being enriched with the conquests of modern science and technology.

The triangle of the Negev is situated between two hostile countries: Egypt and Jordan. Across the southwestern border of the Negev stretches the Sinai Desert, and the Arabian desert is on the other side of its eastern border. The Arabs have transformed more than one flourishing and populous country into a desert; the wasteland in the Arab State is no obstacle to their existence and their independence. The small State of Israel, however, cannot long tolerate within its bounds a desert which takes up over half its territory. If the State does not put an end to the desert, the desert is liable to put an end to the State. The narrow strip between Jaffa and Haifa, 15 to 25 kilometers wide, which contains the bulk of Israel's population cannot survive for long without a large and firmly based population in the expanses of the South and the Negev.

Without the settlement of the South and the Negev this country cannot be secure, and we shall not succeed in attaining economic independence. They cannot be settled without the transformation of the facts of nature, which is not beyond the capacity of science in our day or the pioneering energy of our youth. Science and pioneering will enable us to perform this miracle.

The whole of our achievement in this country is one of the wonders of history. There is nothing supernatural about it; miracles of the supernatural type are not wonderful at all—for if it is possible to create the globe and set it in endless motion round the sun, it is also possible to command the earth or the sun to stand still. Human reason has not yet succeeded—and it is doubtful whether it ever will succeed—in understanding the secret of creation and solving the riddle of existence and eternal renewal. The more human experience and reason learn of the world around us and within us, the more profound grows the riddle, and the further off we are from understanding the eternal secret. But man's experience grows constantly richer; his mastery of his environment and himself continually increases; the instruments which he creates to increase his capacity to examine and understand nature, and in part to gain domination over it, grow more perfect; and the human horizon incessantly expands.

And the most wonderful and most powerful instrument through which man gains the mastery over nature is man himself. The potentialities latent in this wonderful being have no parallel among all the complicated and extraordinary instruments and machines that man has created. And it is only as the result of man's latent potentialities, and the capacity and the will to make use of these potentialities—which we call *halutziut* or pioneering—that we have succeeded in our enterprise in this country, which seemed to be completely incompatible with all the accepted laws and the conventional concepts which existed at the time the enterprise was begun.

Who believed decades ago that Jews who for centuries had lived in towns, and for generations had been strangers to labor and the soil, would become the builders of a country? Who imagined that a people which had been scattered and dispersed for over two thousand years would reassemble in its ancient homeland under foreign occupation and in it renew its sovereign independence? Who believed that a dead tongue, embalmed in songs and books of prayer, would once again become the living tongue of a people which spoke a Babel of languages? Who dreamt that a people oppressed, degraded and helpless for generations would suddenly reveal a heroic spirit and crush a hostile arm forty times its superior in numbers?

The faith—bold and naïve at the same time—which the early pioneers showed eighty years ago, and the force of the creative initiative which they showed in establishing new Jewish villages in the ancient, captive homeland; the pioneering impetus which grew steadily stronger in the course of the last three generations until it achieved the revival of the Jewish State and the brilliant victories of the War of Independence; the daring involved in settling tens of thousands of immigrants from backward countries, who for thousands of years had been foreign to the fragrance of the fields, in the desolate wastes of the South; the cultural, social and economic transformations which took place in the lives of hundreds of thousands of immigrants in two or three generations, transformations unparalleled either in the life of our own people since its beginnings or in the life of any other people in our own day—all these are the fruit of that great human miracle which has taken place in our modern history, and which we call *halutziut*, which is nothing else than the profound faith of man in his power and capacity, and a burning spiritual need to transform the natural order, as well as the order of his own life, for the sake of the redeeming vision.

By virtue of this miracle of *halutziut* we resisted the habits acquired in the Diaspora and uprooted them; we resisted political difficulties and overcame them; we resisted the incitement and hostility of our neighbors and gained the victory; we fought against the poverty and ruination of our country—and rebuilt its ruined places.

Now, in the very hour when we have gained free and sovereign control over all the lands and resources of the State, we have come face to face with the greatest difficulty: the curse of nature and the fate of barrenness and desolation which has held the greater part of our soil in its grip ever since the Creation.

The State, the nation, the youth, the men of science—have now come face to face with the supreme test in the history of our progress toward independence and the renewal of our sovereignty. Only through a united effort by the State in planning and execution, by a people ready for a great voluntary effort, by a youth bold in spirit and inspired by creative heroism, by scientists liberated from the bonds of conventional thought and capable of probing deep into the special problems of this country—only through an all-inclusive onslaught by all the creative forces in Israel, shall we succeed in carrying out the great and fateful task of developing the South and the Negev.

Thirteen years ago a new chapter was opened in the history of the Jewish people. The revival of Jewish sovereignty brought the Jewish people face to face with its destiny—without any intervening barrier. Immediately on the proclamation of its independence the young State had to face the attack of five of its neighbors—and gained the victory. Israel cannot survive without strength and power, so long as the human race is divided into warring blocs and nation lifts up sword against nation. But the profound truth of the supremacy of the spirit, the most incontrovertible proof of which is the long history and the manifold experiences of the Jewish people, remains unchallenged. It is on this truth that the faith of the Jewish people in its future is based, and the supreme test of Israel in our generation lies, not in its struggle with hostile forces without, but in its success in gaining domination, through science and pioneering, over the wastelands of its country in the expanses of the South and the Negev.

Chapter 3

The First Days at Kibbutz Revivim*

Yonat and Alexander Sened

The car was shuddering towards the cypress avenue that in the pale dawn light seemed lower than usual. The red-roofed dining barrack seemed as though it was hiding behind the sand hill, and the group of figures waving their hands before it, merged with the early morning darkness.

In the densely crowded truck's baggage, alongside an assemblage of fuel barrels, work-tools, and folded tents, rested a shining yellow tractor and Menash'ke lay spread out on its wet and chilly tread. He looked toward the sleepy little town. The road was stark between clumps of dark trees, covered by a fine grayish fog.

They stopped for a while near an orange-packing shed, at a side grove. The sun climbed relentlessly, heralding a stifling heat. A person appeared at the broken door, approached the car, handed over a gun to Nahum, smiled and went back. Before he disappeared in the dark shed he turned to the car and called out: "*Good luck.*"

Nahum stuck the pistol in the tractor's took kit. His sun-tanned face was now concentrating and grave— the same expression he had had the day before when Menash'ke saw him as they met before dusk, at the secretary room.

When do we take off Nahum? He instantly sensed why he had been summoned for the talk.

Early tomorrow.

Who?

The two of us and Tuvya.

---

* From Chapter 1 in Sened and Sened (1951). Translated from the Hebrew by Gideon Kressel.

They kept silent for a long moment.

Weapon?

Only one pistol. The wireless equipment will come later.

Is there a police station near by?

Yes, they have a station there, some forty Kilometers South of Be'er Sheva. That matter is kept as a secret. You know. The land regulations. The British forbid it.

Are any of our Hebrew villages in sight?

There aren't any. The distance away from Negbah (then the Southern-most Kibbutz), *is more than 100 Km. The only road leading there is via Be'er Sheva.*

Again they were silent. The knocking of a well pump was heard now clear, as though nearer, when the night had descended.

And water?

A doubtful drilling. Brackish water with chlorine and salt.

He didn't ask more questions. Darkness filled the room. An uncomfortable brief gust of wind was felt in the air. Menash'ke stood up.

What'll be the date tomorrow, ha?

July seventh, 1943, a date to be remembered, isn't it? said Nahum and his voice sounded too solemn, artificial.

So ended their discussion. They were hectically preparing. At the crack of dawn they were ready to go.

The car went on Southward. Bit by bit, deprived of its green color, the landscape turned gray. A British military vehicle passed by, with the chinking of a metal chain dragging on the road behind it. A black driver grinned widely, his teeth blanching.

Approaching Gaza we came across a few isolated Arab villages. Straw and earth-roofed adobe houses with hay sprouting out of their doors; solid walls, sunk in the burning heat's doze.

The main road leading to Be'er Sheva was empty of traffic. On both sides, as far as the horizon, spread a gray-brown plain, marked by a white pathway. A single dark-robed Bedouin strode slowly in a slumbering world. Every solitary shed and green bush on the roadside cried out for attention. Military airports and football fields flung Tuvya into an exhausted state. A tamarisk was observed far on the horizon.

Not a bush, not a real tree, said Nahum.

The heat increased. A thin dust sprung up around, turning their forelocks gray. The wide-open spaces seemed mockingly exposed. The car glided down a slope and passed over a bridge crossing a ravine. Down below burst forth a sign of grass.

Wadi Shari'ah, remarked Nahum, *it borders the Northern Negev.*

They came to a stop and stepped out on the barren and shrunken land surface, all flat hills. Walls white as chalk rose where the road cut through the hills. Depressing monotony spread out around. Nahum plucked a mini-bush, smelled and tasted it. *Pay attention guys,* he exclaimed, but didn't explain.

Back to the car to carry on South-West where they met a group of Bedouin who stood on the roadside, wearing belt daggers, they screamed something towards their car. Menash'ke tried unsuccesfully to decipher from their open mouths whether they threatened or mocked. He saw them as a road-block on their North, separating them from the Kibbutz members, who were now, he imagined, enthusiastically talking about them, gathering by the barracks. The scenery all around was tiring, the road's meandering for hours revealed flatness and nothing new.

Then Be'er Sheva appeared, the Negev capital, surprising with its high-rise trees, surrounding with variety its yellow houses. *S-o, what do you say? Look at this tree crest, forefather Abraham strolls there!* rejoiced Nahum. Tuvya remained indifferent.

Don't you see? There, there! His noble figure, the long sword on his thigh!

Menash'ke followed Nahum's look, trying to adjust the form of the tree's branches to his imagination's description.

The town, its streets and houses dozed. The magnificent Mosque at the entrance and its high and proud minaret seemed to look askance at the few passers-by who moved lazily on the side of the yards, smelling of dust and fire smoke. With considerable effort they found the home of Aminadav, commonly known as Hawaja Ameemn, who dealt with buying lands in the Negev. He, with the custom and the manner of a wealthy Sheikh, was about to join them on their way to the place. Halting by his yard's gate, dozens of Bedouin streamed from gates of houses and shops of the street. Approaching, they formed a thick circle around the car, eyes red from dust and illness, and looked at the unusual scene: *Yahood!* [Jews]

Aminadav appeared at the entrance, very solemn. His plump face, the face of a successful merchant radiated out of his white, shiny silk kuffiyye [Arabic head cover]. Making his way through the crowd with the haughty walk of a demonstrated ruler. He started his little car and moved ahead. The Bedouin ring burst, opening to the roadsides, froze for a second, re-awakened and started pelting the caravan with stones, watermelon peels, and earth clods, whatever came to hand. The cars did not respond. Bedouin ran following them, hanging on the truck's protrusions, trying to sneak out something of the strange objects heaped one on top of the other in every bit of the truck.

Yisraelik squeezed the gasoline pedal to speed up. One by one the looters were driven off empty-handed. The last of them were beaten on falling. Menash'ke heard their guttural screams and tried to disregard them so as not to hear or see.

At the outskirts of the town, the truck came to a stop. Suddenly the engine silenced. Nahum drew the pistol out. Yisraelik rushed around madly. His light, soft hair crest that he used to stroke became dark from sweat and filth and stuck on his face with his effort to discover the silent engine's secret. The Bedouin mob had assembled once again, approaching the cars. Then, hesitating, the mob stopped and noisily discussed their next move.

Tuvya sniffed and blew his nose. *This damned cold, just now!* A clod of earth hit the tractor's roller chain. Its metal sound reverberated and the splinters spread.

Bastards! They closed the carburetor! Menash'ke heard Yisraelik's voice, and immediately afterward the bang of the cabin door closing. The engine sucked the fuel thirstily, and there came the redeeming spurt—they sprung from their spot. Waves of air carried over a polyglot of curses, coming from Yisraelik's cabin. The Bedouin became tired from running after the receding cars. Nahum placed the pistol back in its hiding place.

The spacious desert land spread out in silence. A feeling of detachment from all increased and the perception of the 'Negev' was linked with the sense of the great loneliness and fear of the wilderness. Nahum imagined Eva, his wife, smiling towards her mumbling baby girl, attempting to dash her fears.

The mercilessly barrenness revealed an occasional grayish bush. The dry wind howled. A lone, dark, elongated tent brought to mind a night bird that lands hungry, spreading its wings.

They reached Be'er Al-Dja'ud. There were a few acacia trees by the brown police station, a military camp, barracks and tents, a tiny mosque, and gray cars. The blinding brightness of the chalk hills burnt the eyes. At the sight they stopped to rest, embracing the big cup tap that covered the well. *What a big tap,* said Menash'ke.

Policemen encircled them, one Englishman and two Arabs. They spent a long hour checking their belongings, the English policemen in a rough though sloppy manner, and the Arabs with an aggravating slowness.

What did you bring with you?

Explosives, said Nahum. It's easy to joke when the pistol in not on you.

Do you wish us three to stay and look after you? You can stay here, at the station.

Thanks a lot. They exchanged meaningful looks.

The cars left the paved road behind and started to climb an earth path, meandering through the hills. Nahum pointed out the mound [*Tel*] that was chosen to be their settlement location. At the mound's feet was an elongated concave crater, and a dark opening of a cave.

I'm tired, said Tuvya.

They unloaded the luggage. The cars proceeded Northward and the three of them were left standing alongside their belongings. The heat reached its climax. Airwaves trembled above the burning water container, blurring the sight as they felt a heavy fatigue. *To settle the Negev, well-well,* said Tuvya.

They looked at the wilderness as though requesting it, from its inner self to find the means to overcome itself. The silence of ages was around, not a voice, not a color. No barking dog, not a sign of sprouting grass. Under the metal blue skies stretched lifeless, dying earth, and only here and there sprouted, by a tremendous effort, a faded tiny desert bush.

Better stop this silence, thought Nahum in his heart, making an effort against the despair that was sneaking in. *Well guys!* They began to deal with their movable property.

During the night they watched in turn. Menash'ke napped sitting on a tin box at the tent's opening. A night-bird's scream crossed the whispering desert wind. A howl. At the third watch of the night vigil a heavy fog descended. The water container banged on the unloaded equipment and the amount of dripping increased. Water drips spilt on the earth and changed sounds as the puddle grew in size. One had to fix the container. In case of an onslaught, a possibility was to retreat to the cave for a defense. *"Hanna's checkered-shirt suits her,"* this is a brief recollection when fear takes over his heart. He longs to take a shower, smell a fresh towel, and then to sleep, to pull the blanket over his head....

Nahum appeared at the entrance to replace Menash'ke on guard. From a distance he heard a man's voice, trilling a desert song, monotonous. It sounded as if a single Bedouin was chasing away the demons off his way.

At the crack of dawn, as they were preparing the tractor and the plough for a first plow up, Abu-Tarbush, the fields' guard appeared, riding on his limping mare. He had a dark complexion and fleshy lips, with a thin beard, sharp and protruding. Menash'ke made an effort to understand his talk but soon gave up, hearing the bizarre dialect, bursting with glottal sounds flowing and flowing.

Transferring the water from the leaking container to empty tin boxes and barrels, they stuffed the leak with soap and returned the water to the container. It now had a taste of kerosene. Abu-Tarbush followed their actions, smiling and calling joyful remarks. On leaving the cave Menash'ke saw him plunge his hands into the container. *A morning wash*, rejoiced Abu-Tarbush, turning towards him.

Menash'ke twisted his face. He tried to gulp a second cup of water without gagging. Then he climbed the tractor and directed it to the experimental drilling where their land ended. *Hei!* he cried out, with all his might, to the strange and gloomy space.

No echo returned, only the tractor's engine rattled monotonously. The plough pierced the earth. Menash'ke found it hard to stifle this rising excitement. *Here I return,* he smiled to himself, defensively, *to cultivate the land given to the children of Simon. I am the descendent of Abraham, Isaac, and Jacob, the son of Zvi and Gittel.*

So guys, how is it? shouted Nahum, straining to be heard over the engine's noise. *How is it to plough a field after two thousand years?*

Not bad! answered Menash'ke, returning the prankish look of an accomplice.

Chapter 4

The Pioneer at Kibbutz Sde Boqer*

John Krivine

Rafi Bachrach was born in Hamburg in 1921 and came to Palestine in 1933 with his parents and sister. He worked as manager of a plastics factory in Ramat Gan until the Second World War whereupon he joined the British Army. In 1949 when he was an Intelligence officer in the Israeli Army, stationed in the South of the country he met Avriel Hagai and three years later he was one of the founders of Sde-Boqer.

---

* From pp. 41-46 in Krivine (1991).

If you ask me what was in my mind, personally, when I came to this place, this is my answer. I had a very personal love for this landscape and I didn't want to see it go, so I asked myself what I could do, in my own little way, to justify the Jewish claim to the Negev. After all, I didn't feel that we had any real historical claim on this land as we had, say, on the Galil, Jerusalem, and the Jisreal Valley. I decided that the thing to do was to go and build a permanent settlement there, something that hadn't been attempted as far as I knew, for about 1,300 years.

There was another reason which I know will sound a little bombastic, but here it is. I wanted to show the world that the Jews could do in one generation what a succession of Arab empires had failed to do in fifty. I cannot say with any certainty what my six comrades were thinking when we pitched our tents in 1952 at Wadi Bukka, but this is what was in my heart.

PHOTO OF EARLY GARIN AT SDE-BOQER
Pioneers of Sde-Boqer. 1953. Bachrach is bottom row, far right.
(courtesy Kibbutz Sde-Boqer)

We were a group of about 7 young men, Palmachniks, who all loved this part of the desert. Avriel Hagai was my commander in the army and you could say that he was the driving force in our little garin. He was a tremendous personality who later split from us in order to establish Mitzpe Ramon, thirty kilometers to the South. Establishing Sde-Boqer was not enough for him.

We were completely independent types and there was no stated political objective in what we were proposing. We were told that it was impossible to live there which was completely the wrong thing to tell this group of people. We were more than ever determined and now was added the resolve to do so without any help from our colleagues in the North.

Hagai Avriel

It wasn't enough for us to be just pioneers, we almost had to be explorers. At the last minute, the Army tried to persuade us to go to a place closer to Eilat called Kaat el Krek, South of Machtesh Ramon. They even offered us Ein Gedi, but it was a bit hot for my liking. There was never an undertaking in all the history of the modern Jewish state that was less planned, less thought out, more spontaneous. We would have a farm and raise sheep, goats, and horses. At the end of each year, we would count up the profits and split them seven ways. That was it. Can you believe such naïveté?

The valley was called Wadi Bukka, meaning valley of cattle in Arabic. None of the local Bedouin knew where the name originated but we liked it and it was a fairly precise description of what we intended to do on our farm. So we became known as *Sde-Boqer*—'fields of the cattle-man' in Hebrew. One of our first decisions was to breed and train horses. It was felt that this would be good horse country although I have to say that at the time we had no knowledge whatever of previous attempts to breed horses in this area of the Negev.

We chose this place for two reasons. Firstly it looked like promising agricultural land and, being at the junction of two valleys, we felt that we would be able to catch a lot of runoff rainwater. There was going to be nothing else with which to feed our livestock and for our own needs, so this was a critical factor. Secondly it was situated hard by a Roman road that connected with a paved British road some 15 kms to the North which in turn led to Be'er Sheva. We wanted to know that if we got into trouble, the army could reach us in reasonable time.

Two of our number were killed in the first half year. Barbara Propper, a young Swiss candidate, was murdered by Bedouin while tending a flock of sheep, that was in September and Bambi was killed in November. The Bedouin were trying to scare us away; from time immemorial the desert had belonged to them and suddenly we arrived and pitched camp right on their main smuggling route from Jordan to

Egypt. By now Yehoshua Cohen had joined us with his wife and although it was never discussed, he was held to be the man who killed Count Bernadotte in 1948. Yehoshua, a tough Lehi fighter, went to the Bedouin Sheikh who was thought to be responsible, for a talk and from then on there was no more trouble. We actually lost two more killed in that first year, but not as a result of Bedouin attack.

As far as farming went, all our assumptions proved to be false. When we first scouted Wadi Bukka, it was exceptionally green for the region because there had been four consecutive years of above-average rainfall, and also because since the creation of the state, there had been practically no grazing in this area by Bedouin herdsmen which had given the local vegetation a chance to grow. As soon as we arrived the annual rainfall dropped and our own grazing activities began to deplete the plant life. Also, the soil didn't prove to be as good as we had at first thought. With the help of experts from the Ministry of Agriculture we were starting to master the art of runoff agriculture, but it quickly became apparent to us that in the best of times, water from runoff would not meet the demands of the expanding agricultural concern that we were planning.

The horse ranch was at first very successful. We were breeding draft horses for agricultural small-holders in the hills around Jerusalem where tractors could not work and it remained a profitable business until about 1961 when a small tractor that could do the work was brought in from Germany; we had no choice but to phase out the ranch. In those first years we were driving to Yeruham every day in a tractor in order to bring water in for drinking and washing. Nothing was working out quite the way we had hoped.

Training horses for draftwork in 1958 (courtesy Kibbutz Sde-Boqer)

Then an extraordinary thing happened. The Prime-Minister dropped in on us. It was entirely unplanned; he was on his way back from visiting Eilat with his entourage and he decided to look in on us to see what we were up to. He announced that he would be staying the night, and a year later he came to live with us.

Did it change our lives? You have to understand that we were a group of extremely hard cases, our arrogance only heightened by our hardships and although privately any one of us would have knelt down to kiss the hem of his trousers, there was an unspoken determination not to allow ourselves to be overwhelmed or even influenced by this dominant man. On two occasions he tried to persuade us to take certain decisions and on both occasions he was overruled. For his part, Ben-Gurion showed great sensitivity to the temperament of our group and thus a modus vivendi was created between the fierce young idealists and the ageing Statesman. It really is the subject for a play.

We had no connection with any group or movement. *Stam* (just so), we were independent farmers and this is what he particularly liked. No politics, no bureaucracy, no ceremony, we were simply there under our own steam and he found that irresistible. But we had considerable problems, the greatest being a constant shortage of manpower. We were attracting many young people to live and work with us, but they were drawn by the adventure and romance of the undertaking and most of them eventually got bored and moved on. We desperately needed people who were prepared to commit to our undertaking and put their nose to the grindstone. We knew that with one of the pioneer organizations behind us, we would get the kind of people we needed.

This was an issue about which Ben-Gurion felt passionately and he spoke against affiliation; he wanted Sde-Boqer to be the pioneering flagship of the State, untarnished by politics and compromise. But he was overruled and in 1961, after nine glorious years of struggle and independence, we joined the Ichud movement of Kibbutzim. Were we right? Who can say?

Throughout the diplomatic struggle for the Negev (1948-1956) Ben-Gurion was unshakable in his determination to hold on to it at all costs, I think he was inspired by our example and when I look around me today at Eilat, Dimona, the towns, moshavim, the new roads of the Negev, I feel that I achieved my initial objective to a far greater degree than I ever imagined possible 39 years ago.

PART II

WHAT IS A DESERT?

In Part II we find that the desert has several meanings. It can be a space alive with meaning, or a wilderness, or a garbage dump, or a place for conquest. There are different perceptions, in the Middle East, of the directions of the four winds.

Chapter 5

Midbar, Shmama, and Garbage Can

Michael Feige

Here is a classical Midreshet Ben-Gurion dilemma: what should the garden of a desert home look like? On the one hand, those who appreciate and love the desert tend to choose, naturally enough, the desert plants, which makes their private garden look somewhat like an extension of its arid surrounding. On the other hand, others living and working in the same village want their private gardens to serve more like havens, extracting them from the depressing yellow into colorful flower beds and green grass. The first-mentioned residents convincingly argue that the desert has beauty and lacks water, while their neighbors may claim that surviving in the desert is punishment enough, and at least their homes should serve as contrasting retreat. This seemingly petty argument reflects the in-between nature of Midreshet Ben-Gurion community, stranded between the desert as midbar and the desert as shmama, terms to be discussed here.

The desert assumed a pivotal position in the thought and vision of Israel's first Prime Minister, David Ben-Gurion, and, subsequently, also constructs the way in which the community of Midreshet Ben-Gurion conceptualizes itself. This communal identity, however, turned out to be surprisingly different from the way in which the namesake national leader had imagined the desert. In what follows I want to reflect on the multiple cultural meanings that the desert, especially the Negev, holds in both Israel and the Midrasha.

Like the Eskimos, who know many words for snow, the desert people have conceived numerous words to signify their habitus. The biblical men and women resided mainly in arid areas, and the Bible, whose stories took place mainly in the desert, conserved some of the names it received. They have probably designated different ecosystems in ancient times, and these cultural meanings were practically lost to modern Hebrew language. Now, distinct terms are used interchangeably. The two that I want to concentrate on are *Midbar* and *Shmama*, translatable—inaccurately as I shall show—to 'desert' and 'wilderness.' They are often used together in the same sentence in order to strengthen one another in expressing remoteness and emptiness. I wish to suggest two distinct meanings for them, which are somehow connected to their ancient linguistic roots.

Midbar is a space that holds substance. The term resonates with davar—meaning 'thing', and with dibur—meaning 'talk'. In the midbar, the Ten Commandments—*dibrot* in Hebrew—were given to the People of Israel. It is debatable whether the term can be convincingly connected to *davar* and *dibur*, but it is certainly attached to the act of cultivating cattle, called *midbur*. The midbar, therefore, is defined as an ecosystem through its social functions. It is a space that, so to speak, is alive with meaning.

The opposite is true for the *shmama*, which is defined by absence. The root *Shamam* connotes *Shoom Davar*, meaning nothing at all. Unlike the midbar, the shmama is not an ecosystem, but a space that has none, where human existence was either totally annihilated or never arrived. While in today's Hebrew language the verb *midbur*, desertification, means the transformation of one ecosystem by another one, albeit a catastrophic one, the verb *hashama* means destroying one ecosystem without a defined replacement. The English word 'desert' captures part of the meaning: as a verb it holds the meaning of desertion, leaving one place for an uncertain alternative.

In Jewish, Zionist, and Israeli imagination the desert oscillated between being a meaningful midbar and a meaningless shmama. The place where the nation was forged, received the divine law and went through on its way to the promised land was a midbar, full with historical meanings, even though it is not the actual holy land but rather a liminal space through which the people move on their quest. It is a place of refuge from tyranny and persecution and a place for reflection and the constituting meeting with God.[1]

For the early Zionists, the desert was important not only because of the concept of return to ancient times, but also because it was also considered a shmama, offering an opportunity to create a fresh start without having to disenfranchise former residents and communities. The image of the desert as *tabula rasa* enabled the Zionists to hold two sides of the stick, to arrive to a new land while evading, at least partially, the moral problems of colonialism. The famous Zionist statement of 'a land without people to a people without land' could materialize only in shmama conditions, of a space that has no prior claim placed on it. This utopian ideal was never materialized for various reasons, one of these being that there is no true shmama, devoid of people and culture, in the area in which the Zionists wished to settle.

As the Zionist immigrants started arriving, the symbolism of shmama was paramount in their mind, regardless of the fact that they may have used the term midbar. The desert was conceived as a vast emptiness, waiting—even striving—to be filled by culture and civilization, brought by the Zionist colonizers. As the Zionists saw themselves as modernizers, the desert was considered to be the locus on which modern communities could be established, and where the blessing that the new Jews could bring to the land proven beyond doubt.

The actual desert was not the only type of space to occupy this place in Zionist imagination: the swamps were the northern equivalent of the southern desert, and the wailing of the jackals signified to the early settlers the boundaries of culture and civilization. The Arabs—not only the Bedouin—were also seen as part of the wilderness, waiting to be either transformed or museumized. For example, a new study of Tel-Aviv shows how the Jaffa Arabs were metaphorically 'desertified.'[2] The othering of the local Palestinians as part of the non-developed desert area enabled the incoming Jews to construct their own identity as modern and enlightened. Likewise, they needed the desert-as-shmama to define themselves as bearers of cultured life.

In accordance with prevailing images, Ben-Gurion's fascination with the desert had little to do with its essence—it being a midbar—and much to do with its image as an empty and desolate shmama waiting to be overcome. His famous statements, endlessly repeated by his admirers, all attested to his will to change the desert into something else. If we shall not conquer the desert, so he said, the desert will conquer us. He stated that the Jewish people will be tested in the Negev. In other words, the desert serves as the grounds on which great deeds shall be accomplished, and not a point of reference in itself. He admired the *Halutzim* (pioneers) who went to the desert in order to transform and civilize it and created small enclave communities. His interest in the Nabatim was mainly in their ability to build and sustain large cities and supply them with water, therefore overcoming the harsh realities imposed by the desert.

A famous episode can show how Ben-Gurion regarded the desert. Overlooking the Ramon Crater, Ben-Gurion turned to his aids and told them that the crater should be filled with water. They replied that this cannot be done, to which Ben-Gurion asked: 'says who?' 'The experts,' was the reply. Ben-Gurion commented: 'then find me other experts!' This amusing story is told whenever Zionist use of scientific experts is discussed; it is, however, much more revealing in regards to Ben-Gurion's concept of the desert. Even the magnificent crater held no inherent beauty to him, and held no worth when left on its own.

Another evidence for Ben-Gurion's reluctance of the desert is the biblical verse he chose to place on his desk. All were committed to the transformation of the desert, non to simple attachment to it. Even when he dedicated a verse to his wife Pola, who joined him on his move to Sde-Boqer, he chose to accentuate her sacrifice:

> I remember thee, the grace of thy youth, the love of thy betrothal, when you followed me to the wilderness, to a barren land. *(Jeremiah, 2,1)*

Joining her husband in his desert life merited, according to Ben-Gurion, eternal thanks. In other words, living in the desert did not hold its own rewards, especially not for women.

Not all shared Ben-Gurion's views. In one of the stories told of the Palmah troops (in *Yalkut Hakzavim*, translatable to *A Package of Lies*), Ben-Gurion visited a unit cast in the Negev. He described his future vision and proclaimed that a forest will stand on the arid ground where they are now sitting. Sure, replied one of the young soldiers, and bears shall walk in that forest. His mockery of Ben-Gurion's words and vision was not only based on disbelief, but also on deeper criticism. The Palmah fighters had to train, fight, and practically live in the desert, and they learned to respect the beauty that it had to offer. Their songs, written by Haim Guri, Haim Hefer, and others, are a celebration of the Negev's enchanted mystique.

So, where Ben-Gurion saw *shmama*, the young soldiers offered an alternative gaze, that revealed a *midbar*. When they were released from the army, however, they went to live elsewhere. This is partly because, in the young state of Israel, the concept of the desert as *shmama* ruled supreme. Development towns were built in desert areas with the idea of not only developing their population, but also transforming the physical environment around them. The immigrants populating the development towns saw themselves as cast in the far periphery, and generally speaking, the magic of the desert was lost on them. A new movie describing life in these desolate towns is called '*To the End of the World and then Left*' (*Sof HaOlam Smola*). In the hardship and bitterness of their lives, it is small wonder that the incoming immigrants found little time to marvel at their surroundings. Anthropologists have showed that, as development towns searched for an identity that will extract them from their peripheral position, they created religious centers around saint veneration.[3] Their cultural history, rather than their physical environment, was the anchor around which they forged their Israeli identity.

In moving to the desert, Ben-Gurion wished to recenter Israel. His statement was not that the desert is already a center, but that pioneering zeal, his and others, can make it one. Few people, however, chose to follow him to the Negev, and even when he was Prime-Minister his government invested very little in Israeli south.

Two areas took precedence, and eventually determined the future of the Negev. The first was the Coastal Plane, developing intensively with the cost of land and housing constantly rising. 'Between Hadera and Gedera' became a phrase that captured the growing human density of the strip of land with which the Negev could hardly compete. The second was Judea and Samaria, occupied by Israel in the 1967 war. After the eruption of the Gush Emunim movement in the 1970s, and the election of consecutive right-wing governments, much investment went eastwards, and the Negev found itself again far from the hearts and minds of Israeli policy-makers.

Through the years, the Negev became the actual and metaphoric garbage can of Israel. All the institutions and social functions that were not wanted in more central areas were dumped in the seemingly endless planes of the far and unseen south. The Dimona nuclear plant is an obvious example, but so are army camps and training grounds, jails, and garbage storage places. The shmama meaning of the desert was enhanced, yet the Ben-Gurion narrational logic of developing and cultivating the shmama, became empty words, used manipulatively by politicians to claim the continuance of the founding father's legacy. Significantly, the desert lost the meaning that Ben-Gurion, and Zionism in general, wished to apply on it, as emptiness waiting to be salvaged. Israel's desert was emptiness waiting to be used and abused, a problematic back yard, with no defined future embedded on an inspiring national ethos.

As stated before, Ben-Gurion went to the desert in order to start its transformation, to cultivate the shmama. His namesake village, Midreshet Ben-Gurion, was created in accordance with his wishes to hold a cultural fortress in the middle of the great nowhere. His ambition to create an academic center, a combination of Oxford and Yavne, partly materialized—I say partly because very few academics (notice I did not say none) in the Desert Research Institute or in the Ben-Gurion Research Institute see themselves either as wise as the sages of Yavne or as world-esteemed like the scholars of Oxford.

Unlike Ben-Gurion, most residents of the Midrasha arrived with at least mixed feeling regarding the desert. Most follow their professional interests or their families, not necessarily their heart-felt desire to find a shmama and transform it into something else. Many feel a deep affinity to the desert, and appreciate what it has to offer, such as a refuge from the hectic city life, an opportunity for reflection, not to mention unique sights and fine weather. Transforming the desert would obliterate the very motivation that brought them to Midreshet Ben-Gurion in the first place. Many of today's Midrasha residents strongly endorse 'green' ideology, which in this context, ironically, means keeping the yellow and screening the green.

In other words, again ironically, many of the Negev residents are critical towards the image of the desert propagated by the famous founding father. It is a criticism based on experience and knowledge, a sense that the Ramon Crater is beautiful just as it is, and if there is a cause worth fighting for, it is its preservation rather than filling it with water, not to mention building a casino on its edge. The criticism is ambivalent, as most residents would certainly appreciate some development and investment, more people arriving to the Negev, and the south better connected to the center.

As the Midreshet Ben-Gurion residents conceptualize the desert, their desert, they see it concomitantly as a midbar and a shmama. They distance themselves from the noise, pollution, and density of the city into the midbar, represented and embodied by their village. But on the other hand, their village itself is a refuge from the harshness of the shmama around them. A certain way of understanding how the Midrasha builds on previous images of the desert and offers a new and rewarding way of advancing towards new options, is to see how this community, positioned between and betwixt, negotiates between various possibilities of constructing its existence. For example, what should the garden of a desert home look like?

Notes

1. On the various meanings of the desert in Zionist imagination, see: Yael Zerubavel, (2004), 223-236, "The desert as a mythical space and memory site in Hebrew culture."
2. Sharon Rotbard, 2005.
3. Eyal Ben-Ari and Yoram Bilu, (1997), 61-84, "Saint sanctuaries in Israeli development towns: On a mechanism of urban transformation."

Chapter 6

The Conquest of the Desert and the Settlement Ethos

Yael Zerubavel

"*The Conquest of the Desert*" was the official title of the first international exhibit that the State of Israel sponsored five years after its establishment. Prominent Israeli leaders, including President Yitzhak Ben-Zvi, Deputy Prime- Minister and Minister of Foreign Affairs, Moshe Sharett, other members of the Israeli Cabinet and the Knesset [the Israeli parliament], top government officials, heads of national agencies, and representatives of settlement organizations participated in the official opening in Jerusalem in September 22, 1953. The ceremonial event was also attended by foreign dignitaries and UN representatives as well as leaders of the various religious communities. Only three countries officially accepted Israel's invitation to take part in this fair, but the participation of five hundred companies from fourteen countries and four UN agencies contributed to its international scope.[1] The exhibit was designed to display the agricultural, technological, and scientific accomplishments of the young state that had recently emerged from a difficult war following the declaration of independence and was facing the challenge of building its foundations as well as accommodating the continuing influx of immigrants with scant resources. A bilingual Hebrew/English catalog issued for this event featured the national as well as international significance of the exhibit by including numerous greetings by state officials and participating organizations.[2]

The choice of defining the Zionist achievements in terms of 'conquering the desert' may seem surprising given the scope of the tasks facing the young state. Yet a close analysis of the symbolism attached to this concept reveals its broader meaning for modern Israeli society. Jews' long exile from the land was believed to have turned the ancient homeland into a symbolic desert. The Zionist mission of national renewal therefore aimed to counter the double negative impact of exile—on the people and on the land. Zionist ideology of the pioneering era thus perceived nationalism and the transformation of the landscape as historically and symbolically linked. As the lyrics of a popular song of the Zionist pioneering era articulate this symbolic connection, "we return to the land to build it and be rebuilt in it."[3]

President Yitzhak Ben-Zvi articulated Zionism's degenerative view of Jewish history[4] that regards Antiquity as a golden age and linked centuries of exile with the destruction of the landscape of the ancient homeland:

> During all the time that Israel lived on its land ... we find a picture of unceasing activity ..., our ancestors engaged in constructing wells and giant ponds ..., fashioned terraces on the hills and planted them with corn and orchards. They dug ditches and laid pipes, thus widening the areas under cultivation .... When the land was conquered by desert tribes, camel drivers, and shepherds, *the desert once more pushed back the cultivated land*. Settlement shrank and the wasteland expanded; for the Bedouin made his livelihood mainly in wild growth and not in cultivated plants. [Emphasis added, YZ].

Ben-Zvi defined the agenda of the young State of Israel as continuing the Zionist efforts to conquer the desert:

> Israel's future lies in intensive agriculture and industry. Our State cannot be satisfied with the sparse settlement that existed in the country at the time of the Ottoman regime.... It is up to us to save what has been destroyed, to extend the irrigated areas, to plant forests on the hills, to introduce new corps and to establish new industries. It is up to us to extract the utmost from the desert with modern working methods.[5]

Within this context, 'desert' does not refer to a specific geographical region identified as such by scientific criteria. Rather, it is a broader cultural category that marked the space outside of the Zionist settlement as 'desert' [*midbar*] or 'a barren landscape' [*shemama*]. The two terms, which were interchangeable in the framework of the settlement agenda, were often used as a pair [*midbar-shemama*] to highlight the underdeveloped character of the landscape.[6] The act of 'conquering the desert' thus indicated a profound transformation of the desolate landscape into a cultivated land that was part of the civilized Zionist space.

The Zionist settlers carried with them a romantic European image of the Promised Land as the biblical land of milk and honey, and earlier depictions of the country shifted between such over-idealized portrayals to grim depictions of the unfamiliar landscape.[7] The poets of the pioneering era articulated the difficulty in facing the Middle Eastern climate and landscape. Thus, Yitzhak Lamdan writes in his famous poem '*Masada*' that the modern encounter with the desert poses a threat for the survival not of Ishmael (as the Bible indicates) but rather to Abraham's Jewish descendants; while the poet Avraham Shlonsky alludes to the feeling of being uprooted from the European landscape and experiencing the suffocating heat in a desolate land.[8] Moshe Beilinson, the editor of the Socialist-Zionist newspaper *Davar*, goes further in defining the move from civilized Europe to the desolate land of Palestine as an act of great courage and personal sacrifice.[9]

This early view of the landscape as barren, alien, and foreboding was reproduced in the educational materials of the 1950s. Thus, the description of the landscape around Rishon Letsiyon, one of the First Aliyah's agricultural colonies, as "desolate, barren, mournful and still" and evoking emptiness and associations with death, was reprinted in a textbook for the fourth grade.[10] Similarly, educational brochures produced by the Jewish National Fund reprinted descriptions of settlers' accounts of their first encounters with the untamed landscape and efforts to 'conquer' it. Thus, a settler describes the "difficult and depressing feeling" he and his friends experienced at the first sight of the barren Judean mountains, being used to "the large open space, the green meadows, the limitless view of fields with crops" in the Ukraine, while another writer refers to "the wild landscape" that greeted the Zionist pioneers "with all its cruelty," remarking in conclusion: "Indeed, a desolate and neglected land." (JNF 1955:35, 47) Ben-Gurion's depiction of the landscape echoes the same view: "We inherited a desolate and destroyed country, and more than a half of its territory is an empty and gloomy desert. In the northern part too there is a lot of barren land, rocks, and sands."[11] Early Zionist films, such as *Oded the Wanderer*(1933), *Sabra* (1934), and *Avodah* (1935) showed images of the desert or of barren landscapes and the Zionist pioneers' efforts to find water sources, build settlements, and cultivate the land.[12]

The 'desert' was the territory surrounding the Hebrew Settlement [*Yishuv*] and Hebrew settlement narratives typically describe the hostile relations between them. The desolate landscape and the harsh conditions that the Zionist pioneers faced turned the settlement process into a long and difficult struggle against the desert environment. These antagonistic relations with the environment, its nature and inhabitants were often framed in military terms such as battle, assault, war, struggle, conquest, victory, and defeat. The "conquest of the desert" was therefore only one among a host of expressions that drew on the term "conquest" to address various aspects of the pioneers' settlement agenda: The "conquest of labor," the "conquest of guarding" and the "conquest of shepherding" referred to the goal of becoming agricultural and construction workers, guards, and shepherds employed by Hebrew settlements to make them self-reliant and avoid the employment of Arabs in these roles. Similarly, the challenge of draining of swamps in order to eliminate the risk of malaria and increase the cultivated land was identified as the "conquest of the swamps," and the construction of a port in Tel Aviv was hailed in a popular song as an act of conquest.[13] The "conquest of the mountain" expressed the agenda of building settlements in the mountains in the vicinity of Jerusalem and the Galilee, and cultivating their rocky landscape.[14] An overarching expression relating to "the struggle between the cultivated land and the desert"[15] articulated a similar conception of the relations between the settlement and the desert environment. The reference to the 'The Wall and the Stockade' [*homa umigdal*] method of founding new settlements as the "settlement assault"[16] points out the conflation of military strategies with settlement planning that was designed to expand the Zionist hold over the territory.

These concepts were particularly popular among members of the Second Aliyah and Third Aliyah, and were supported by other military concepts such as the 'people legion,' 'conquest groups,' and 'work battalions' to indicate groups that saw their calling in being mobilized to respond to acute needs of the settlement movement, following the model of soldiers called to duty.[17] A young-adult novel that became part of the canon of the Hebrew pioneering literature, Eliezer Smolly's *The Frontiermen*, tells the story of a Zionist pioneering family who moves by itself to a new frontier. When a visiting friend appeals to the father to leave the isolated farm post and join his friends' collective settlement for his family's safety, the man refuses to do so by evoking a soldier's obligation to continue his battle to the bitter end: "I'm a soldier, and the battle doesn't scare me. On the contrary, it adds to my courage—and [what's more,] we'll win."[18]

These proto-military concepts took hold within Zionist settlement rhetoric and were later incorporated into the Hebrew educational literature of the late pr-estate and early state periods, shaping and reinforcing the settlement ethos.

The prototypical settlement narrative also emphasizes the scarcity of resources as another dimension of the struggle for survival in the process of rebuilding the land. The lack of sufficient food and water, the recurrence of plagues and diseases as well as the Arabs' hostility posed immediate problems that threatened the settlers' well being. Hebrew educational literature of the prestate and early state periods featured the settlers' determination as a key to the Zionist success in spite of these problems and as a model for the young readers. Some narratives took this educational message further by instructing children of their obligation to carry out the pioneering mission and its spirit of courage, commitment and persistence. Other narratives presented a similar message by providing examples of children who took the lead in rescuing their settlements from a situation of hardship or an eminent danger. Thus, for example, children set out on their own to look for water sources and find a hidden spring in the desert, thus bringing critical help to their settlement.[19]

Every accomplishment in the process adds to the ultimate success in the prolonged struggle between the settlement and the desert. A JNF educational brochure presents the idea that "every portion of land from which stones are removed, every field that is plowed, implies a great achievement." (1955:37) Even setbacks are seen as temporary retreats only and as tests that eventually strengthen the settlers' resolve to go on. In the youth novel *The Frontiermen*, each chapter describes another episode or a challenge in the struggle to build the foundations and maintain the farm in the face of successive problems: lack of resources, natural disasters, mistakes, health issues, and growing tensions with the Arabs. As the story reveals, however, the slow progress and the setbacks serve to reinforce the settler family's vision and commitment. Toward the end of the story, when Arabs set the forest and the farm on fire, the settler watches the devastating scene of destruction of his longtime efforts. Engulfed by enormous despair he considers for a moment to take his own life, yet as his elder son joins him, the father-son team finds their old plow and begins to plow their land again. The story thus ends in a symbolic gesture of recovery that articulates the message of a total commitment to the settlement process in face of all odds.

The settler-protagonist in this novel, who had been a guard before he decided to settle down with his family and build a farm, reinforces the image of the Zionist pioneer as a settler-warrior. His words quoted above—"I'm a soldier, and the battle doesn't scare me"—disclose his readiness for sacrificing his life for his vision. The settler-warrior image, shaped in the early decades of the twentieth century, found its symbolic expression in the figure of Yosef Trumpeldor, the Zionist hero who had died in the defense of Tel Hai, a frontier Jewish settlement in Northern Galilee, in 1920. Trumpeldor's total commitment to the Zionist ethos of settlement and self-defense was articulated in his famous last words, "it is good to die for our country," and Tel Hai emerged as a myth of never abandoning a Jewish settlement during the prestate years and continued to be central to Israel of the early state period.[20]

The 'desert,' which marked the exterior boundary of the Jewish settlement, was clearly a dynamic category. Given the Jewish Settlement's continued expansion from the center toward the periphery during the prestate period, the Negev desert and the Galilee emerged as the primary frontiers and the focus of the settlement project during the 1940s–1950s.[21] Following the foundation of the state, then, the 'desert' became an interior frontier while the political and educational establishment enhanced the emphasis on the 'conquest of the desert' as a key component of Israeli national ideology. The selection of this theme as the title of the first international exhibit was therefore neither puzzling nor out of the ordinary within the context of the 1950s but rather emblematic of its prominence in Zionist national rhetoric.

The desert continued to be defined as the frontier of the settlement and the struggle against it as leading the way to Jewish national renewal. The linking of settlement and defense with the mobilization of the youth for this agenda led to the establishment of the *Nahal* framework combining military service with the settlement mission in 1949. Similarly, the *Gadna* high school youth were described as following the footsteps of the early pioneers in promoting the ethos of settlement, labor, and defense in their dedication to making the desert bloom.[22] Nonetheless, Ben-Gurion's call to youth to get mobilized to settle the Negev in the name of the Zionist pioneering spirit brought to a limited response.[23]

Hebrew curriculum continued to promote this message as an important part of its patriotic education that carries forward the pioneering spirit that had been shaped during the prestate period. Textbooks for primary schools published in the early state period thus included entire sections devoted to the theme of the conquest of the desert and its variations, addressing both the Zionist pioneers' settlement history and the challenges that the young state faced in this arena. Earlier texts, as was mentioned above, were incorporated into the 1950s textbooks and new literature articulating similar themes continued to be produced during this era. Textbooks extended the representation of the challenge of settling the Negev desert, including settlers' personal stories, poetry, fiction, and songs along with essays.[24]

A new generation of Hebrew writers depicted the challenge of confronting the desert. A children's play thus repeats the view of the barren landscape of the land and its association with exile: "For many years the mountains stood empty and barren... covered with only low bushes, dry thorns, and stones—plenty of stones...." The narrator comforts the young audience that "the place is sad these days but you should not become sad since the land is good and trees and beautiful flowers will grow there."[25] A teacher in another play tells his students: "Once the entire Negev was settled and populated, and there were many settlements, towns and villages filled with the people of Israel... Jews were exiled from their country, and the land became desolate, the desert dunes conquered the cultivated land. The water springs became dry as well. This situation lasted for many years, decades, centuries. And the entire environment turned into a desolate desert [*midbar-shemama*]. Until the time became ripe, and we the pioneers have returned to the land of our fathers...."[26] A popular song by a young song writer, Hayim Hefer, calls to the youth to go to the desert: "Go, go to the desert, the roads will lead [you]/... To the desert, a land without water,/ Ahoy, you, my land, we've returned to you" (JNF, 1953:212). A book titled *Man Subdues the Desert*, published in 1953, draws heavily on military rhetoric: "The desert is facing us as an enemy, and you cannot assault the enemy without knowing its nature and power. The desert conquered the Negev and didn't want to abandon it.... To study the enemy from a close range, to learn about the qualities of this region where the struggle would take place—this is the task that the scouts face." The text goes on to refer to the first three small settlements built in the Negev in 1943.[27] New works of fiction go on to describe those early settlement days of the 1940s, revealing the human drama of young settlers as they encounter successive difficulties and challenges.[28] A local paper of Be'er Sheva, the capital of the desert, describes the desolation and neglect that the Hebrew settlers had found in the Arab town and how they struggled with the sand, the heat, and the dust in their effort to transform the desert into a green spot (Yaacobi, 1955).

In the Zionist settlement discourse, making the desert bloom is a sacred goal that promotes national redemption. Working the land, plowing, seeding, and planting are thus more than practical steps toward 'the conquest of the desert, and green represents the achievement of victory in this battle. A popular Hebrew song that became part of the youth movement canon praises the plow, the hoe, and the hayfork that help create "a green flame" that lights up the landscape.[29] The settlement process included the tasks of laying the groundwork for the settlement, such as constructing new houses, paving roads, digging wells, advancing production, and developing technological skills and methods to improve its economic base. The glorification of mechanical instruments and machinery that contribute to the settlement and construction work was an important theme of early propaganda films (see, for example, the film *Avodah*) and recurs in Hebrew poems and songs.

A popular song thus glorifies the sprinkler and describes how the water pipes, the pump and the sprinkler now help bring water to the dry land of the desert and transform it. The battle theme is implied in the speaker's warning to the Negev desert that its days are numbered (Mohar, 1983). In the popular *The Road Song*, by the poet Natan Alterman, the short verses and the harsh sound of the Hebrew words reproduce a staccato-like rhythm of working with a hammer, and convey the power of the tools that the workers use in the road-paving process: "Hit hard, Hammer/ Rise up and plunge down/ Roads of concrete/ We stretch in the sands./ Wake up, wasteland,/ Your sentence is cut. / We are coming / To conquer you!" The speaker uses the plural first person to underscore the collective nature of this work: He and the hammer he uses, are only instruments within the larger scheme of the settlement project, and the process of road paving is an aspect of a broader battle between the settlement project and its war against the desert: "The asphalt pot is hot/ The hand is bloody./ This is how Man/ Combats the desert."[30] In a similar vein, the Hebrew novel *An Enterprise in the Desert*, published in the mid-1930s (Ever-Hadani, 1931), revolves around the heroic image of an engineer leading an effort to build an industry in the desert, near the Dead Sea. The novel describes the challenges, setbacks, and progress in bringing the message of construction to the desert. The theme of construction is also central to Avraham Shlonsky's poem *Against the Desert* (1965:311-17). The speaker turns to the camel, an icon of the desert, and warns it that it would be mobilized to carry concrete in service of construction, thus indicating its submission to the Zionist settlement process.

The JNF highlighted the immediate tasks it faced in the 1950s as part of the larger vision of "making the desert bloom." Its advertisement in the exhibit catalog specifies the goals to make the land of the mountains and the desert fit for agricultural production along with its forestation projects and the draining of swamps.[31] JNF Posters provide a visual interpretation of the meaning of 'victory' over the desert, displaying images of new and modern settlements, plowed fields, trees and flowers.

The same visual image of the conquest of the desert is presented in a Hebrew textbook in an illustration that juxtaposes the wild barren landscape filled with thorns and rocks with the landscape of rural landscape and a sprinkler spraying water on the cultivated ground (Ariel, Blich, and Persky, 1958:183).

Jewish National Fund Poster, 1953

Logo of *The Conquest of the Desert: An International Exhibition (1953)*

The logo of the 1953 state-sponsored exhibit depicts a worker's hand holding up a flower with a long and straight stem that has the design of a paved road. The logo conveys the idea that planting and road paving are two complementary aspects of settling the land and part of the Zionist plan to conquer the desert. The establishment of new settlements, the planting of young forests and orchards and working the fields were means to transform the desert landscape into the civilized Zionist space. Making the desert bloom, or turning it green, emerged as a source of national pride and as the embodiment of patriotic faith. Conversely, the featuring of barren landscapes ran the risk of being interpreted as an admission of defeat in the struggle against the desert, and hence subversive to the Zionist enterprise.[32]

'The conquest of the desert' was thus a major theme in Israeli culture of the prestate and early state periods and deeply rooted in Zionist collective memory and national ideology. It was selected as the major theme of the first international exhibit sponsored by the State of Israel because of its significance for the national secular Hebrew culture and its symbolic message of national recovery. It is therefore noteworthy that the sponsors of this event made a deliberate effort to extend its significance beyond the Israeli nationalistic framework and highlight its universalistic message. Thus, along with the representation of Zionist history and the new society's achievements in conquering the desert, the speakers and the catalog attempted to associate the theme with the strive for progress, a theme that represents the future trajectory of mankind. In his coverage of the opening event, the daily *Ha'aretz* reports that that President Ben-Zvi hailed the exhibit as highlighting the success of construction over destruction at a time of a global race of armament (1953, *Ha'aretz*, September 23,1). Deputy Prime-Minister and Minister of Foreign Affairs, Moshe Sharett, underscored the universal themes of "increasing sources of livelihood for the present population and bequeath a broader basis of existence to coming generations" and the importance of scientific research and capital investments for the cultivation of areas that were once considered permanently arid and uninhabitable. Furthermore, he stressed the role that the exhibit played in promoting international cooperation in the effort to achieve these goals (Sharett, 1953:1). Similarly, Dr. Avraham Granott, the Chairman of the Directorate of the Jewish National Fund, explained the title of the exhibit as referring to "man's incessant grappling with the powerful elements for survival and development," and addressed the theme of a constructive struggle for progress (JNF, 1953:90) The emphasis on scientific and technological achievements offered a broader interpretive framework that highlighted Israel's claim to represent the enlightened and civilized world in its efforts to colonize the desert. The words of A. G. Black, the Chief of Food and Agriculture Mission in Israel, echoed the military rhetoric of war between nature and culture, this time from a global perspective: "The *conquest* of the *unconquered* forces of nature has at all times been a challenge to the peoples of the earth." The goal, accordingly, is "to *harness* the Desert in the service of Mankind" [emphasis added, YZ] (JNF, 1953:16).

The emphasis on the universalistic message and the participation of international companies in this project were also used to obscure the political implications of holding the exhibit in Jerusalem, which Israel declared its capital. This may explain why countries that had not recognized this act refused to take part in the exhibit. A cartoon in the daily *Ma'ariv* features the boyish image of 'Srulik,' the iconic representation of Israel in cartoons, extending the flower-logo to Uncle Sam, who turns up his nose in a symbolic act of disapproval.

The United States of America bans the exhibit The Conquest of the Desert
Cartoon by Dosh (Kariel Gardosh), Ma'ariv: 1953 September 22:4

Only Finland, Belgium and Luxemburg officially took part in the exhibit, but Israel played it down by featuring 22 international flags at the entrance, including those of states that sent documentary films or had objects presented in the exhibit through Israeli firms. The participation of the United Nations was similarly highlighted both in the exhibit and in the catalog that featured greetings from UNESCO, the Food and Agriculture Organization, World Health Organization, International Labor Organization as well as World Meteorological Organization.

The broad message of the exhibit as representing civilization and its progress was further promoted through a variety of cultural events, ranging from musical and dance performances to various symposia (1953:29-31). The success of the exhibit in featuring Israel's achievements extended it well beyond 1953, turning it into a permanent exhibit sponsored by Israel's Center for Tourism, the Jewish National Fund, and the Jewish Agency. Although in reality the settlement of the desert, in its narrow sense, lagged behind this vision during those years, 'the conquest of the desert' remained a central theme in Israel's self-representation during the 1950s and provided the context for presenting much broader claims in terms of Zionism's past achievements and future aspirations.

Notes

1. "The Conquest of the Desert Exhibit Opens Today in Jerusalem," *Ma'ariv*, Sept. 22, 1953, 1 [Hebrew]; "The Conquest of the Desert Exhibit Opened," *Ha'aretz*, Sept. 23, 1953, 1-2 [Hebrew]; N. Urian, "We Go to the Exhibit," *Ma'ariv* Weekend Supplement, Oct. 2, 1953, 2 [Hebrew].
2. *The Conquest of the Desert: An International Exhibition* (a bilingual catalog). Jerusalem, 1953.
3. For a more extensive discussion of Zionist collective memory, see Yael Zerubavel (1995). On the centrality of the phrase "we return to the land to build it and be rebuilt in it" in Israeli literature and culture of the early settlement years, see Eric Zakim (2006:1-22).
4. On the decline narrative in collective memory, see Eviatar Zerubavel (2003: 16-18).
5. *The Conquest of the Desert: An International Exhibition* (1953:5-7) [English Section].
6. Note that the Hebrew title of the exhibit is "*kibbush ha-shemama*," which may be translated as the conquest of the barren land or the wilderness. *The Conquest of the Desert* is the official translation promoted by the sponsors. The interchangeability of these terms is apparent in the comparison of the Hebrew and the English sections of the catalog throughout.
7. Yaffa Berlovitz (1992, 1996); Yigal Zalmona (1998). In his study of Hebrew geography textbooks, Yoram Bargal (1993:137-46) attributes the transition from the romantic descriptions of the land of milk and honey to a desolate land to the post-World War I period.
8. Yizhak Lamdan (1971 and 1972:56-58). Avraham Shlonsky (1958).
9. Moshe Beilinson article marking the 25th anniversary of the Second Aliyah, which was published in *Davar* in spring 1929, reprinted (Naor, 1984:71-73). Naor also reprints the poet Rachel's angry critique of Beilinson's glorification of this act as sacrifice.
10. M. Meirovitch (1957:117).
11. David Ben-Gurion, reprinted in JNF, 1955: 6).
12. The film "*Oded the Wanderer,*" 1933, directed by Nathan Axelrod, was produced in Palestine; "*Sabra,*" directed by Alexander Ford, was a co-produced in Poland and Palestine in 1934; "*Avodah,*" directed by Helmer Lerski, was produced in Jerusalem in 1935. See also Ella Shohat (1989:15-53); Hillel Tryester (1935:187-217).
13. See the expression of "conquest of swamps" in Nahum Gavrieli, (1934:28); Y. Bargal, (1993:147-48); and "*The Port Song,*" the lyric of which was written by Lea Goldberg hailing the new Hebrew port (built in the late 1930s) is reprinted in Yoram Tehar-Lev and Mordechai Naor (1992:32-33).
14. See JNF (1955) and David Benvenisti (1959).
15. The Hebrew phrase "*milhemet ha-yeshimon veha-mizra*" was used as a title of Avraham Reifenberg (1950), and appears in a somewhat modified form in Moshe Sharet's Hebrew introduction in the exhibit catalog "*milhemet ha-yeshimon veha-midbar*" (*The Conquest of the Desert: An International Exhibition,* 2) (1953). Similar references to "war" can be found in Yisrael Betser(1937:131); and in Shlomo Kodesh (1972).
16. Elchanan Orren (1987).
17. For the use of these terms, see *The Guard Anthology* (1937); Yaacov Goldstein (1993). On the borrowing of military terms to connote success in colonizing the land see Gershon Shafir (1996:45-90) and Yoav Gerlber (2003).
18. Eliezer Smolly (1964:65), modified here to reflect more closely the original Hebrew (1975:57).

19. A children's play instructs children that they should not be intimidated by their young age, urging them to get mobilized to the task of making the desert bloom, and highlighting the importance of willpower in this process. See H. Tehar-Lev (1959); Rivka and Meir Benayahu (1955); Moshe Unger (no year: 63-69.) See also the important role of the children in the family's settlement saga in Smolly (1964).
20. For an extensive discussion of the Tel Hai myth and the image of Trumpeldor, see Zerubavel (1995:39-47, 84-95). See also David Tartakover (1991) for a prototypical story of the young pioneers' readiness to die in the face of a direct danger of malaria, in Shmuel Dayan (1958).
21. Bargal (1993:137-138, 150-151); Ruth Kark (2002); Mordechai Naor (1985); Dvorah Hacohen (1998).
22. B. Eytan (1958); Yitzhak Nishri (1985).
23. On David Ben-Gurion's criticism of the decline of the pioneering spirit and his personal commitment to the settlement of the Negev, dramatized by his joining the young kibbutz of Sde-Boqer in 1953, see Zeev Zahor (1994:195-210); Yehiam Weitz (1988); on his call to go to the Negev, see Ben-Gurion (1997:174-187).
24. See the source book, *The Negev: A Reader* (JNF, 1955) that presents an extensive selection of literary and scholarly sources on the desert. Other textbooks published in the 1950s include special sections devoted to the conquest of the desert. See, the section entitled "The Conquerors of the Desert" in Gabrieli and Avivi (1950:220-243); see also "The Conquest of the Desert" in Ariel, Blich, and Persky (1958).
25. Uriel Ofek (1959:11-12).
26. Unger, "*The Water Festival*" (no year). The story is told about a kibbutz in the Negev, and relates to the same era as the other texts quoted here.
27. Berta Hazan (1953); a section reprinted in *The Negev: A Reader* (1955:248). Note that in the quote the author uses the Hebrew term "midbar."
28. S. Yizhar (1945, reprinted 1978); Yonat and Alexander Sened, Kibbutz Revivim members published an autobiographical novel (1951, reprinted 1977).
29. The song "*Watch, Look, and See*". [Shuru, Habitu U-re'u] by Zalman Chen (1983, II:109).
30. According to Yoram Tehar-Lev and Mordechai Naor, Alterman's poem became a popular song of the pioneering era and although it was written in the 1930s addressing the experience of paving roads in Tel Aviv, the poem has been associated with the earlier, more romantic period of road paving in the Galilee by members of the Third Aliya's "labor battalions." See Tehar-Lev and Naor (1992:20-21).
31. See JNF Advertisement (no. 135) in the catalog (1953).
32. When the first full-length Hebrew film, "*Oded The Wanderer*" (1933), was issued, a critic protested that it displayed too much desolation. "Where is the renewed and constructive land of Israel? [...] the blossoming orchards, the sprinklers?" Quoted in Shohat, (1989:28). See also my article (2000).

Chapter 7

The Perception of the Four Winds

Gideon M. Kressel

Before and After Holocene

A common belief has it that people approach deserts and thus experience the view and life rhythm in them, rather than that deserts approach people and impose their conditions and rhythmic ordeals on them. Research has shown that both developments take place, are noticed, and leave measurable records. For people, experiencing life in deserts entails the crossing of borders that stretch along the fertile (precipitated) zone, which they do sometimes forcibly, but most often at will. The diffusion of desert conditions implies dispersal of aridity into previously fertile zones, a process that forces those human groups that cannot cope with the change to vacate in search of something better.

A change of climate that transformed fertile zones into arid ones was the essence of the Holocene (lit. warm era), beginning some 12,000 to 10,000 years ago. Prior to the Holocene, traumatically remembered, was the Alluvium, long years of rain and floods (*mabbul*) that decimated the numbers of living throughout the Northern Hemisphere ('the end of all flesh'). Legendary traditions have it that only one 'righteous man' and his family survived the ordeal. "Blameless in his generation, Noah walked with God" —The bible survivor of the flood (Genesis 6: 9). Other Noah-like figures are Utnapishtim of the Gilgamesh epos[1] and several others, less-known protagonists who were the heroic survivors of floods in their own areas (Frazer, 1890). That time when the present-day fertile areas spreading from Europe Eastward (the North) were flooded, the present-day deserts spreading Southwards enjoyed sufficient precipitation to make them rich with flora and fauna, thus facilitating human life. They were the blessed places on earth, which enabled the gathering of foodstuffs and hunting of small game to live on. The Bible has perpetuated the indelible impression left by the fortunate South in its narrative of Adam and Eve in 'Paradise' (Eden) which came to an abrupt end. The human race was then expelled out of it and forced to till the land to make a living. Climatic changes forced the animals to wander away and the human hunters and gatherers to follow them to the banks of standing water (lakes) or of the region's rivers. The 'Neolithic Revolution' implied for the first time production, rather than the gathering, of food.

Viewing the contemporary borders of arid districts as proofs of stability of the divide flanked by sown and desert lands since the week of creation is of course erroneous. Flint tools and other stone-age remnants scattered on the face of the Mid-Eastern deserts suggest that this space was thickly populated prior to the Neolithic Revolution. Archaeologists have learned to estimate the importance of pre-historic evidences beginning in the late 19th century, after centuries of poring over historic documents. Palaeontologists of the evolutionist schools, attentive to discoveries made by geologists and climatologists were the first to draw conclusions concerning stone-age cultures in today's wilderness.[2]

The Four Orientations after the Holocene

Once the land strip of the 30–20 degrees of altitude leading from the Sahara in the west to the Arabian Peninsula in the east turned into desert, the precipitated North got the image of the blessed land and the South was considered the cursed. In the Semitic languages an etymological connection exists between the names of the four winds: North, South, East, and West, and the names of the orientations forward, backward, right, and left. Until then 'left' in Arabic meant North (*Shmaal*); the traditional expression for the 'South" was 'right' (*Yaman*), which is also the name of the ancient kingdom on the edge of the Arabian peninsula, until today retained in the Hebrew word '*Teiman*.' Such a semantic pattern is cohesive only when one is facing East, with North to the left, South to the right and West at one's back.

Facing East endows the four cardinal points of the compass with significance for a worshipper of the sun, the moon, and the five planets—together 'the seven Wanderers.'[3] 'Rising' here is suggestive of birth or rebirth. Turning one's face eastwards to pray implies the quest for life or rejuvenation. Worshipping eastwards (and not westward where the horizon is also touched by the Wanderers) makes sense, because adoration of the moving celestial entities developed parallel to the humanization of the mythic lore in attributing to these bodies personal features. According to ancient mythology, the rising of these heavenly bodies symbolizes birth, and their setting – death. The cyclical rising and setting is suggestive of the resurrection of the dead, with east symbolizing the newborn and west the temporary passing.[4] The Hebrew phrase '*be-'arov yamav*' (literally 'at the evening of his days') refers to an old man, and equivalent expressions can be found in many languages.

Also in Arabic etymology, facing West means to go astray. One proverb makes the connection between going west and sacrificing one's social commitments as follows: Dishonesty (telling lies) likens the young man who went west, with the old man whose contemporaries passed away — that is, both are free from bonds of social commitments and tell any story they fancy.

The connection between south = right, and north = left is also imbued with a spiritual value, which comes to the fore in mythology and rites. The ritual preference of the right side as the provenance of purity, opposite the left which stands for defilement, is manifest to this day in the eating habits observed in certain oriental countries. The right hand is reserved for eating and forbidden in any connection with the toilet, and the left is used when attending to bodily functions and prohibited from handling food.[5] Inculcation of such habits is brought about by punitive methods, where a parent will slap the left hand of a child when his hand reaches out for the food. Allusions to the superiority of the right hand are numerous in the biblical context, as in Jacob's (Israel's) blessing of Ephraim and Manasseh; Israel stretched out his right hand and laid it on the head of Ephraim, who was the younger, and his left hand on the head of Manasseh, crossing his hands, (for Manasseh was the firstborn, Genesis 48: 11). "Your hand will find out all your enemies. Your right hand will find out those who hate you." (Psalm 21: 8)

In as long as South and Right stood for the blessed, the symbolic link evoked no question, but since the Holocene, when the South became the pole of aridity (hence a curse), the cleavage between the civilized (*khadara*) and wilderness grew throughout the Middle East. The power that acts in separating the functions of the hands and the two sides of the body as expressions of purity and its opposite, is integrated in the myths of North and South. South (right) stood for order, justice, and success; in opposition to North (left), which represented evil, the unexpected, the distorted, and the hapless.[6] The right stands for the path to life, and the left for the woe of death. Whoever breaches the accord, e.g. reaches for food with his left hand, realizes that he is risking his life.

Similar traditions have survived, and although they are today interpreted in rational terms with no resonance of their heathen origin, the fact is that the origin of these traditions harks back to idolatry,[7] and cannot be dismissed. We may not have the answer to the question as to what the impetus was to discontinue, first within a small circle of Hebrews, and finally to abolish the direction of prayer towards the East. It may have happened on grounds of a moral imperative, since heathen rituals go along with human sacrifice. The notion of the immorality of human sacrifice that has been ascribed to Abraham Ben Terah, the first to hold the knife when he desisted from sacrificing his son, slowly gained a foothold in these cultural areas.[8]

How the change in the direction of the prayer came about is more palpable. First, an alternative myth was put forward which connotes a change in the image of the deity by detaching him from idolatry of the sun, the moon, and the five planets: Mercury, Venus, Mars, Jupiter, and Saturn. Simultaneously, a new ritual foundation was laid and new sanctuaries for worshipping were founded, which retain the abstract presence of the master of the Seven. Later, and respectively the direction of prayer was adjusted anew towards the dwelling of the spirit of God. With the Israelites creating the Tabernacle, a focus of orientation was established, which was still movable. King Solomon's Holy Temple superseded the Tabernacle to become a magnetic pole for worshippers. This was clearly no simple transition, and it didn't take place overnight. Still in the year 593 AC, at the time of the prophets, Ezekiel arrived at the Holy Temple that had existed for several centuries and saw worshippers, their backs towards the temple, facing the rising sun.[9] Ezekiel attests that the rite of child sacrifice (to Moloch or Baal) continued (in the Valley of Hinnom, Ezekial, 16:20-21) up to his time.

More than a millennium after the Jewish Temple was built, the consecration of the Ka'aba in Arabia determined a new direction to face at prayer. Believers north of Mecca face the desert as they pray, and no longer the rising orient. Indiscernibly, on setting that the prayers should look forward (*Iqball*) towards Mecca, a connection is born between South (and desert) and the sanctified. Most Muslim pilgrims go southward on visiting Mecca. "Going forward," meaning to follow an orthodox (literary meaning 'the straight way') track, leads southward.

Conflicting Orientations

Increasingly warming, the Holocene exacerbated the living conditions in the south of the Middle East, while the once dreadful North, the source of threatening waves of chill and onslaughts of nomadic tribes of the Central Asian steppes,[10] relaxed. Now it was the inhabitants of the desertifying South who broke out into the fertile zones. Intending mainly to extend Arab (etymologically the people of the Arava = steppes) inroads into the sedentary zones, they brought their native desert to their vanquished Others.[11]

Contrary to the social climate at the river basins of the Euphrates, the Tigris, and the Nile basins, where people for the first time began to domesticate fruit trees and crops, and "eat bread by the sweat of their brow" the frustrated desert shepherds and their claims of extortion spoke ill of their lands of origin and changed the attitude towards the South from positive to negative. Desertification remained an ongoing process, leaving these areas barren and they came to symbolize a curse.

A proverb known among Bedouin in the Arabian Peninsula says: "Go North for a year and don't go South for even one day" (*Shamel sana' wa-la tqabel yawm*).[12] Depletion of the land led to a decline in population, but in spite of the exodus, life did not improve for those who remained, and who had to fight each other for their livelihood. Scarcity and internecine wars embittered their lives, which again led to a change in attitude towards the South. The traditional conception of historic

Yemen as a haven of abundance ('*Arabia Felix*') faded before the exuberance of Damascus and Baghdad. Imperceptibly, a new word for South found its way into Arabic: '*Janub.*' Derived from the same root are *jaaneb* (pl. *Jawaaneb*), meaning edge or side, and also sideways and negligently; *Janab* meaning far off; and *Janaaba* contamination. *Ajnaba* is to be in a state of defilation; *ajnabi* (*pl. ajaaneb*) is foreign, suspicious, removed, and in fact all that related once to the North.

With Islam adopting Mecca as its holy center, bestowing heavenly distinction to the faithful, travel to this place seemingly contradicted the course of benediction. However, the southern position of Mecca was interpreted in the eyes of the believer as a crucial part of the blessing to the pilgrim. The enervating travel from north to south is necessary for the liminality[13] and the purification, which prepares the pilgrim for the blessing from Mecca. Like the oasis that draws its grace from the wilderness around, so is the divine grace for the pilgrim (*Haj* pl. *Hujaaj*) which rewards him for afflicting himself with the ordeal of the way.

Further north, in Asia and Europe, from the beginning of the Common Era and until the Industrial Revolution, the North remained viewed as gloomy and threatening.[14] "The land of snow and night" clearly alludes to the underworld. Negative connotations tainting the North are evident in the indigenous folklore, uttering longing for the warmth of the sun-rays of the South. Parallel to the barren desert belts emerging in the south, a milder climate was underway towards north. Glaciers melted and facilitated conditions for human life beyond the tundra and further into the Arctic zone, contingent on humans' improving adaptation for survival to harness natural conditions to their benefit.

Towards the end of the middle-ages, the northern peoples surpassed the South in technology and economic achievements. From here on stems the change in the popular view that now tends to attribute creative thinking to the cold North and a laid-back easy-going way of life to the hot South. The nature of Northmen is believed to be forged by the chill that renders them composed, even-tempered, thinking types, whereas their southern counterparts are perceived as slack, daydreaming, and at the same time impulsive, sanguine, and vengeful. Where previously Northmen were considered coarse and wild, gradually the repute of the South passes, and the North is now credited to be the cradle of all inventions, of human development, and modernity. Later, physical attributes, color of skin and hair, characteristic of the northern man (the white man), became linked to proficiency and orderliness, opposite the colors of a southern type, which suggest thoughtless spontaneity.

Dissonance, the Compromise, and the Resonance

If deserts are dryness and the divinity engulfed by desert, then an introspective problem is posited to the believer (*Torah*, the law of Moses, from Sinai). "Semites had no half-tones in their register of vision," wrote T. E. Lawrence (1926 [1921]: 36). "They were a people of primary colors, or rather of black and white, who saw the world always in contour. They were a dogmatic people, despising doubt. There were assertions, not arguments, so they required a prophet to set them forth. The prophets' life were after a pattern. Their birth set them in crowded places. An unintelligible passionate yearning drove them out into the desert, where they lived a greater or lesser time in meditation and physical abandonment; and thence they returned with their imagined message articulate, to preach it to their former and now doubting associates"[15] (Lawrence, 1926:37).

Dissonance felt in town-life propels prophets to deserts whence they return feeling better, purified, carrying with them a resonance. Out of a double negation comes the rectifying message. Righteous, all right, but after a short time, usually forty days, they come out of it. Being rejected out of deserts confirms that this is not the place to live. Social living creates the problems they do, not in the desert, in town, and now they (the prophets) are back in town to teach that two wrongs make a right? An axiom is a compromise, saying that living aloof and alone in the desert can purify (though not everyone of course), but on returning from the desert, a righteous person's (prophet's) speech resounds like the voice of God.

"The essence of the desert" said Lawrence (1926) "was the lonely moving individual, the son of the road, apart from the world as in the grave." The desert cannot be ignored; it parts the settled population of the Fertile Crescent from the Nile basin and in that way obliges people to cross it under duress. The desert forges the essence of the customary that is both Arabic and Muslim and brings out good qualities like hospitality, frugality, modesty and bravery (Ibn Khaldun, 1967:249 ff).

Prosperity, Progress and bettering the image of the East

The economic decline of Yemen, the corner and the pearl of the South, which until the Arab conquest was renowned for its wealth and enjoyed the Latin name *Arabia Felix* demonstrates another aspect of what we have been discussing. 'Felicity' is related to wealth and stability. Geographic conditions contributed to this area's wellbeing, contrasting with its far-stretching, withering surroundings. The trade route between India and Europe, passing through Yemen, contributed further to her wealth. But the demand for her products declined. Moreover, as the Arab settled the southern and eastern shores of the Mediterranean and conquered the trade routes to Europe, Yemen lost its prestige and thus the last thread of communication between South and the source of bounty was severed.

Once during a drought the children of Israel left the Levant to survive the famine and reached Egypt. There the economic stability was the result of an agriculture based on irrigation and independent of the rainy season. In this case redemption was found in a movement westwards. Today, thanks to the discovery of crude oil, the economic salvation for the Middle-Eastern countries is in Iran, Iraq, Kuwait, Qatar, Abu-Dhabi, Bahrain and the Saudi Coast, all in the East.

Centuries of industrial revolution with its resulting social, economic, political and military development would widen the gap to the Middle East. The economic decline of the East, relatively and absolutely, deepened the dependence of the Middle East on Western products, loans and contributions. Imperialism and colonization ensued, and although the colonial period didn't last long, it left its impact. The national independence that the countries of the area since gained, did not heal ailments, on the contrary, it has worsened them. Gradually the area lost its attractiveness even in the eyes of the natives themselves, who emigrate in growing numbers towards north and west, to Europe and the New World. In other words emigration from the desert lands to Europe is a mental move westwards.[16]

The connection between the four corners of the globe and value preference, for good and for bad, has changed course through the times and it has been demonstrated that its direction can be overturned following heavenly influence, religious impetus or, lately, economic progress. It has also been demonstrated that a developed economy in itself is not sufficient. The oil fields discovered under the desert sands in the Middle East—leading to relative wealth for some millions and incredible wealth for a few—did not lead to a broadening of the mind. People from the countries with the greatest wealth, Saudi Arabia and Kuwait and the other emirates of oil seek vacations "there" (in Western Europe and in the US) and if possible permanent settlement. The West is criticized for its permissiveness, but it is sought after as the place to recuperate.

It is freedom that sets the direction for those leaving their countries of origin, seeking their fortunes far away. Like the Afro-Americans in the US who during the second half of the 19th century fled northwards, away from the enslaving South, following the hope of liberation, the West has become a magic symbol, although the globe is known to be round and no absolute West exists. Flocking Northwards to Canada and the US from Central and South America is a search for the redeeming spirit of the West. People emigrate to improve their economic lot, but even more so to get a taste of civic freedom in these countries, not known in their countries of origin. Northwest today stands as a model for imitation and envy; forgotten is the fact that this was not always the direction of progress. Freedom and quality of life did not always dwell in these areas.

One exception worth singling out in this context, is the case of Singapore in the equatorial Far East. Singapore is hailed as a model of perfection, unique in its kind, which is relevant to our discussion. Like the other 'Asian Tigers,' countries within the culture area of Confucius, the social-economic success of Singapore is stunning, and this country has long since caught up with the West. Singapore stands for diligence, and this in a climate that is not conducive to an industrious effort. The hot and humid equatorial temperatures have been blamed for the backwardness of the South and the motivation to break away from these areas. The success of the North has been ascribed to the temperate climate, which supposedly stimulates activity. Nevertheless here we find success in a completely unexpected location, with no natural resources, but with diligence, initiative and creativity.

We find a maximal investment in social wellbeing, education and culture, all without compromising the private space of the individual. Social involvement in family planning, restricting the birthrate to one or two children per family—all this has turned Singapore, in the eyes of its neighbors, into a model state, situated right on the Equator.

Insight, ability to obtain capital, and a flair for making it useful can make the difference.

Notes

1 On the ancestral reminiscence of Utnapishtim who found eternal life, who is the prototype of Noah. See Scharf-Kluger (1991).

2. For this wealth of paleological findings, see Marks (1976, 1977).

3 The 'wanderers' are the seven heavenly bodies that daily rise and set: sun, Moon, Mars, Mercury, Jupiter, Venus and Saturn. Ever on the move (animated) they become sacred and their number, seven, became a widely accepted unit of time, i.e., a week.

4 e.g., in English context, to go West means to die.

5 On the pre-eminence of the right hand and the connection of death and the left hand, see Hertz, (1960).

6 See e.g., "sinister", which connotes adverse, bad, dishonest, oblique, etc.

7 The seven wanderers were rated by their light force. The smallest of them, Saturn (=Cronos=Shabtai) was placed as the seventh, which stands for Saturn's-day (Saturday) or Shabbat. Since the distancing from idolatry, the Hebrew interpretation has it that Shabbat means cease from labor.

8 The monotheist perceptions struggled foremost against the pagan custom of human sacrifices.

9 "And he brought me into the inner court of the house of the Lord, And behold, at the entrance of the temple of the Lord, between the porch and the altar, were about twenty-five men, with their backs to the temple of the Lord, and their faces towards the east, worshiping the sun toward the east" Ezekiel 8:16.

10 "Out of the North an evil shall break force." Jer. 1: 14.

11 cf. Ibn Khaldun 1967 [1382].

12 See also T. E. Lawrence 1935 [1926]: 35.

13 cf. V. W. Turner 1969; 1975; 1979.

14 Yearning for the South, the lands of warmth, is uttered in poems and songs.

15 See also Borg 1999: 121-151.

16 Paradox; Morocco's Atlantic shore is West of Britain. Going from Morocco Mediterranean shore to the shore of Spain, France or Italy are a move from South to North and from West to East.

PART III

INSPIRATION

Recorded here are some of the ways that the desert around the Midrasha has inspired religion and the work of photographers, painters, theater directors, writers, sculptors, and poets who live in the community. There is also an account, by a linguist, of the color categories used by the Bedouin to describe their livestock.

Chapter 8

Religion and the Desert

Yigal Granot

Anthropology teaches us that people's environment shapes their culture. Accordingly beliefs endorsed by inhabitants of deserts differ from those endorsed by residents of fertile zones.

Archaeology of prehistoric eras shows that beginning with the Holocene era (8,000–12,000 BCE) harsh climatic changes have occurred that brought about aridity to the previously precipitated desert belt stretching from the Atlantic Ocean through the Sahara in the West to Iran and Pakistan in the East. Forced away from dry lands, humans began then to domesticate flora and till plots on precipitated lands.

Change of maintenance patterns affected anew the ancient (pastoralists) configurations of creed. The phenomena of nature that amazed nomadic pastoralists, gave vent to belief in an almighty force that shaped the landscape diversely. Archaeological surveys in the Negev (Negev, 1986) indicate that ancient worshipping rituals were performed by people confronting stelae. Stelae were taken as the deity's home (Gen. 28; 18-22). Standing, vertical pillars were dedicated to the idea of masculine God (Nevo, 1991). Plump, round, and squat rocks stood for the feminine deity. Erected pillars are commonplace in the desert. The oldest one observed, from the 11th millennium BCE (before the common era), was found in Rosh Zin (Zin Head).

Stelae represent the strength, stability, and durability that are the qualities of life lacking in deserts. Such sturdy rocks inspire one to deal with all daily risk-taking moves (cf. Eliad, 1963). Rude stelae answered as well the non-iconolatry principle we find in the Bible (*Deuteronomy* 4:16). No attempts were made to shape the stones or sculpture them.

Ancestor cults persisted in the area throughout the Bronze Age. Tombstones or heaps of stones (*tumuli*, in Arabic *rujma* pl. *rujam*)[1] are placed on top of mountains. High mountains were sacred, perceived as belonging to the sphere of Gods. The spirits of the dead were used to connect their pleading descendents to the realm of the Almighty. An echo of this belief (*Deuteronomy* 12:2) is the name '*El-shadai*,' meaning 'God of the mountain.' '*Shadau*' in Acadian means a mountain. Placing *tumuli* on hilltops reinforced the trend to reach and affect, on praying, the divinity in its highness (*Genesis* 31: 45-48). In addition, Negev archaeologists find worshipping arrangements like stone walls; the longest of which is the K-line that relates Mount Rammon and Mount Rommem, some 4.6 kilometers long. Its assumed role was an open temple. Until this day Bedouin are seen praying at square arrangements of stones (Israel and Nahlieli, 1998:146).

Many feminine monuments were located in Near Eastern deserts, most of them face East, the place of the rising heavenly bodies, viz., the orientation of birth (contrary 'to going West,' i.e., to set, that is to die). Stone arrangements represented the three Goddesses, daughters of the pre-Islamic Allah. Records of ancient rock paintings found in the Negev also indicate religious matters: deification of hunted animals (mainly wild goats) to importune, via the deity, the hunter's further success. Fertility, assigned to an encounter of feminine and masculine symbols, is worshipped to assure the siring of children.

Later, painted symbols were developed to represent letters and words. Nomadic pastoralists, who were also engaged in cross-desert trade, came in touch with sedentary peoples who had developed the knowledge of writing.

Literate Bedouin were among the first converts to Christianity, then to Islam, which did not eradicate paganism, and remnants of the ancient beliefs survived through the ages. As much as desert winter-pasture enabled pastoralism, there were rarely permanent settlements.

First remnants of permanent, rural settlements appear in the Northern Negev beginning in the 6th millennium BCE. The prevalent worshipping pattern in these sites was one of idolatry; clay and stone sculptures of human figurines indicate a transition away from the imagery of herding in the steppes. Arad, a town State in the North Eastern part of the Negev, reached its acme during the early Bronze Age (3050–2300 BCE). Excavations made in Tel-Arad and in small villages in its vicinity discovered a mix of farming and shepherding, as well as traces of religion. A stelea was found in the temple of the late Judaic era (the 7th century BCE) that resembles the Holy Temple in Jerusalem.

Houses of Negev villages during the Middle Bronze Age 1 (2300–2000 BCE) were constructed round as in the desert, and square after the style of building in the north. The guess is that their inhabitants were partly settled, hence they were not completely nomadic, but continued to subsist mainly on stock breeding, which brought them into contact with villagers living in the settled North. Their pattern of burial has been continuously of the *tumuli* kind. Next to them (as along the Yeruham ridge) can be found altars for sacrificing animals in commemoration of the dead. The sites are planned facing east or west, i.e., the rising and the setting sun. The K-line faces the point of the sinking sun on the year's longest day, which resembles the Egyptian practice at that time.

During the Late Bronze Age (2000–1200 BCE) or the Canaanite era, there is evidence of a transition of desert tribes to sedentary ways of life. Adopting agriculture and moving away from shepherding entails various readjustments, but still the worshipping patterns were slow to change. The introduction of farming to arid lands did not promote the spread of feminine cults to the area of masculine creed. Evidence has been found in the Hurvat Halukim in the Negev Highland, where Judaic pottery was discovered alongside a Negev piece, indicating the encounter of the two traditions did not affect one another in this place.

In the 4th century BCE the Nabateans spread their influence over a vast area, including the Negev. Although they based their economy on trade of incense and spices (not on livestock breeding), the Nabateans exhibited a different brand of desert culture. At its center there was sun worship. A pantheon of deities was headed by a male god named *Dushra* ('the one of Mount Se'ir') and a female Goddess named *Uzzah* (power-full). The two were represented by small, abstract stone symbols that were carried along in traders' caravans and worshipped whenever they reached a place to stop (Wenning, 2001; Patrich, 2002).

The Nabatean cult and its pantheon had a formative influence on Islam. For example, the *Ka'aba* (black stone of Mecca), which at one time related for sanctification to the Nabatean prime deity *Hobal*, became central in the pilgrims' ritual honoring Allah.

Also the rules that command believers to abstain from the drinking of wine began among the Nabateans, and were later endorsed by Islam. On the other hand, morning sacrifices to the sun, or the burial habits practiced by the Nabateans were modified, and later on discarded, when they intensified commercial contacts with Jews, Greeks, and Romans, and were influenced by their customs. Inhibitions in regards to construction of stone homes came to an end when their trade dwindled, once the Romans captured the shores of the Mediterranean Sea and the Nabateans became more settled.

Subordination to the Roman Empire at first reinforced the cult of the Nabateans' necropolis. After a first burial, the bones of the dead were collected and brought to be interred in public sites. These sites were later taken over by the living. When forced to minimize the caravan way of life and settle for good, they employed their necropolises for dwelling.

The Nabatean customs were influenced by pagan Greek, then Rome, and later, Christian Byzantium. Churches appeared in due time bedecked with crosses, as well as signs of ancient traditions of pagans and herders' deities, as can be observed in ruins of the Negev towns Avdat, Shivtah, Khalassa, Nizanah, Mamshit and Ruhebba.

Christianity, tolerant as it was, did not reign for long, and once the Arab Muslims occupied the land, the Nabateans, it seems, were assimilated among them and disappear from history's arena. For two to three centuries, between the 7th and the 9th centuries, archaeologists have revealed evidence of a Mosque and a Church coexisting in one and the same place, as in Shivtah. Also a Mosque coexisting with a pagan temple, as in the 'lost city'at Halukim intersection, where the names of Muhammad, Moses, and Jesus are mentioned alongside pagan stelae, and where *tumuli* burial cites were in use.

Millennia of moderate paganism mixed with monotheism of various sorts shaped the form of Islam in the Negev continuously until the modern era. Negev Bedouin who practice Islam are now more orthodox than they ever were, but to this day their customs are saturated with pagan traditions.

Note

1. See Bar-Zvi, Abu-Rbi'a and Kressel 1998.

Chapter 9

The Arts

Photographs by Arie Bar Lev

Photographs by Arie Bar Lev are included in two books about the desert (*Amar*, no date, and *Bar Lev*, c. 1998). We reproduce here seven photos of the area around the Midrasha.

A view of the canyon looking down from the plateau where the Midrasha is located.

The pond at the spring that supplied water for the area in olden times.

Yosef Amar, the promoter and publisher of the book on *Desert Poetry* (no date) notes that "the photos of Arie Bar Lev, impressive and inflaming, are esthetic and sensitive first-class experiences, among them rises outbursts of the eternal nature melody, of the works of creation." In the book on *Desert Illusions* it is recorded that Arie Bar Lev's "color photographs are an expression of his fascination with nature in the Negev."

The wadi flooded by winter rains.

Camels

Ibex

Vultures

Chelmoniot

Angels in the Desert

A visit with Binah Kahana by Gretel Rieber (2004)

Translated from the German by Wolfgang Motzafi-Haller

> In the desert live the angels and the demons. But to the mortal eye they can only appear in material shape. So, you walk through the desert and suddenly a small sand whirl arises, and a small sand-hose circles you once, twice, and shoots up into the sky. And you think you just saw a sand-hose. This you think the first time, the second time, and at the third time the sand-hose is already somewhat familiar. Suddenly you realize who she actually is: She is a small child of the desert. She is still small but one day she will be a heavy sandstorm, and then you will retreat from her back into the house and you will shut all windows and from behind a window you will see how the air turns yellow and red, from the sand, and the sun turns blue. The sun gives off a blue light through this red sand and the light that strikes the ground is violet. There you see what's meant with ultraviolet. At once you realize, it was a small angel, whom you have seen, and she greets you with this violet sunray that draws a checked pattern in front of your feet. You become friends. She returns again, and again the blue sun sends her greetings. Always again the violet light, always again returns the sandstorm.

Binah Kahana, who, in her house in the Midrasha tells me about the meetings with the angels and demons of the desert, wears today a white silk dress, that casually falls to her feet and that covers her arms; light-pink silk roses decorate the taken up seam.

The blond woman with green eyes and open smile has an almost saucy Berliner accent that does not seem to suit her, just as the dress doesn't suit her work.

Bhina Kahana is a painter, and her work clothes are not jeans but in summer pastel colored silk dresses, in winter often gold-brown velvet dresses with numerous delicate, silk-rose adorned petticoats. The garments she designs, sews, and decorates by herself. Also her jewelry from gold and pearls she makes from her own designs. Her unusual working dress surprises me. Her work is prayer, divine service, she says. Painting is for her a congregation with spirituality, with the biblical persons who she paints. For Moses, Solomon, and David, and for this congregation she wants to be dressed appropriately.

The prevailing bright colors of the large format paintings that are displayed on the walls of the very sparingly furnished house in the Midrasha, in the Israeli Negev desert, seem to fade into infinity. Desert colors, sand colors: Gold, a very bright yellow, a light stone green, the pale blue of the wintry Negev sky, much into reddish leaning ochre, bright orange, light pink, also sparingly put Chinese red, yellowish white, Umbra, traces of violet, some black. At first sight almost abstract forms, but then one realizes that here with astonishing power, stories are being told, biblical stories.

The Berlin-born painter lives in the south of Israel with her husband, the writer Chaim Noll. In the past few years, she has, here in the desert, rediscovered her Jewish roots.

As a child I was named Sabine and I grew up in the house of a very well known artist. My father saw his task in illustrating the world literature and creating them in bibliophile books. He was a very educated man, who devoted all his life to the art of illustration of most diverse techniques. He had a great library. From childhood on I busied myself with books and particularly with images. That was my life: My father sat at a writing table and worked, and I lay on my belly in his office — in front of me, picture books. And I looked at these images and when I had a question, I could ask him. He answered them in great detail. He talked about the stories to which these pictures belonged, about the Bible, about the legends, about the ancient Greeks, about the ancient Romans. Yes, that was my childhood.

Sabine lived with her parents and three siblings in East-Berlin; there she also met her future husband, Chaim Noll.

I have studied art in East-Berlin, at the Art Academy in Weissensee, which has a very turbulent and interesting history, in which many members of the resistance against the Nazis were teachers – which was however later on regulated by the communists – and therefore, especially for the very gifted students, it was often very hard to work freely. But I got there a profound education.

Then I started to study for a Masters degree at the academy of the arts. For three years I was able to concentrate in my work, receiving a small stipend. I was also able to travel extensively. I was often and for long periods in Russia, in Moscow and Petersburg. There I met the most interesting artists and I gathered important artistic experiences. I was in Yugoslavia, Poland, in Czechoslovakia — in all these countries that were accessible then.

But when I perfected my knowledge and abilities, I discovered that this world would be too limiting for me. This was one of the reasons why my family, my husband, I and our two children finally left East Berlin.

I thought I was going to a country that did not exist. I felt that I was leaving this world and going to the next one. After our plane landed and I stepped into the hall in Tel Aviv, there stood my son to welcome us. Only at that moment could I believe that this country exists. First we went north, to a kibbutz. Later we graduated in Netanya from an Ulpan, a language school. I then attended a nine-month long conversion course. The conversion to Judaism was a great spiritual adventure, and it caused a deep transformation in my art. The rabbis were so fair to alert us in advance; it's going to be a difficult psychological process. And they were right. It was very, very exhausting but it also was happy and wonderful. It is difficult to understand Israel coming from Europe. This small country finds itself in the center of events, in the center of worldwide tension zones. One experiences this personally. It throws one in all sorts of conflicts. I have lived here in this country now for almost ten years and I have not left it since I arrived, that's how much I am still captivated by the process of return, the recovering of the spirituality, which I experience here.

Binah Kahana, as she is called today with her Hebrew name, and her husband both devoted themselves increasingly towards biblical and religious subjects. Binah Kahana paints scenes out of Exodus, paints Moses who beats water out of rock, the young David, and women of the Bible.

> I wait for the inspiration. I wait until I am called. Therefore I always must be ready like our father Abraham was. When god called upon him he said: "Here I am." And then I start working. And when its time, I don't care anymore about time. Out here in the desert there is very little distraction. One can work in an unusual concentration. The colors changed, the subjects changed. I occupy myself here with the desert and with man in the desert, with our forefathers and-mothers, and with the Bedouin who now live here. I love them as our relatives who stayed, like we once were, Nomads who move through the desert with their tents and herds. That's how the Hebrews lived here thousands of years ago, here in this area. The landscape that surrounds me is biblical ground. One can learn from the Bedouin quite practical things as well, how one has to live here, starting with that one must not be rushed in the desert, to the custom to drink tea with green mint all day long.

Binah Kahana does not exhibit currently nor does she sell besides from time to time to faithful collectors who have valued her work for a long time. Currently she turned towards a new field: the traditional technique to punch, to hammer, and to enamel finely rolled gold plates and thus creating jewelry, cups and small wall pictures.

For almost eight years the couple have lived in the Midrasha in the Negev, at the rim of the overwhelming Wadi Zin, a bizarre landscape of bare mountains, in the evening light wrinkled beige-pinkish velvet of stone. The Zin wilderness is a biblical location, often mentioned in the five books of Moses, as a site of the wandering Israelites. Some years ago Ben-Gurion, the founder of the new Israeli state, lived at Sde-Boqer. He is also buried here, very close to Binahs house. Binah Kahana tells:

> About two years after our arrival in Israel we traveled one early morning to the Midrasha, and here I experienced my first morning in the desert. This is an unmatched experience. One essentially understands only here what the sun, the earth, and human beings really are. I went to the grave of Ben-Gurion and I caressed the stones and told Chaim, what a fortune it would be if one could live here. Earlier we traveled a lot but from here we simply don't get away any longer. This place captivates. It is a magic place. One does not realize how time passes. In this place one works from morning till evening. One day challenges the next. Here is essentially paradise, I often think. But one does not see it, it is concealed in invisibility. If you watch the mountains attentively for a long time one detects in them all shapes and colors of the world – the sources of architecture, of painting, of science. Here, city-folks, born in Berlin, turn into children of the desert.

Now, the two are building their own house. The first private house of their restless lives, that here, in Israel has found its base.

(Reprinted with permission.)

Theater

Ofra Faiman

When asked about the special experience one can expect from working on theater in the desert, after 26 years in the Israeli Negev Desert, I have chosen to point out various angles of looking at it, that have made it worthwhile and significant for me:

a. The desert as a source of inspiration.
b. The need to overcome isolation.
c. The need to create as an occupation.
d. The urge to excel despite the isolation.
e. The informality in working relations as a symptomatic phenomenon.
f. The ability of putting things in a different perspective.

I shall relate to these points, but not as titles.

I first came to the desert, to live in a small community, following my husband. He had just accepted the task of setting up a solar energy research group as a part of the Blaustein Institute for Desert Research in the Midrasha. Occasionally, I like to tease him by quoting the biblical verse: "Follow me to the desert, to a barren land," which is known around here as Ben-Gurion's humorous command to his wife some years earlier, when she had to follow him to live in the desert, upon his leaving the government and joining our neighboring Kibbutz Sde-Boqer.

My mission did not necessarily touch upon studying the meaning of deserts, neither was it associated with improving living conditions in deserts, as was that of most of the scientists who came here. Rather, having been nourished on art, theater and education, I decided very soon after settling the two of us and our three young children, to devote my creative ability to offering educational work to the community, which was in a transitional state at that time: People were leaving and new ones arriving—a bit like a train station.

I volunteered to teach drama and theater at the newly created high-school for environmental education, and at the same time, began my lengthy attempts to convince the founders of the school about the importance of teaching theater studies as an integral part of the curriculum at that particular kind of school. I also suggested to the local regional council that I start a theater group for adults, to include our community but also members of neighboring kibbutzim and villages. This would be a constructive step to breaking the isolation and separation between the various settlements.

So now I had two groups: a group of teenage high school students and a colorful group of adults, both were excited about working in theater. On the other end of the line, there was a large local community with a high level of expectation for theatrical performances at an accepted level.

An interesting episode comes to mind that illustrates the excitement some people shared thanks to our existence. It was one of the first theatrical adventures of our "Adult Theater Group of the Negev"—a temporary name (temporary for almost 20 years!)

The first play we presented at a local theater hall, (which until then had only hosted theater and dance groups from the center of the country—at a very high cost!) was called *Kinneret, Kinneret*, by the late Israeli poet and playwright, Nathan Alterman. The play dealt with the life of a group of pioneers who had settled in the Jordan Valley at the beginning of the 20th century at a place they called Kinneret. This is the Hebrew name for the Sea of Galilee, and an appropriate title for the first commune that settled not far from that lake. This same commune was later to found the first kibbutz, which was called Degania. The simple task of living for this group of young people, in that particular place and at that particular time, was an almost impossible mission. They were newcomers to the country, mostly from Europe. Furthermore they were mainly students who had left their university studies in order to fulfill a dream of coming to live in a true homeland. They suffered from malaria and a difficult climate, from Arab gangs who violently objected to their presence in the land, and from the extremely hard physical work they had to perform on difficult soil. It was nothing like what they were used to.

Their dream of creating a new society with high moral values and aspirations for social change was worn down by the stubborn land, by the deaths of close friends—either from malaria or from their Arab neighbors, and by the extremely hard work. Those who survived became heroes, and created an ideal model for the new pioneers who were to follow them from Europe to the new land. Alterman's play is based on these historical facts, but it also tries to shed light on the dramatic and human aspects of conflicts between various members, and upon the conflicts, dilemmas and personal involvements within the group. There was love, jealousy, a mysterious death, conflicts with parents, with the general working conditions, and so on.

People in our theater group were able to identify with the characters in the play from their first reading. Although they belong to a different generation of *Kibbutzniks* most of our actors were also pioneers who had settled around the late 1940s in a different part of the then barren land—the isolated Negev Desert. To some extent, of course, the Negev is still barren, if not as isolated as it once was.

In order to develop the right feeling towards the place and the living conditions that our characters in the play had to face, we spent a weekend in Kinneret (i.e. in the ruins of what remains from the old settlement). We actually lived over there, in the same old building that the Kinneret people had lived in. We slept on that same floor, and cooked together like the heroes of our play. We relived the experience of pioneering in that part of the country almost 80 years previously. This helped a lot, later in rehearsals, and became apparent from the way people acted their parts.

I remember a comment made by one of the founding members of Kibbutz Revivim (in whose theater hall we used to perform, and from where most of the group members came) after our first night. He said that watching the play the night before had moved him very much because it had brought back to him the kind of feelings they, the veterans of the Kibbutz, had all experienced when the first fruits of their kibbutz orchard had first appeared on the table in their communal dining hall, so many years back! It was the same feeling of achievement and success against all odds. This comment touched us deeply and connected all of us with the original motivation we had had when we began working on that play.

The identification with Genesis and with pioneering touched us all, as it was relevant to most of us, reminding us of the first days of our own settling in the Negev Desert. People started relating and sharing experiences from the 'good old days' and asking themselves about changes in their life style and about how far the dream of the beginners had progressed thus far.

For me personally, it was the closure of a circle in my own family saga. There was something there that evoked in me a kind of longing for my parents' and grandparents' pioneering days in our newly-born country. It was a part of the family stories I grew up with, and which connected me with my newly experienced desert adventure. It somehow helped me in understanding my fantasy and fascination with Genesis and pioneering, my attraction to living in the desert, and possibly even my reason for having chosen this particular play for our group.

Another incident comes to mind, that happened during the first year of our life here. The kibbutz next door approached me with the offer to help them write and direct their 25th anniversary play. I started my investigation with a period of intensive historical reading and searching in the kibbutz archive. There was a lot to learn about the kibbutz past, the connection between the present and the past of these people who had settled along the wadi's low soft mountains, resting like enormous elephant legs from time immemorial. It was important for me to work with the members of our neighboring kibbutz in order to create a contact between two settlements who are isolated neighbors. Also, I nurtured particularly warm feelings towards these people who had chosen the same desert that we chose to live in 25 years later!

Wadi Zin is one of the places where the biblical Children of Israel wandered during the 40 years on their journey to the Promised Land. It is vast, strong, bare, embracing and, at the same time, inviting. I take my daily walks, down to the wadi, to the Ein-Avdat water spring, always starting at this point, where the kibbutz pioneers wove their dream. It is as if I want to pay a tribute to the founders of Sde-Boqer for having chosen such a magnificent spot for us to live in. It has historical and traditional meanings for me, but also spiritual ones having to do with the relationship between me and the God who created this place and invited me to come and live here and enjoy its bareness and fullness at the same time. I consider it a true privilege.

When working with my high-school students on the play *Antigone* by Sophocles, I tried to use my spiritual relationship with the desert as my personal interpretation for the play. Rehearsals took place outdoors. My original intention was to perform it in the open air, in a nearby natural amphitheater. However, for reasons I need not go into, the performance of the play for the school community had to take place in an indoor space, against all my expectations.

The concept for the play belongs to the desert: The Greek palace was in the desert; the body of Polynices, Antigone's brother, was left unburied in the desert for the play's heroine to discover; Antigone wants to escape to the desert; she is punished and left alone to die in the desert; etc.

The openness of space in our desert left room for the actors to experiment with behavior in an unknown space, and enabled us also to create another era, where deserts were vaster and had a more significant effect on human beings. The students were asked to collect desert stones as props for exploration; to grind flour and spices; to sharpen tools as weapons and as musical instruments. At a certain moment we brought masks into our work, for the chorus. They were made by the students themselves, from local desert sand.

For me as the director and educator, there was always the danger of losing control and of allowing diffusion into our work. When students became carried away, they wandered off, but somehow, at the end of the day, the parts and the story brought everybody back together. The need to express themselves in a stylized, unrealistic, manner was rendered easier by working in that open and surrealistic desert space that was all around us. This we achieved through our desert work. The performance was a great success in the community, and also elsewhere.

At an annual national youth theater contest, this performance received very high marks and approval. Soon after, we were invited to perform it for other schools as well. This helped us bring our students out of their isolation—as Sde-Boqer is far from the center of the country. It brought them together with other students from other schools in the country. This was not a policy thought about in advance, but in the event, the point became clear, how important it was for the students to make contact outside of their far-out-of-the-way school.

This brings me to another point I mentioned above, isolation in the desert. I believe that being far away from where 'the action' is commonly held to be, stimulates our basic need to excel.

Being excellent in their attitude to work, helped our students in coming out of this remote and unknown place, and connecting in a very special way with themselves and with their spectators elsewhere. They knew they were going to be 'very good' with their 'very special performance.' But in fact they were excellent: better than when performing at home, and also they became 'that special group from the desert!' Other people became interested in them, and in the place they came from. This opened doors for new acquaintances and friendships.

During all these years I have lived in the desert, I have come across many artists, writers and poets who love to come here and create. When speaking to some of them, you realize they often come here to the desert seeking a place of refuge. All they want is to escape from the routine demands of their life and sit somewhere where they can do their artistic work peacefully without being interrupted. Most of them take off just a short period of time in the desert, to pause from the flow of their lives, and then return home, where there are more people, more noise, and more disturbances.

For me, living and creating in the desert are a need and a way of life. In a certain way it is a means for putting things in perspective. It gives you a different sense of proportion. When, each morning, you face this eternal view of rocks, mountains, sandy passes toward the distant horizon, frolicking ibex, sparse vegetation—this emptiness invites you to start something. You then realize everything else is just a passing event. Life in front of our desert dwarfs the unhappiness around us, and gives it another dimension of time and space. It gives us freedom to create and helps us avoid commercialism. I enjoy this freedom and my creativity is enriched by it.

Literature

Chaim Noll

Chaim Noll asks[1]: Is the desert—hidden from our unbelieving senses—the Garden of Eden? At least, desert is a place, giving man back what he has lost in our days: his task and meaning. Re-discovering the significance of human life turns out to be essential in a time of destruction of nature, ruin of the resources, crises and catastrophes, and subsequently the growing self-contempt of man. This self-contempt, the feeling that human life is bereft of content, the estrangement, loneliness, anxiety of modern man threatens the survival of the entire creation. One of these threats is the desert.

In view of that, a new start in the desert is—beyond all practical reasons—a kind of therapy. Being exposed to the pressure of unrestrained elements, of wilderness, of permanent challenge, man has to summon up all his strength neglected by the spoils of a misled civilization. Man in the desert has to live up to a higher level of power of resistance, spiritual fulfillment, inner balance. The desert seems to have healing powers. As, some decades ago, the English poet Wystan H. Auden wrote in the prophetic lines: "In the desert of the heart let the healing fountain start."[2]

In the ambivalence of the desert—as an end of the line and a starting point in one—we find one of the eternal cycles of human life. The apparent end turns out to be the beginning, the decline bears the revival. Man in the empty desert is a beginner, he develops a more optimistic, future-orientated psychological structure than man in crowded, contaminated conurbation. It makes a big difference for self-esteem and mental health, whether a person is living in a lethargic mass, caught in dangerous, destructive habits, manipulated by media, mislead by populist politicians, or acting as a moving power at a place still to discover.

For years I have been occupied with the literature of the desert. I read and research the literary evidence of human struggle and self-assertion throughout centuries and millennia. One of the old expressions for desert is *arava*, an Aramaic word meaning frontier or border zone, a place, a situation, were the spheres meet and mix with each other. *Arava* means—aside of other derivations as *aravi*, the Arab, or *erev*, the dusk—also confusion or bewilderment, a state of mind often caused by the wilderness, the desert. Indeed, at first glance desert is confusing. The confusion can go into both directions: enchantment or fright. Both are based on alienation, for what is alien enchants or frightens much more than what is our own. For instance, the first sight of a landscape never seen before. The awareness of vast expanse and emptiness. The abolition of all we are accustomed to. A totally different proportion between human ego and environment. The apparent loss of our own dimension.

In the desert, there is too much or too little of all. Too less visible difference, variety, support for the searching eye, too much secrecy, mystery, premonition hidden in obscurity. An incessant expanse spreads in front of our eye throwing us out of the framework of the parceled out pictures. Mercilessly the infinite is indicated, just in front of us, nevertheless out of reach. In drastic immediacy a world shows up, alien, evasive, not submitted to our will. Here, in the unlimited, we feel our limits more than elsewhere. The first glance causes confusion, perhaps a kind of recognition, the strange idea of having been here before. Not everyone—this my experience with first time visitors—is happy about it. There are people who withdraw instantly, turn at the heel and flee.

Deserts, as literature from all periods of human history let us know, are places of death, of exile, scenes of decline and catastrophes of civilizations. The Greek-Roman view on desert was predominantly negative. Typical for its general abhorrence is the portrayal of desert and desert people in Herodotos' novellas or, half a millennium later, in Roman poet Lucanus' famous opus *Pharsalia* or *De Bello civilii* (The Civil War).[4] The imprint of the Greek-Roman picture on European literature is still dominant in the Middle Ages or later, although the negative picture had its reasons mainly in political actualities and the geo-strategic situation of the Alexandrian and Roman Empires, both bordering to and always threatened by fiercely fighting desert peoples.[5]

In fact, the desert border zones were the cradles of civilization. The development of higher cultures had its beginning in frontier areas where desert and water meet, along the Nile, in the deltas of Mesopotamia, at the Mediterranean coast of Canaan. Writing and science, religion and law of the later Western empires have their origins here. The Middle Eastern deserts were the scene of survival and tradition, of written records and the early awareness of man's historicity. Because of the ups and downs they had witnessed in the political play between the great powers of old, the desert peoples gained the knowledge of transitoriness and doom, of hope and new beginning. In the soil of these cultures rests the mystery of our Becoming.

Beside the political danger that the Greeks and Romans felt from the old desert cultures as Egypt, Judea or Persia, there was always a hard pressure of the so-called 'Eastern religions' on Greek-Roman polytheism. This was evident in numerous complaints of Roman historians and philosophers, and finally, with the triumph of Christianity, victorious. The Christians, a religious sect coming from the Judean desert, proved right the forebodings of Roman authors looking suspiciously on the province Judea as a deadly peril for Roman religion, lifestyle and *mos maiorum*, despite Judea's decline at this time, leading to its political breakdown in the year 70. *Victi victoribus leges deterunt*, Roman philosopher Seneca truly predicted, "In the end the victims will conquer the victors."

The break between the Jews and their own offspring, the Christians, coinciding—about the third century—with the integration of Christianity into the system of rule of the Roman Empire, brought Christian literature under the influence of Roman thought habits, so that its pictures of the desert—despite Jesus being born and always living in a desert environment—became ambivalent. We find evidence of the growing indifference, even abhorrence towards the topic desert in pre-mediaeval texts about pilgrimage to the Holy Land, Crusaders' poetry, novels about traveling heroes or Christian chronicles.[6] With the European humanism of the renaissance area the attitude towards desert changed again, especially when the study of Hebrew language and the original Hebrew Bible became customary among European thinkers of the time. An example is John Milton's famous poem *Paradise Lost*, published in 1667, with its astonishing geographic knowledge and detailed descriptions of the Biblical deserts, written by an author who never in his lifetime had been in a desert and was already blind when the poem was recorded. With the Enlightenment and the modern age, especially in the 18th and 19th century, desert became a subject of growing interest in European literature, even of longing and romanticism.

There have always been—and will probably ever be—lovers of the desert as well as those who feel an inexplicable dislike. The question is, whether we discern in the meeting of the extreme something productive or not, a potential of unusual possibilities, a symbiosis of the still undiscovered with our human capacity to discover. Nowhere is appearance as deceptive as in the desert. Nowhere is the clandestine, the invisible, of such influence. The barren soil turns out to be a vessel of unexpected surprise. A little water only, and the sand, lying moribund in the heat, is covered with delicate green, crowded with micro organisms and insects. In the shadow of these tiny plants and creeping lichens the sprouts of bigger and stronger ones will thrive. Man becomes the catalyst, the connecting entity, a crypto-creative instance.

Being conscious of that function is the exact opposite to the feeling of human life being bereft of content, of being minute and insignificant that spreads among people in modern Western societies. Man in the desert discovers his own importance. This sensational process is a leitmotif of world literature: from the *Mosaic Books* to Saint-Exupery's memories *Wind, Sand and Stars;* from Sumerian cuneiform tablets to Thomas Mann's *Joseph* novels; from the report of Egyptian traveler Sinuhe in the 20th century before Christ to T. S. Eliot's poem *The Waste Land* in the 20th century of Christian era. Desert literature spans a period of about five millennia. It became the subject of my interest and analysis, my contribution to modern desert research. I know that I am a pioneer in this field. In the stereotypes of the West, of academic literary science in Europe or North America, desert is still considered a topic out of the world.

The parable of the desert, its being *All-in-Nothing, Infinite-in-One*, the *World in a Grain of Sand*, was expressed by 18th century English poet William Blake in his poem *Auguries of Innocence* in four eternal lines:

> To see a World in a Grain of Sand
> And a Heaven in a Wild Flower
> Hold Infinity in the palm of your hand
> And Eternity in an hour

It is the metaphor of a world still to discover, a world of nothing but sand and sky, brought into formula by an author who never saw a desert with his own eyes. Also, the German writer Wilhelm Hauff, English poet John Milton or French novelist Honoré de Balzac (to whom we owe the most beautiful descriptions of the desert, the deepest declarations of love for this landscape), had never been there. Hauff pictured Middle Eastern deserts in his fairy-tales *Die Karawane* (The Caravan), published 1825; Milton in his translations of Hebrew Psalms and his own poems in the second half of the 17th century; and Balzac in his novella *Une passion dans le desert* (A Passion in the Desert) of 1830, with descriptions so accurate and impressive that one cannot help ask from which source the authors got it. It is a mysterious phenomenon, showing that we all contemplate the desert, know about it from olden times, and that desert is a part of the essential, eternal program of man.

Desert research is an optimistic science, generally supposing that the human race will survive the catastrophes and challenges of our troubled days, generally in accordance with the Biblical promise given immediately after the flood to Noah and his sons, the promise of being spared of another overall cataclysm destroying mankind as a whole.[7] In accordance as well with the predictions of the psalms and the prophets about a future blooming of the desert, especially in the land of Israel, inhabited again by its ancient owners, the Hebrews or Jews.

The concept of human revival in the desert is an alternative to the usual Western thought habits and life-style of our days. It means the reduction of standards to the approximate nothing, a readiness to work without having demands in advance, a new start completely out of us and the given actualities of Creation. This approach to life is just the opposite of what is usual today: egotism, consumption, wastefulness. It seems, just the waste land helps to cure man from waste. From perilous habits leading to the self-destruction of our civilization.

Modern desert research was developed especially in Israel and the United States, countries with recent settlement in arid landscapes triumphing over apparently overwhelming hardships. Desert regions are those with the highest growth of populace in North-America,[8] a fact proving that there are not only the well-known negative reasons as flight, exile or expulsion, but also positive motives to turn to the desert. In the United States desert life became fashionable during the last decade among those who look out for an alternative lifestyle. It may become a trend in other countries, too: frustrated inhabitants of big towns discover the desert's clean air, open spaces and relatively affordable housing.

He who exposes himself to the extreme climate, the dangers and hardships of desert life, is a believer in the possibilities of man. Most of my neighbors in the academic community of the Midrasha in the Negev are natural scientists and non-religious, but they are different from most secular people today: they believe in the future. They assume there will be no general disaster finishing man's history on earth, and it will be worthwhile to prepare new programs of revival for hard times to come. When human history moves in cycles, as the Talmud states, desert is the cyclic return of a situation man has already gone through and managed successfully. We only have to remember. We have to look back to the knowledge of former man, to the oldest sources of wisdom and literature. To those that came from the desert.

Notes:

1. This is a selection of the last one third of a lecture by Chaim Noll at the Hebrew University of Jerusalem, The Franz Rosenzweig Research Center, May 7th, 2006. A German version was published in Noll (2006).
2. Auden, W. H. In Memory of W. B. Yeats, quoted from: W. Schmiele, 1985:306.
3. Evenari, M. (1982).
4. cf. Chaim Noll (2000), Die Wüste als literarischer Topos von der Bibel bis zur Moderne (The Desert as a Topic of Literature from Biblical to Modern Times), Lecture Series, Ben-Gurion University of the Negev, Be'er Sheva.
5. The Persians, a desert realm, were among the permanent enemies of the Greek, later the Roman Empire. A people with a desert background also the Phoenicians/Carthaginians, Rome's arch foe for centuries. Also North African desert princes became threatening, for instance the infamous Yoghurta. First century C. E. was dominated by increasing tensions in and influence by the province Judea. Altogether, from a geo-strategic point of view, deserts were the problematic, dangerous frontier zones of the Rome-centered ancient world.

6. The literature of the late ancient world did generally not picture wild landscapes, as v. Humboldt noticed („Den Griechen und Römern… schien fast allein das gemächlich Bewohnbare anziehend in der Landschaft, nicht, was wir wild und romantisch nennen"), cf. Friedlaender's, 1922 . Burckhardt (1928) noticed that this lack of interest was typical for European mediaeval literature as well.
7. Genesis 8, 21, and 22
8. American statistics, quoted by Time (October 2005), give the following numbers: growth of populace during the last decade: in desert state Arizona 53%, Nevada even 87%.

Sculpture

Ezra Orion

Powerful formation forces dated to the last 5 million years (pliocene and pleistocene) forged the mountainous plaits of the ground, lifted the southern part of the Sinai and deepened the whole of the Dead Sea. Geo-sculpturing as such is a continuous process, to this very moment. The kinds of living species of flora and fauna that evolved here ever since the last tectonic elevation, the withdrawal of the sea shore, and the growing continental aridity. Climatic fluctuations have gradually changed these species with the preference given to the aridity-fit. Natural selection where adaptation to acute desert conditions gave the preference to those species who survived. Some hundreds of specimens of Pistachio and Red Tamarisk on the chains of the Negev and Sinai mountains give evidence of the once wetter conditions that prevailed here still some 1,000 years ago.

The Presence of Mankind in the Negev Highland

The earliest remains of living human beings in this part of the world are dated to approximately 100,000 years ago. These were groups of hunters and food gatherers whose social array was of small bands. They produced flint tools, which they gradually improved so as to better serve their usefulness. What is now arid used to enjoy precipitation typical of a Mediterranean climate, and the surface of the earth was covered with woods that provided game.

About 10,000 years ago, man domesticated wheat and barley and agriculture began. At that time also livestock were domesticated and pasturing began to replace the dependence on wild game. Mankind took a more active role in the adjustment to the changing climatic conditions. Continuous improvement of culture is evident in the transition of human home-sites in the Negev and the Sinai through the milestones of the neolithic, bronze-age, ancient Judaic, Nabatean-Roman-Byzantine and the ancient Arabic. The process leading from nomadic to sedentary life and from rural settlement to urban life were always mixed with one another.

Desert group, iron
(Photograph by Wolfgang Motzafi-Haller)

Knowing that we are a link in a chain of events, in a continuous development implies that whatever we do is an inseparable part of a bundle of processes. So I feel. How can I express my feelings or utter it in a manner that engages my soul, hence transfer its excitement to others?

Note:

From Ezra Orion's book *Sculpturing: A Bundle of Processes* (1995: 57-62). This excerpt describes what is on his mind facing the Negev Plateau, where he lives. Thought of the micro universe that surrounds him shapes his aspiration to leave his imprint on it that would sign the passing moment in the long process. Reflect the impact that the environment leaves on an artist's soul.

Sculpture

Dalia Meiri

Landscape sculpture, for me, is a dialogue between the landscape and myself—between all the factors with which the area supplies me: the shape of the relief, the rock, the wildlife and vegetation—and my personal wishes. I never approach a project ready prepared for the first meeting with the area. The initial stage is the impression through experience, sense, which leads to the learning of the various components. In the wake of this, associations arise, memories and connections, bringing ideas. This all comes together through spending time in the area. I do not believe in ideas which come from hasty acquaintanceship. I do my work with the open landscape in stages, where between these stages I check the proportions and the ratios on site. The forming plan is solely one of ideas and many things change during the actual work on site. Elements move from here or there. Certain pieces become unnecessary and I decide not to use them, in contrast to those I add or change. As my elements gradually become additions to the landscape my standpoint becomes sharper regarding their relationship to the landscape near and far. From which direction and how will the viewer approach them and what visual journey I want him to experience on his way to the sculpture and inside it.

The landscape is big wide and very strong in its forms and I have no pretensions to compete with it, not in size or form. Nor do I have the aspiration to imitate its complexity of configuration and material. My place on the landscape is the human dimension—that niche in nature which leaves room for man, for the order and logic specific to him. As man changed the landscape with his physical, natural powers, the traces he left were in correct proportion to his size and importance in nature. Today, when the means are, as it were, unlimited: bulldozers split the mountains, tractor shovels carry huge rocks and cranes place them in every possible position, I feel bound to be careful and not to exaggerate with force. There is no reason to run away from technology to romantic use of ancient tools but care must taken that the golem does not turn against its master.

Every landscape has materials which make it unique. In order to integrate properly into the substance and shade of the area I try to use local materials. Every locality has traces and remains left by man throughout history. When I learn about the area this is also an important part of understanding its unique characteristics. The understanding mans' confrontation with the landscape through the ages for the functional needs of housing and staying alive and for ritual needs, this also helps me to clarify for myself what my place in the landscape can be.

The desert is an extreme landscape. The sparse earth and vegetation leave it in geological nakedness and exposes to me the strong inner skeleton which builds it from within and styles its outer shape. The *Machtesh* (crater) exposes to us the layers of hard rock, inclined, arching, the remains of an anticline which emptied from within. In contrast to many landscapes typified by their horizontal, laid, lines containing natural or artificial perpendicular elements – the Machtesh is special in its strong diagonals which create a feeling of insecurity and excitement of danger.

I chose diagonals as the central motif for my work on the rim of Machtesh Ramon. The work is built of a number of groups of flat rocks, each characterized in a different order and in a sense that it is trying to stimulate. Two fundamental issues arise in the different groups. On the one hand the diagonal rocks leaning like the sides of the Machtesh create a feeling of falling and imbalance and on the other hand the rocks leaning and meeting like huge tents and creating human balance. The work is divided as follows: one series of structures, taller, long in length along the Machtesh cliff and creating a continuous line parallel to it. Other series are laid in lines perpendicular to the cliff and create continuity of space in the direction of the approach road.

The last series is arranged parallel to the first and restricts the whole layout with very low structures almost level with the ground.

Note:

From Meiri (1998:42).

Poetry

Elaine Solowey

Desert Song

The music is the patient wind

The iron silence of the hills

The mute expectant emptiness

The shattered wheel of stars

The strange grey hush that comes with rain

The brittle flowers of the dust

Blue glowing dusk when darkness falls

The chill that touches bone

And vanishes from sun-touched lands

In silver heat, a shimmering

Of sand that coils in serpent's tracks

Across the valley floor

Sand Music

Coming fiercely from the south

Like voices of a chorus

A litany of scorching wind

A paean of sand and fire

Strums the ridges like a harp

Bows dunes like a viol

Sets the iron in my walls

Humming like a lyre

Shivers cymbals of flat glass

Mourns in cracks and corners

Strikes the fence posts

Like small gongs

Plucks the barbed wires

Snare drum rolls across plowed fields

Flutes among the date palms

A whisper on the dry bleached plain

A trumpet in the wadi

Sandstorm I

The mountains dim and blur
All colors fail the curve of the horiozon
In waves of hissing smoke
The air sings and the sands
Begin to blow
The sun glows in a haze
Of burning grey
A blaze of sullen amber
The wind's voice
Is a river
Among stones

Sandstorm II

Seen through sweat sting in the eyes
Like tawny silk a ripple
Dune and hill
Change with the rush
Of a wind like heated metal

The mountain scoured away
The sky scratched to dull pewter
The sun fades to a haze
On the battered grey horizon

All the known is unfamiliar
Every landmark alien
I am lost in my own garden
Under trees bent by the wind

Poetry

Arie Issar

People of the desert

Such are the people of the rocky desert,
such are the folks of the parched land
who descend at sunrise into the dry gorge
to look for a spring for a source of water,
ascend at sunset, thirsty, worn out
and in their eyes the flash of rebellion.

Such are the people of the rocky desert,
such are the folks of the parched land
who defy the commandment of their idols
disobey the orders of their priests.

Such are the people of the rocky desert
such are the folks of the parched land
who hit the rock with their hammers
who force the stone to bring out water
to save their kin from famine and starvation,
their flocks from drought and death.

Such are the people of the rocky desert
such are the folks of the parched land
who lead their clans over non-trodden trails
towards a new land to be conquered,
towards a new god still to be created.

Question marks

Crying crows tore black scraps
from the blue transparency
enfolding the cliffs of the gorge of Zin
challenging the proud serenity of the desert rocks
walls and towers of thundering silence.

Crying crows painted black scornful question marks
on vistas feigning knowledge
of secrets of eternal chaos
of secrets of infinite desolation.

And a wanderer gathered a few hours of light
into his satchel of wondering
to carry with him during the hours of dusk
during the hours of gloom and souls
to illumine the darkness of the caves
as the certainty of the sun dies out
as the perplexity of the years of the nebulas
slowly, slowly encompasses existence.

The face of a rock

There is nothing more in the face of a rock
than a rock
and nothing more in the spring of water
than water
and in the whisper of the wind
nothing more than wind
and in the colors of sunset
surely just another sunset
and in a man
just a human being
which is a rock
and a spring of water
and a whispering wind
and a breathtaking
unique colorful... sunset.

Bedouin poetry from the Negev

Translated by Alexander Borg

These vernacular Arabic poems were originally recorded from native poets and reciters in the sixties and seventies in the Negev desert in southern Israel by Mr. Sasson Bar-Zvi, an outstanding connoisseur of Bedouin lore. They were subsequently made available to the Arabist, Professor Alexander Borg of the Ben-Gurion University who transcribed them in phonetic script and translated them into English.

I

A poem of vengeance

nār al-ḥatab tíniṭfi u nār galbi dawām,
waḷḷa ya ʿamm layy taḥt al-arδ̣ iʿδ̣ām
ḥalaft ma ʾartāḥ wala athanna min manām
ḥatta ʾağla l-ʿār u ʾasidd ad-damm bid-damm,
ḥatta ʾağīb aθ-θār u ma ʾašūf frūḥ u ʿār.
al-yamīn yirmīh u ʾana bi kull māli ʾafnīh.
ya nğīb aθ-θār u niδbaḥ ʾaʿādīna
ya nmūt u nδ̣all ʿa-bakrat ʾabīna
u nutruk aθ-θār la xālig al-lēl w-an-nhār.

A wood fire goes out but the flame in my heart endures.
By Jove, my friend, bones [call out] to me from beneath the earth.
I swore I'd neither rest nor indulge in sleep
Until I wiped out shame, requiting blood with blood.
I swore to wreak vengeance and eschew mirth and women's company.
My right hand will bring him low and I'll annihilate him with all my means.
Either we attain our vengeance and destroy our foes,
Or we die becoming like all the rest,
Relinquishing vengeance to the Creator of night and day.

II *A poem about a sad divorce*

lāh Xalaf ashartani u māni k-an-nās
w-aḥramtani yabūy liδδ al-manāmih
ʾabkiy w-ana galbi min al-ġibin miḥtās
ithawwatatni hmūm lōn al-ğammāmih
xalli al-bika l-alli tḥāfir lih bil-fās
ma yinbiki ʾalli hū bi-ḥāl as-salāmih
—ʾabki ʿala ʾaṃṃi ma bakēt ʾaṭrāf an-nās
ʾabki ʿala ʾalli laδδin li-ṭaʿāmah
yōm aṭʿamatni lugimtin ma bha ġmāṣ
ʾaxēr min ʾalli rafīʿtin ʾīdāmah
—ṣaḥīḥ wlēdi ğawābak ʿala r-rās
ma dūn ʿaṭf al-ʾaṃṃ ḥubb u ḥašāmah
mār ʾaṃṃak kama rīmītin b-rūs al-aṭʿās
tigṭuf min an-nuwwār ġāyit marāmah
ḥaṭṭat ib-rās abūk tisʿīn wiswās
wa-la warraθatni ġēr an-nadāmah
hāδa ğaza ʾalli gāran ib-ġēr migyās
yindam wala ġērih ʿalēh an-nadāma
mağnūn man yibni bētih bala sās
yinhār walaw yaʿṭīh kull ihtmāmah.

Desist O Khalaf, you keep me awake – and I've become like no other man!
Son, you deprive me of gratifying sleep.
—"I weep and my heart is rent with sorrow,
Cares, grey like a desert pigeon, crowd upon me!"
—"Keep your tears for one awaiting burial;
There's no sense bemoaning one who's well!"
—"But I weep for my mother; not just for anybody!
I weep for that the taste of which was my delight!
A mere morsel of her bread, unseasoned
Was better than a dish flowing with butter!"
—"True enough my little boy;
But, like a gazelle, your mother roamed the hilltops
Plucking flowers to her heart's content,
Filling your sire's head with a hundred woes.
She bequeathed me nothing but regrets—
A just recompense for one who weds below his station!
He rues his act, and repentance is his sole prospect.
Only a madman builds a house without foundations;
It'll crumble no matter how much care he bestows upon it."

III

A poem about a camel mare

tartaᶜ bil-furᶜa tišrab karaᶜ
ma tᶜūz ġarf gidḥān
ṭawīlt al-ḥanḥūn ṣafra rafīᶜah
tiğmil ğamīl aδ̣-δ̣abi lin šāf sulgān
šdād ṭagg fi xulg rāᶜīh
u dwērᶜin ᶜala l-mitin markāh
w-iᶜδ̣dārha nagš al-banāt al-milīḥih
u mnaggaytih min θamānīn dukkān
u-ya xrayyiğha min ṭayyib al-ᵓisim malyān

She grazes on a slope and drinks from rain puddles;
No need to scoop out water for her with bowls!
She's long-necked, light brown, and slim,
And races like a gazelle that has caught sight of dogs.
Her saddle, at a mere tap, follows its rider's whim,
And the leg-rest hangs on her flank.
Her headband was embroidered by pretty girls
With threads picked out of eighty shops.
And lo, her fine saddle-bag's full of her good name.

IV *Love poems*

1

xšēmak ṣabb ʾafēmak δabb
al-girš al-maṣri saddādi
ya ḥasrit galbi ya Dalāl
w-al-kull mrawwiḥ ʿa-blādih

Your little nose is shapely, and your dainty mouth pouts
An Egyptian piastre could cover it.
It's a pity, darling Dalal
That we had to part, each going his way!

2

ʾalli salāni u ʾana bnayyih
ṣabiy ma xaṭṭ lih šārib
ʾahlah u ʾhēli ḥasūdiyyih
gōṭar maʿ al-ğēš yḥārib

When I was young, a boy consoled me,
His moustache not yet sprouted.
But his folk and mine were envious,
So he joined the army and went to the front.

3

šabbahtki l-al-iġzayyil fil-ḥamādih
makḥūlt al-ʿēn ġufla ma ʿalēha wsūm
al-galb ʿaṭšān u ṭālib šurbit mayyih
u brīg fuxxār ib-ʾīd al-maṭrabāniyyih
ṣubb al-ibrīg w-isgīni gurδa u tilgāhi
w-illi zaraʿ ṭayybih yibaššar ib-šarwāhi

To me you're like a young gazelle in the plain,
Dark-eyed, care-free, without a taint.
The heart's thirsty and yearns for a draught
From the earthenware jar in the charmer's hand.
Pour it out to quench me, and your loan will be requited!
The doer of a good deed can expect a just recompense.

V

A poem on meanness

ǧīnālak ʿal-Uḥēdiy,
zayy ma hagēna lagēna.
yōmin wigifna ʿa-frāših
ʿayya la-ysallim ʿalēna.
gāl: ʾintu ya ṭēr al-gibliy
ma ʾakθar lōǧitku ʿalēna.
al-bakraǧ makfi ʿan-nār
w-iǧrābih ma fīh ḥabbih.
biḥuṭṭ al-imrāy fi yaddih
w-al-mūs byilʿab ʿa-xaddih.
u bētih šarāg al-Mašabbih
ya Faʿūr al-Uḥēdiy
bil-ǧubba w-al-xazarān;
ya Faʿūr al-Uḥēdiy
imġaddiy δēfih ib-musḥānih;
la ṭabb maʿ ʾahl al-māris
la-gaṣṣu šanabah maʿ ilsānih.

We came to your Wuḥaydāt tribe
And discovered what we surmised!
When we presented ourselves at his tent,
He refused to greet us.
He said: "You folk from the south,
Hang around us far too much!"
The coffeepot is upturned on the fire
And not a grain of coffee's in his pouch.
Holding a mirror in one hand,
He goes on plying the razor on his cheek.
His tent is east of Mašabbih.
"O Faʿūr of the Wuḥaydāt,
With your flowing robe and bamboo cane,
O Faʿūr of the Wuḥaydāt,
Feeding your guest with a pestle!"
Had he chanced on men of substance,
They would surely have lopped off his moustache and his tongue

Chapter 10

Linguistic and Ethnographic Observations on the Color Categories of the Negev Bedouin[1]

Alexander Borg

1. Language, Culture, and the Bedouin

There is an extensive literature on Bedouin in several western languages— beginning roughly from the early decades of the 19th century (e.g., Burckhardt, 1829)— attesting to a sustained interest in their way of life on the part of ethnographers and anthropologists in Europe and America. The last decade has seen a revival of research activity on cultural aspects of Bedouin, especially in relation to elements of their orally transmitted traditions currently threatened with obsolescence, such as their poetry (Sowayan, 1985; Bailey, 1990; Kurpershoek, 1994) and their customary law (Stewart, 1988, 1990). Oddly only scant attention has been devoted to the more general question of 'language and culture' in relation to these nomads in the research paradigm of linguistic anthropology.

With a few notable exceptions, past work on the language of Arab nomads has addressed itself almost exclusively to formal analysis of sound patterns, grammar, and lexicon (cf. Marçais, 1908; Boris, 1958; Blanc, 1970; Palva, 1976; Al-Muzaini, 1982), and the linguistic particularism of Bedouin communities has ordinarily been presented exclusively under the rubric of Arabic dialect geography Given the Bedouin's distinctiveness concomitant with their nomadic way of life, it would appear desirable to complement conventional linguistic study of their vernaculars by examining their language from the perspective of cultural ecology, for indications of 'the processes by which a society adapts to its environment' (Steward, 1968:43).

The cultural distinctiveness of Bedouin from settled Arabs is sometimes explicitly adverted to by native observers. In his study of the Negev Bedouin conducted during the period of the British Mandate—when this group was admittedly appreciably closer to its traditional way of life than it is today—the ethnographer and one-time governor of Beersheba, Aref Al-Aref (1934:16), remarked impressionistically that 'they represent a race of people whose methods of living, whose laws and customs and whose outlook on things, material and spiritual, are in marked contrast to those of civilized communities.'

The present essay on the color terms of the Negev Bedouin proposes as a research objective the hypothesis that certain linguistic categories encoded in the vernaculars of Arab nomads represent cultural isoglosses setting Bedouin speech communities apart from sedentary Arabs in these regions.

The propensity to overlook the cultural dimension of Bedouin Arabic is arguably a product of ethnocentricity on the part of western researchers—still the principal investigators of spoken Arabic—since dialectal subvarieties of European languages are not ordinarily expected to deviate significantly from their acrolects in the domain of semantic categorization.[2]

Lucy and Shweder (1981:159) have observed that

> ... cultures that have had equivalent amounts of time to evolve a color lexicon vary enormously in the number of basic colors ... in their linguistic repertoire.

Arabic colloquials spoken by Bedouin groups are known for their archaizing tendency at various linguistic levels, most transparently perhaps, in the lexical sphere, which invariably displays a rich stock of words relating to their special way of life and desert habitat. The Bedouin's color paradigm is one such conservative semantic domain.[3]

Most contemporary Arabic dialects spoken by sedentaries show the maximal set of eleven basic categories, following the trend of Modern Standard Arabic, itself influenced by European languages (Monteil, 1960:219):

> JERUSALEM ARABIC: *abyaḍ* 'white' | *aswad* 'black' | *aḥmar* 'red' | *axḍar* 'green' | *aṣfar* 'yellow' | *azraʾ* 'blue' | *bunni* 'brown' | *ramādi* 'grey' | *zahri* 'pink' | *burtuʾāli* 'orange' | *lēlaki* or *banafsaji* 'violet' (own observation).

The most archaic version of the Negev Arabic [NA] color paradigm comprises the first six basic categories in the Berlin and Kay evolutionary sequence: *white, black, red, green, yellow,* and *blue*. In effect, this means that over a rather extensive period of 1500-odd years intervening between the pre-Islamic period and the present day, the diachronic process that yielded NA has occasioned only minimal change at the level of basic categorization of the color continuum: the addition of just *one* new category to the pre-existing five reconstructed for early Arabic (cf. Fischer, 1965:237).

With its relatively small basic color paradigm of six terms, the Arabic vernacular spoken by tent-dwelling Bedouin in the Negev exemplifies the expected evolutionary stage in the lexification of color associated with small- and medium-scale societies (Witkowski, 1996:221). However, the stability of the Negev Bedouins' basic color system over time is also plausibly ascribable to cultural factors specific to the Bedouin way of life, in particular, the impact evidently exercized by ecology over their color categorization.[4]

2. Color Research on the Bedouin

Fischer reconstructed for Old Arabic [OA] five basic color categories: *abyaḍ*, 'white,' *aswad* 'black,' *aḥmar* 'red,' *axḍar* 'green, blue,' and *aṣfar* 'yellow'—an evolutionary stage implicit in the diachrony of color paradigms in many present-day varieties of colloquial Arabic, sedentary and nomadic. As for the categorization of the OA color continuum and the semantic content of its basic categories, Fischer (1965: 381) states:

> Im eigentlichen Bereich der Farbigkeit werden nur drei Grundfarben unterschieden: 1. Grün-Blau = Dunkelfarbigkeit (*axḍar*), 2. Rot-Braun (*aḥmar*), 3. Gelb-Braun (*aṣfar*). Die Qualitative Differenzierung der Farben ist also viel geringer ausgebildet als diejenige, die in den uns geläufigen Farbwerten rot, gelb, grün, blau, violett und braun ihren Ausdruck hat. Die Feststellung, daß die dem System der aar. Farbwörter zugrundeliegende Farbauffassung nur sehr grobe und summarische Unterscheidungen trifft, wird noch dadurch unterstrichen, daß das Aar. ... auch innerhalb der einzelnen Grundfarben keine qualitativen Farbtöne oder Farbnuancen differenziert. Farbwörter wie 'purpurrot, karminrot' oder 'gelbgrün, türkisgrün', die einzelne Farbwerte innerhalb der Grundfarben charakterisieren, haben im Aar. ... keine Entsprechungen.

In defining the meaning patterns of these Old Arabic color categories, Fischer significantly stresses the marginal role of chromaticity, and emphasizes the importance of brightness contrasts:

> Diejenigen Farbbezeichnungen, die den generellen Farbwörtern *axḍar*, *aḥmar*, *aṣfar* untergeordnet sind und die einzelne Farbtöne bezeichnen, differenzieren allein den Helligkeitsgrad der Grundfarbe, nicht den Farbwert.

The highly restricted role of hue differentiation within individual categories ascribed here to the Old Arabic stage of the Bedouin color system is suggestive in the present context. In this paper, I will try to show that though NA has gone some way towards diversifying the content of its basic categories, these are, on the whole, still sparsely lexified in the speech of tent-dwelling Bedouin. In fact, an overview of the NA color paradigm reveals two noteworthy trends:

(a) the core of the lineally inherited color paradigm in this vernacular encodes principally the hues of livestock, terrain, and vegetation;

(b) the majority of level-2 color terms[5] define a somewhat restricted area of the color solid: specifically, in the domains of red and yellow, and along the achromatic continuum between white and black.[6]

Concerning color usage of modern Bedouin, there is a concise but informative paper by the Swiss orientalist Johann Jakob Hess, *Die Farbenbezeichnungen bei innerarabischen Beduinenstämmen* (1920), based on fieldwork conducted among the Central Arabian ʿUtaybah Rwūge tribe and, apparently, the first scientific investigation of vernacular Arabic color terminology. Hess's objective was to document this group's color paradigm and to determine, with the help of the *Code des Couleurs* (Klincksieck and Valette, 1908), the precise chromatic values of the 50-odd color names elicited from his Bedouin informant.

Interestingly, from the viewpoint of the present study, Hess observed a cultural bias, which he regarded as self-explanatory, in the ʿUtaybah tribe's categorization of color concepts: in particular, a systemic skewing towards yellow and brown hues and a paucity of terms for green and blue:

> Wie schon gesagt überrascht die Reichhaltigkeit der Benennungen, aber ebenso der Umstand, daß unter ihnen die Bezeichnungen für die gelben und braunen Töne vorherrschen, während die Sprache für Grün und Blau nur spärliche Ausdrücke hat ...

In the tradition of cultural ecology, he added: 'wohl ein Einfluß der Wüste' (Hess, 1920:75).

Roth's 1986 study of the elaborate color inventories of North African Arabic-speaking nomads on the basis of the available field data relating to the Marazig Bedouin in Southern Tunisia (Boris, 1958), the Bedouin of Zaire (Loubignac, 1952), and the nomadic sheep herders of Djelfa in Algeria (Lethellieux ms.), underscores the cultural salience for pastoralists of color terms encoding their natural world. Beyond these formal studies on the color terminology of Arab nomads, data on Arabic color terms for livestock are sometimes appended to monographs and shorter studies of specific Bedouin groups (cf. fn. 21).

The present study has two aims: (a) to provide a preliminary description of the Negev Bedouin's color paradigm; and (b) to discuss cultural aspects of their color terms in the light of the relevant linguistic literature on color.

3. Field Methodology

The fieldwork for the present study was conducted among tent-dwelling tribesmen from the ʿAzāzmih confederation encamped in the Negev Highlands, south of Beer-sheba.[7] Color terms were elicited in a naturalistic manner in the course of informal interviews held in Arabic in which I posed as a learner of their Negev Bedouin dialect.

Informants were ordinarily consulted in the *šigg* or men's section of the tent, which generally proved congenial because questions could be directed to the immediate realia of Bedouin life, and because Bedouin women could also be consulted. An aggregate of about thirty Bedouin were interviewed.

All my Bedouin informants are, in western terms, completely illiterate, though many can recite or improvise in their traditional poetic genres. They are, at any rate, unaccustomed to participation in research projects of the kind undertaken here. I have therefore avoided making systematic use of color charts or special color kits like the Munsell color chips. Attempting to elicit from Bedouin, with the aid of materials completely extraneous to their culture, the type of discriminatory judgments that can reasonably be expected from persons with formal schooling has the drawback of inducing informants to adopt a reflective attitude at variance with what Whorf (1941:134ff.) characterized as the modality of 'habitual thought,' and of imposing on them the western notion of 'color.' Furthermore, certain meaning patterns of Bedouin Arabic color terms relating, for instance, to texture, are not elicitable by means of color chips; thus most of the Bedouin's terms for colors of livestock would not have been obtainable in this formal manner.

In my fieldwork, I have tried to record "the visual-quality attributes taken from descriptions of specific items of the natural and synthetic surroundings" (Conklin, 1955:190) of the Bedouin, and the meanings of color terms elicited were determined primarily by reference to the hues of camels, sheep, goats, terrain and vegetation, and to those of garments, rugs, and household goods generally found in Bedouin tents.

4. Some Formal Features of NA Color Terms

Tight formal constraints determine the canonic shapes of words in Arabic, reflecting the extensive iconicity operative in its lexical structure (Justice, 1987, *passim*). Lexemes encoding level-1 color terms in NA ordinarily have three distinct morphological shapes corresponding to verbal, nominal, and adjectival status. Membership in these grammatical classes is signalled by conformity to one of the canonic forms *CCaCC*, *aCCaC*, *CaCāC*, respectively:

byaḍ̣δδ̣	'to become white'	*abyaḍ̣δ*	'white'	*bayāḍ̣δ*	'whiteness'
swadd	'to become black'	*aswad*	'black'	*sawād*	'blackness'
ṣfarr	'to turn yellow'	*aṣfar*	'yellow'	*ṣafār*	'yellowness'

Lexemes for level-2 categories tend not to have verbal equivalents, and usually generate only adjectives. The standard canonic forms for native color adjectives in NA are: *aCCaC* (m.), *CaCCá* (f.) and *CuCC* (pl.): *azrag, zargá, zurg* 'black.'

Readers conversant with Classical or vernacular Arabic will note that certain masculine color terms cited throughout this study deviate from their OA etyma in that they tend to show a secondary vowel [a] dissolving word-internal *CC* clusters with a velar, pharyngeal, or laryngeal consonant in root-medial position. The new syllabic attracts lexical stress, and the preceding stem vowel—now in an open pre-stress syllable—becomes liable to optional deletion: OA *aḥmar* 'red,' *axḍar* 'green' > NA *(a)ḥámar, (a)xáδ̣ar*. These secondary forms are the authentic NA reflexes of the *aCCaC* scheme, but many speakers freely resort to the shorter *koiné* forms imbibed from urban Arabic. Feminine color adjectives (< OA *CaCCāʾ*) show raising and fronting of the final vowel **āʾ* > *iy* after historically plain (i.e., non-velarized and non-back) consonants: *šahabíy* (< *šahbāʾ*) 'grey, light blue,' but retain the low vowel after velarized or pharyngeal consonants: *bēδ̣á* 'white f.' Pausally, this final *-á* is arrested by an automatic glottal catch which will not be marked here: *samrá* 'dark f.' (= [samráʾ]).

Color terms displaying other canonic shapes are secondary, more recent lexicalizations usually deriving from noun forms referring to objects showing the color in question: *sakaniy* 'grey' (cf. *sakana* 'ashes').[8]

5. *The Basic Color Categories of Negev Arabic*

The most archaic basic color system I have noted among tent-dwelling Negev Bedouin—the focus of the present study—partitions the color solid into the aforementioned six categories corresponding to Stage V in B&K's 1969 evolutionary sequence:

abyaδ̣	'white'
azrag	'black'
aḥámar	'red'
axáδ̣ar	'green'
aṣfar	'yellow'
ašhab	'blue'

Figure 1. The basic color categories of the Negev Bedouin

In reality, an indefinite number of color systems coexist in the usage of the NA speech community, currently undergoing the later stages of a sedentarization process and acculturation to urban linguistic norms. Idiolectal variation seems to correlate very roughly with the speaker's age, gender, education, or degree of urbanization. Fig. 2 illustrates the correlation between color categorization and age in the usage of two Bedouin speakers: Salmān, about fifty years old, and ʿĪd, twenty-four.

Color Categories	SALMĀN	ᶜĪD
Red	*aḥámar*	*aḥámar*
Brown	*aḥámar*	*bunniy*
Black	*asmar/azrag*	*aswad*
Orange	*aṣfar*	*birdigāniy*
Grey	*as̆hab*	*ramādiy*
Blue	*as̆hab*	*azrag*

Figure 2. Some age-related differences in color categorization among the Negev Bedouin.

The younger speaker, ᶜĪd, has a more 'modern' color system than Salmān since the latter groups 'red' and 'brown' together in a macro-red category, whereas ᶜĪd contrasts *aḥámar* 'red' with *bunniy* 'brown.' Also, for Salmān, 'orange' is non-basic and is subsumed under *aṣfar* 'yellow,' whereas it is a distinct category in ᶜĪd's idiolect. For 'black,' ᶜĪd uses the sedentary term *aswad*, ordinarily avoided by Bedouin speakers (cf. §7), and for 'grey' and 'blue' he has two distinct categories as against Salmān's single term.

Urbanized Bedouin speakers are liable to shift imperceptibly from one system to another in their responses to formal questioning. On being requested to name the hue of a light-colored sheet of brownpaper, ᶜĪd Ibn Darrāj (50's), a speaker in his 50s, first ventured *δahábiy* 'golden,' a common level-2 term for this hue, but then shifted to its superordinate term *aṣfar* 'yellow.' He followed this up with *aḥámar* 'red' and finally settled on *gahawiy* 'coffee-colored, brown.' The hesitation between 'yellow' and 'red' evidently reflects the indistinct boundary between these two categories at low levels of saturation. Whereas the first two terms presuppose a color paradigm at stage IV or V, the last term probably pertains to a system with incipient 'brown.'

Bedouin women generally employ a more precise and more differentiated color language than men.[9] Their attentiveness to color is no doubt enhanced by some of their traditional activities in the household: weaving rugs, tent partitions, and embroidery (Biasio, 1998:139f.).

White (*abyaḏ, bēḏá, bīḏ, abayyiḏ*) vs. Black (*azrag, zargá, zurug, azērig*)[10]

From a generalizing standpoint, very light shades of several hues (yellow, pink, grey, etc.) tend to be classified as white by NA speakers. The poles of the white/black continuum are encoded by the expressions *abyaḏ guḥḥ* 'pure white' and *azrag ġaṭīs* 'deep black' (cf. *ġaṭas* 'to immerse'), respectively; the qualifiers *guḥḥ* and *ġaṭīs* do not co-occur with other color adjectives.

The OA term *abyaḍ* (~ *bayḍ* 'eggs'; Fischer, 1965:96) conveyed both brightness and hue values without differentiation (Ducatez and Ducatez, 1980):

Old Arabic (Fischer, 1965)
abyaḍ 'hell, leuchtend, weiss' (p. 243)
azhar 'leuchtend, strahlend hell, strahlend weiss' (p. 249)

and 'whiteness' was commonly attributed to objects characterized by transparency, reflectance, or luminosity, as in the following quote from the 9th century traditionist Al-Bukhārī, referring to water (cited from Fück, 1955:70): *māʾuhū abyaḍu min al-labani* ['Its water is whiter than milk'].

A lexical residue of terms for brightness survives in the NA terms *awδaḥ* and *ašʿal*, which now simply designate 'white,' i.e., light-colored camels. The other NA hyponyms of 'white' include the camel colors *ašgaḥ* and *abraṣ* 'off-white,' and two covert terms for the lighter hues of desert terrain: *baraṣa* 'light-colored sand' (Bailey, 1984:56), a cognate of the aforecited camel color *abraṣ*, and *raġamūn* 'white bedrock of limestone showing through a thin layer of loess.'

For the 'black' category (which also comprises very dark hues of brown, blue, and green), there are three near-synonyms occurring, to some extent, in complementary distribution: *azrag, asmar,* and *aswad,* the unmarked term here being *azrag.* Cognates of *azrag* in Modern Standard Arabic and many contemporary Arabic colloquials encode 'blue.'[11]

In NA, the term *azrag* can occur interchangeably with *asmar* in general contexts but, as in other Arabic vernaculars, *asmar* is the usual designation for dark skin color short of black. A black person of African ancestry is ordinarily *azrag.*[12]

The word *asmar* is common as a level-2 term for black camel hair, and its nominalized form *samār* is a generic terms for goats in the expression *bayāδ u samār*, literally, 'whiteness and blackness' (i.e., 'sheep and goats'). Other hyponyms of 'black' include *adġam* 'completely black (donkey),' and the covert color term, *yaḥāmīma* 'a blackish hill or mountain' (Bailey, 1984:56) ~ OA *yaḥāmīm,* sg. *yaḥmūm* 'a black mountain' (Lane, 1863–93: 638).

Color symbolism restricts the use of the NA term *aswad*, ordinarily avoided by the Negev Bedouin on account of its association with the notion of *taswīd al-wijih* 'blackening of the face' in their customary law (cf. §7 below). Euphemistic substitutes for the lexeme *swd* 'black' have been noted in several parts of the Arab world, e.g., *azrag* or *axḍar* recorded by Hartmann (1899:85) for Libyan Bedouin.[13]

Red—*aḥámar, ḥamrá, ḥumr, aḥēmir*

NA *aḥámar* 'red' < OA *aḥmar* (cf. Hebrew *ḥómer* 'Lehm, Ton,' akkad. *emēru* 'gerötet sein,' etc.; Fischer, 1965:116) is, for the most conservative speakers, macro-red, ranging over pink, purple, Bordeaux, light brown and, sometimes, orange. The best example of red is 'blood-red,' called *aḥámar gāṭiᶜ* 'deep red.'

The most stable simplex hyponyms of red are predominantly in the brown area and denote mainly colors of livestock: *aḥámar* 'reddish brown (camel),' *amġar* 'light reddish brown (camel),' *adham* 'dark red (goat),' and *adkar* 'greyish pink (camel)'; the last term, meaning simply 'pink,' can also apply to a red sky after sunset and to the chalice of the desert annual, *šilwih* (Bailey and Danin, 1981). Redness as an element in the coloration of goats is implicit in NA *adraᶜ*, *aᶜáṭar*, *aġbaš*, and *asfaᶜ* (cf. fig. 3 below).

Level-2 terms for more conventional hues in the red category occur mainly in women's usage and tend to define the areas of pink and brown, possibly indicating incipient categorization around these points:[14]

> *zahriy* 'pink' (cf. *zaher* 'flowers, blossoms') > Palestinian *zahri* 'rosa' (Bauer, 1957: 246) | Damascene *zahᵊr* 'pink' (Stowasser and Ani, 1964:173) | *ᶜinnābiy* 'bright pink' < Egyptian Arabic *ᶜinnābi* 'reddish brown' (Badawi and Hinds, 1986:604) | *gaháwiy* 'coffee-colored' ~ NA *gaháwah* ~ Modern Standard Arabic *qahwah* 'coffee.'

Certain neologisms (including loans from Modern Hebrew) are used exclusively by young speakers:

> *mirᶜiz* 'pink, purple' (< Aram.) | *aškalyūṭi*, literally, 'grapefruit pink' < Mod. Heb. *eškolít* 'grapefruit' | *kikāwi* 'light brown' < Mod. Heb. *kakáw* | *šuglātiy* 'dark brown' < Mod. Heb. *šókolad*.

Urbanized speakers with a stable 'brown' category ordinarily resort to the koiné term *bunniy* 'brown' (> NA [bánniy])—mostly unfamiliar to older informants as a color name. Oddly, younger speakers tend to extend the use of *bunniy* to purple, which must be an innovation in NA. In general, the labeling of the derived colors, pink, purple, and brown by speakers of this vernacular is in a state of flux.

The Negev Bedouin attribute redness to the human skin in race classification. Light-skinned Bedouin, usually individuals of Egyptian peasant extraction, are customarily referred to as *ḥumrān* 'red ones,' in opposition to *sumrān* 'dark ones' (people of genuine Bedouin ancestry).

GREEN—*axáḏ̣ar*, *xaḏ̣rá*, *xuḏ̣r*, *axayḏ̣ir*

The focal area of NA *axáḏ̣ar* < OA *axḍar* (~ OA *xaḍir* 'sprossendes Grün, Vegetation'; Fischer, 1965:8) is the color of grass, called *axáḏ̣ar ᶜišbiy* 'grass green.' A few speakers have B&K's GRUE category extending across the green-blue continuum, but this usage seems to be marginal in the Negev. A stable GRUE category does, however, occur among Bedouin in the Sinai peninsula. On being asked to name the colors of two oil cans—one green, the other blue—a middle-aged speaker from the Mzēnih tribe in Nuwayba‘ (Sinai) designated the first, *axáḍ̱ar* 'green,' and the second, *axáδar baḥariy* 'lit., sea green,' continuing the OA category, *axḍar,* glossed as follows in Fischer (1965:306):

> Das Wort bezeichnet die den ganzen dunklen Farbbereich umfassende Grundfarbe, sowohl 'grün' als auch 'blau.'

Old Arabic here concurred with other ancient Near Eastern languages, such as Sumerian, Akkadian, Ancient Egyptian, and Hebrew (Baines, 1985:284),[15] and with a commonly reported cross-linguistic lexical typology. Within the Arabic *Sprachraum*, a GRUE category has also been noted for the Arabic dialects of Upper Egypt (Rivers, 1901) and the Sudan (Reichmuth, 1981).

Most NA terms for different greens are lexically compound terms usually entailing the mention of a concrete object: *axáδar baṭṭīxiy* (lit., water-melon green), *axáδar zētiy* '(olive) oil green,' both referring to dark shades of this color, and *axáḍ̱ar luksiy* 'light green' < *Lux* (soap). Khaki has the odd name *dukrun,* probably from *Dacron* (name of textile), the material of police and military uniforms.

In the domain of horse colors (not treated here), the term *axáḍ̱ar* conveys the meaning 'grey': *faraṣ xaδrá ḥamāmiyyih,* literally, 'a pigeon-grey mare.' A similar usage is found in Sudanese Arabic (Reichmuth, 1981:61) as a sheep color:

> *axadar* —'verschiedene Grautöne; ein häufiger Typ mit Oliv-Einschlag galt bei den Informanten am Atbara-Fluß als *axadar*, ...

The same usage occurs in rural Egyptian Arabic in relation to the donkey: *jḥēš xēdir* 'ein grauer Esel' (Behnstedt and Woidich, 1999:369).

Harold Conklin's celebrated 1955 study of color categories in Hanunóo, a language of the Philippines, highlighted the salience in this language of nonchromatic meanings of green conveying notions of freshness and succulence of plant material. Oddly De Haas's 1954 study of the lexical coding of the semantic spectrum of moisture in Classical Arabic overlooks the green category and the possible diachronic semantic interface between OA *xḍr* and the term *xaḍila* 'be moist, wet.' Old Arabic emphasized this aspect of the green category. Thus, in the twelfth Sura of the Quran (45-46), where the seven green ears of corn are contrasted with the seven wilted ones, the color term *xuḍr* 'green (pl.)' is opposed to *yābisāt* 'dry (f. pl.)' which is not a color term.

The semantic association of greenness with moisture and succulence is also well developed in modern Arabic vernaculars, both nomadic and sedentary. Marçais (1911:281), for instance, glosses Maghribi *xḍar* < ᵓ*axḍar* as follows:

1. «vert» 2. «pas cuit», en parlant du pain, des legumes, de la viande; ainsi à Tlemcen, Nedroma, Alger. Par contre, à Constantine et chez la plupart des ruraux, on emploie ce mot en parlant de la viande ... mais non en parlant du pain.[16]

The wide geographical distribution of this semantic usage across the Arabic *Sprachraum* intimates cultural continuity with Old Arabic usage as exemplified in the language of the Qurʾān:

Cairene *axḍar* 'fresh, not salted or cured (of fish); damp, moist': *il-hidūm lissa xaḍra* 'the clothes are still damp' (Badawi and Hinds, 1986:254) | **Dathina** *xḍr* 'être vert et ensuite avoir de l'eau (terrain); *axḍar* 'mouillé, humide': *θawbī axḍar* 'mon vêtement est mouillé' (Landberg, 1920:606) | **Aleppo** *ǧəbne xaḍra* 'fromage frais' (Barthélemy, 1935–54:207) | **Palest. Ar.** *ʾaxḍar rabīʿ* 'junges Frühlings' (Bauer, 1957:143), *damm ʾaxḍar* 'frisches Blut' (Fischer, 1965:306, fn. 3) | **Upper Egypt** *ṭūb axḍar* 'ungebrannte Lehmziegel' (as opposed to *ṭūb ʾaḥamar* 'gebrannte Lehmziegel'; Behnstedt and Woidich, 1994:292)[17] | **Yemeni** *ʾaxḏ̣ar* 'damp, moist, humid, wet' (Piamenta 1990: 130).

The same meaning pattern can be noted in the dialect of the Negev Bedouin as in the following gloss of *ʾaxáḏ̣ar*, by a native speaker:

al-kilmih fīhā maʿāni kθīrih. fīh ʿišib ʾaxaḏ̣ar, fīh duxxān ʾaxaḏ̣ar, fīh al-ʾawāʿi bitḥuṯṯhum fil-mā u tġassilhum, fīh ʿindak kbāš u widdak tnazzilhum aṣ-ṣūf, widdak tġassilhum l-ikbāš—al-ikbāš xuḏ̣ur 'The word [green] has several meanings. Grass is green, smoke is green, and clothes [too], when you immerse them in water to wash them. [Or] you may have sheep to be sheared and you might want to bathe them—the sheep are green (i.e., when wet). '

Though often considered an exotic trait, this semantic pattern finds close parallels in a number of European languages:

grüne Häute 'undressed skins' | *grüne Hering* 'fresh herring' | *green meat* 'not cured, unprocessed' | *green cheese* 'unreife Käse' (Betteridge, 1978:1083, 280) | *green mortar* (freshly set but not completely hardened) | *green bricks* or *pottery* (not fired) (RHD, 620).

In fact, Ancient Greek *khlôros* also encoded 'freshness' outside the context of foliage and could refer to fresh fish (i.e., not salted), freshly picked fruit, and even fresh cheese (Liddell and Scott, 1996) as in Aleppo *jebne xaḍra* 'fromage frais' (Barthélemy, 1935–54:103).

Secondary terms combining the meanings 'green' and 'succulent' also occur in Old Arabic, e.g., *aġyanu* had a rather wide range of meanings conveying luxuriance[18] in addition to its basic color sense:

> green or green inclining to blackness, ... and [its fem.] *ġaynā'* is applied to a tree as meaning green, abounding with leaves, having tangled, or dense, branches and soft, or tender: and sometimes it is thus applied to herbs: or [applied to a tree] it signifies great, having wide shade, ... (Lane, 1863–93:2320)

These examples recall Conklin's paper (1955) on non-chromatic information—freshness and succulence—transmitted by the 'green' category in Hanunóo, a language of the Philippines. This point has been taken up by Lyons (1999:16) in relation to Ancient Greek χλωρός:

> Of particular interest to us here is *khlôros,* which is used more particularly of plants and foliage. It was this word that I had in mind when I said that Ancient Greek was similar to Hanunóo. Standard dictionaries of Greek will say that *khlôros,* like the English word green, has two meanings, in one of which it denotes a colour and in the other of which it can be paraphrased by such words as fresh, unripe or even moist and full of sap, according to context. But this is not so. The colour-term sense of *khlôros* is inseparable from its more general sense in which it is used typically, to describe fresh, green foliage.

As already noted, this usage finds close parallels in certain sedentary Arabic colloquials, e.g., Aleppine and Cairene.

YELLOW—*aṣfar, ṣafrá, ṣufr, aṣēfir*

OA *aṣfar* (~ *ṣufr, ṣifr* 'Kupfer'; Fischer, 1965:116) comprised "alle gelblichen Farbtöne vom hellsten Gelb und Beige bis Orange und gelblich Dunkelbraun" (Fischer, 1965:358). For the Negev Bedouin, *aṣfar* extends from bright yellow to light brown and ordinarily includes orange. 'Yellow' and 'red' in NA enjoy a close systemic proximity, both colors being frequently associated in descriptions of lighter shades of brown in animal pelts. The best example of *aṣfar* most often cited is the color of egg-yolk *(ṣafār* or *maḥḥ al-bēδa).*

The color term *aṣfar* is applied to light brown camel hair, and to the dark yellow hue of turmeric (*kurkum*), used by the Bedouin for flavoring home-made butter *(samn).* The Bedouin's ethnobotanical term for the yellow *Senecio glauca* L and for the almost orange *Calendula arvensis* L derives from this lexeme: *ṣfērá,* literally, 'yellowish' (Bailey and Danin, 1981:159). Paleness of the complexion is also 'yellow.'

Common NA hyponyms of *aṣfar* are: *δahabiy* 'golden,' applied to duller hues located between yellow and light brown, and the koiné term *aṣfar lamūniy* 'lemon yellow' (< *laymūn* 'lemon'). NA has no special term for 'orange'; one informant described this color as *zayy al-kabrīt* 'like sulphur,' and *zayy al-fuxxār* 'like pottery.' Urbanized Bedouin speakers use the koineized term *birdigāniy* < Palestinian *burtʾāni* (< Modern Standard Arabic *burtuqālī* 'orange-colored'). Just as NA *axáδar* 'green' can connote freshness of plant material, so too, the lexeme *ṣfr* can allude to desiccation: *warag miṣfarrāt* 'dry leaves.'

Blue—*ašhab*, *šahabíy*, *šuhub*, *ašēhib*

NA *ašhab* designates the continuum from 'grey' to 'light blue.' Young speakers generally place its focus in blue, but older speakers in grey, its original meaning in Old Arabic:

> *ašhab*—of the colour termed *šuhba* 'a [gray] colour in which whiteness predominates over blackness ... ' (Lane, 1863–93: 1608–9)

Thus the emergence of grey in Old Arabic and NA preceded that of blue, reversing the order postulated for these colors in the earlier version of B&K's evolutionary sequence. In the realm of natural colors, *ašhab* can refer to greyish animal pelts: camel-hair, 'the rusty grey coat' of the wolf (cf. Jarvis, 1951:95), to birds' plumage, such as that of the chukar *(Alectoris chukar*; NA *šunnāra)*, and to the color of dust. This term is also applied to nondescript colors of low chroma, such as that of faded garments; it thus approximates "a category of desaturated, non-vivid, or 'bad' color," which "usually contains grey and a diverse collection of hues that never attain high saturation" (Kay *et al.*, 1997:33; MacLaury, 1999).

Common hyponyms in this category are: *ramādiy, sakaniy,* both meaning 'ashen, grey' (~ *ramād*) and *sakana* 'ashes,' *adxan* 'smoke grey' (~ *duxxān* 'smoke'), and *raṣāṣiy* 'the color of lead' (~ *raṣāṣ* 'lead').

Certain cultures conventionally ascribe quintessential blueness to sky color. On clear sunny days, my Negev Bedouin and Mzēnih (Sinai) informants refer to the sky as *abyaḏ* 'white' (*abyaδ zayy al-labanih,* literally, 'white like milk').[19] Terms for 'sky-blue' are used by younger speakers: *samāwi* 'sky-colored, light blue' (cf. *sama* 'sky' < OA *samāʾ*).

Many NA speakers have the term *ṣīniy* 'deep blue (lit., Chinese).' The papers by Powels and Warburton (1999) agree in tracing its diffusional pathway in relation to the introduction of 'blue-on-white' chinaware cups used by the Bedouin for coffee-drinking possibly as early as the 17th century.[20] Another hyponym of *ašhab* in the blue domain is *nīliy* 'indigo-colored' (cf. *nīlih* 'the indigo plant'), traditionally used by Bedouin women as a dye.

Young NA speakers lexify more color points than their elders within the blue domain, including very dark shades that older speakers classify as black: *ašhab milḥiy* 'light blue,' *ašhab kuḥliy* 'dark blue,' *ašhab ġrābiy* 'blue-black' (cf. *ġrāb* 'crow')—suggesting that the blue category is probably ripe for a formal split into fullfledged 'blue' and 'grey' in their variety of NA.

The name and meaning of the category 'blue' in the dialect of the Negev Bedouin furnish a striking isogloss setting this group apart from Arabic-speaking sedentaries in the region, 'blue'—commonly encoded as *azraq* and semantically akin to 'blue' in western languages—being a well-established category in Modern Standard Arabic and in many spoken vernaculars.

The color blue is rather well objectified in the Negev Bedouin's material culture, partly because of its prophylactic character in the Arab perception, and partly because of its symbolic significance. Blue beads *(kuššāš)* or items of clothing are usually worn by children as protection against the evil eye *(ʿēn saww;* cf. Shinar (1999:181). Earlier, blue embroidery was the norm for unmarried young women (Weir, 1989:139); today a blue girdle is often worn by older women past child-bearing, especially in mourning.

6. Natural Colors

Fischer (1965:380ff.) classified the color terms of Old Arabic into three kinds comprising (i) genuine color terms, in effect, concentrated in the red, yellow, and green areas of the color solid; (ii) brightness terms in the areas of white, grey, and black; and (iii) semantically diffuse designations.

This last group comprised terms lexifying complex stimuli only partially defined by hue: e.g., *axṭab* 'dunkelfarbig (blau, grün) und hellfarbig gefärbt' (Fischer, 1965:321), which could apply as well to the juxtaposed yellow and green hues of a colocynth as to a combination of light and dark plumage (Fischer, 1965: 240, 323; 381).

Particularly noteworthy in this context is OA *azraq* (> NA *azrag* 'black), which Fischer (1965:54) glosses: 'blinkend, glitzernd, schillernd' in reference principally to heavenly bodies, the glint of steel, the sparkle of water and eyes; hence, a sensation of brightness combined with movement. As already noted, this term later came to mean 'blue' in Classical Arabic and many spoken vernaculars. Its evolution from a brightness to a hue term replicates a well known shift attested in the color paradigms of several other languages (MacLaury, 1992; Casson, 1997).

This type of lexical usage is difficult to document in fieldwork and I have not recorded color terms of this kind in NA. In her color research on poetic texts in Southern Tuareg, Drouin (1989:1) has indicated the utility of this type of genre for retrieving cultural categories relating to color that informant interviews often fail to elicit.

A dominant idea in the present paper is the salience of natural hues in the color categorization of the Negev Bedouin. Thass-Thienemann (1968:291) noted that

> Beyond one's own body, the color display of animals, then of plants and minerals, may serve for naming color qualities.

NA speakers habitually resort to the natural hues of desert terrain and fauna to calibrate color judgments: *baraṣa* 'the color of loess,' *baraṣa mamṭūra* 'the darker color of loess after a rainfall,' *zayy as-sakanih/ar-ramil/l-iblād* 'like ashes, sand, earth'; *zayy aδ-δ̣abbiyyih* 'like the lizard (= pink)'; *zayy aδ-δīb/ zayy aθ-θaᶜlab* 'like the wolf/fox (= rusty grey).' As already noted, some informants resorted to circumlocutions of this kind in attempts to characterize conventional synthetic hues for which NA lacks an appropriate color term, e.g., orange.

This usage highlights the unmarked status for NA speakers of natural hues concomitant with their referential stability, being associated with very familiar objects and therefore devoid of the open-endedness, arbitrariness, and unpredictable distribution of synthetic colors.

The core of the Negev Bedouin's hyponymic color inventory comprises a fairly elaborate nomenclature relating to animal pelts (livestock and desert fauna), exemplified in fig. 3. These usually denote the coloration of a salient part of the animal's body (head, shoulders) or a pattern on its skin.[21] Besides encoding color properties, these terms serve as classifications of types of livestock.

aṣbaḥ	'black with white head (sheep, goat)'
adraᶜ	'with a reddish brown head and shoulders (sheep)'
aᶜáṭar	'white, black and red (goat)'
aġbaš	'black, with white and red markings (goat)'
asfaᶜ	'black, with reddish brown head and ears (goat)'
aġarr	'black, with a white spot (blaze) on the forehead (goat)'
adġam	'completely black (donkey)'
akḥal	'with white or reddish head and black rings round the eyes (goat)'
abrag	'variegated (sheep, goats, dogs), mottled (snake)'
anmar	'spotted (dog)'
aḥáwa	'grey with light-colored belly (donkey)'
adᶜam	'black-headed (sheep)'

Figure 3. Color terms for livestock and desert fauna used by the Negev Bedouin

In §1 I referred to the stability over time evinced by basic color categories in NA; this seems also to hold true, to a considerable extent, for level-2 categories encoding animal colors; thus most NA terms in fig. 3 have OA cognates:

LANE: *aṣbaḥ* 'a black colour inclined to redness' (1643) | *adraʿ* 'having a black head, the rest being white' (872) | *muʿṭira* 'red she goat' (2078); *asfaʿ* 'black tinged or intermixed with redness' | *ġurra* 'a blaze on the forehead' (2240) | *adġam* '(a horse) of a colour inclining to blackness' (887) | *kuḥl* 'antimony' (2999) | *abrag* 'having two colors' (191) | *numra* 'a spot or speck of any colour whatever' (2853) | *ḥuwwa* 'a brown colour' (661), etc.

Certain terms listed here are also used outside the domain of animal pelts and designate the colors of landscape, and some occur as lexical components in descriptive toponyms: *Wādiy al-Aḥáwa* (Sinai; Stewart, 1986:52).[22]

6.1 Camel colors

In referring to camel colors, the Negev Bedouin can either adopt a generalizing viewpoint and resort to basic terms—in their parlance, *asmāʾ rasmiyyih* (lit., 'official names')—or a particularizing one, and employ more specific terms. When I asked Salāmih, a 50-year-old camel herder, to name the most common colors of this animal, he stated: *ál-bil, fī ḥamrá, fī samrá, fī bēδá* 'there are red, black, and white camels.' This three-way classification, confirmed by other speakers, no doubt continues a folk taxonomy reflecting the relative frequencies of these three varieties of *camelus dromedarius* in the region.[23] Dalman (1987:148) notes appositely about the camel in Palestine:

> Das Gewöhnliche ist ein rötliches Gelb (*aḥmar*) … am seltensten [ist] weiß *(auḍaḥ)* oder schwarz *(amlaḥ, aswad, asmar)*.[24]

Figure 4 displays some of the most common specific terms for camel colors used by the Negev Bedouin. The precise meaning of some of these words is somewhat elusive and the glosses provided here are meant to be only suggestive:

awδaḥ, waδḥá, wiδiḥ	'white'
ašʿal, šaʿalíy, šiʿil	'white'
ašgaḥ šagḥá, šuguḥ	'off-white'
abraṣ, barṣá, burṣ	'light-colored, off-white'
amġar, maġrá, muġur	'light reddish brown'
aṣḥab, ṣaḥabíy, ṣuḥub	'reddish brown w/a black stripe along the back'
adkar, dakrá, dukur	'greyish pink'
arxam, raxmá, ruxum	'reddish brown with light colored breast and legs '
aṣfar, ṣafrá, ṣufur	'yellowish brown'
adġaθ, daġaθiy, duġuθ,ašhab, šahabíy,	'grey'
šihib. adxan, daxaníy, duxun	'grey'
azrag, zargá, zurug	'dark, black'

Figure 4. Some camel colors of the Negev Bedouin.

Etymological and semantic parallels obtaining between camel terminologies in several Bedouin Arabic dialects spoken in various parts of the Arab world presuppose a common historical origin, plausibly in ancient Arabia. The following display includes some OA cognates for the words in fig. 4 with their meanings:

> NA *awδaḥ* 'white' ~ OA *wāḍiḥ* 'strahlend weiß' (Fischer, 1965:10) | NA *ašʿal* 'white' ~ *ašʿal* 'a horse having the whiteness termed *šuʿla* (= a firebrand)' (1564) | NA *ašgaḥ* 'offwhite,' cf. OA *raġwa šaqḥāʾ* '(froth) that is not of pure white, but coloured' (1580) | NA *amġar* 'light reddish brown' ~ OA *amġar* 'the colour of red earth *(maġra),*' (2726), etc. (Lane, 1863–93)

Fischer (1965:242–3) expresses some doubt concerning the existence of a stable nomenclature for camel coloration in Old Arabic and states that genuine color terms for this animal were restricted to what he calls

> einige besonders auffällige und einige besonders wertvolle Rassen, die an ihrer Färbung erkenntlich sind ...,

among which he includes terms for the light-colored varieties (*aʿyas* 'weisse Kamele,' *ādam* 'fast weisses, hellfarbiges Kamel,' *aṣhab* 'blondes Kamel'). Interestingly, the first four NA terms listed in fig. 4 all refer to white or light-colored camels. I have been able to document only one color term for the dark variety.[25]

In his thought-provoking remarks on color terms for animal furs, DuQuesne (1996, passim) suggests that their lexification in various languages is more than a matter of mere functional labeling. In fact, ethnographers generally experience some difficulty identifying the perceptual cues underpinning indigenous color nomenclatures for animal pelts, and defining the meanings of specific terms. As far as camel colors are concerned, my Bedouin informants' attempts at glossing them seldom amount to more than vague approximations: *bēn al-aḥámar w-al-azrag* 'between red and black,' or *byiṭʿi ʿala l-ašgar* 'it approaches fawn,' for the camel color, *amġar.* When I inquired about the difference between *awδaḥ* and *ašʿal,* both designating 'white,' one informant volunteered: *kullu bigarrib baʿδ̣u* 'they are very similar,' which is not very enlightening.

Two main difficulties bedevil the discussion of camel colors for the researcher: first, grasping the perceptual cues underlying the Bedouin's taxonomy, and second, translating the native color terms with some degree of accuracy into a foreign language. On examining samples of camel hair carrying different color labels, the non-native observer is struck by the subtle contrasts distinguishing between the lighter varieties, for which no adequate, simplex lexical equivalents appear to exist in English and other western languages. The belabored English definitions for the color 'camel' in *Webster's Third New International Dictionary* (1971:1321) illustrate this translation problem:

(a) a variable color averaging a light yellowish brown that is slightly redder and very slightly less strong than khaki, yellower and less strong than cinnamon, and yellower and duller than walnut brown;

(b) a brownish gray that is lighter than average chocolate, redder, lighter, and stronger than taupe ... or castor, and redder than mouse gray.

By and large, definitions of color terms are misleading since they obscure the fact that communicating with colors involves above all situational intelligibility rather than mere labeling accuracy (Lucy, 1997:323). This point is brought out in an observation on the camel terminology of the Āl Murra Bedouin of the Empty Quarter in Ingham (1990:74):

> It will be noticed that the normal translation of such words as *ṣufur* 'yellow,' *ḥumur* 'red,' *zurug* 'blue' is not of much use in understanding the color of camels. As with all other specialized vocabularies it is first necessary to be able to observe the referent, i.e., the camel, and then to learn the cognitive system associated with it.

This comment echoes a remark in Turton (1980:326) on terms for cattle colors used by the Omotic-speaking Mursi cattle herders of Southern Ethiopia:

> Although *hurai* and *lele* were also used of cattle, I did not get a clear idea of the precise discrimination they were used to make. *Hurai* was used of animals that looked to me identical with others called *biley,* although I was assured there was a difference ...

6.2 *Natural vs conventional colors*

Another issue arising vis-à-vis the color systems of pastoralists is whether and to what extent, these groups attend to and formally lexify colors outside the range of hues relevant to what B&K designate as "areas of high cultural interest" (1969: 141). These authors recognize an evolutionary stage in the diachrony of color systems, at which peoples close to nature may ignore basic color categories in favor of non-basic ones encoding the natural colors of their ecology:

> For example, to a group whose members have frequent occasions to contrast fine shades of leaf color and who possess no dyed fabrics, color-coded electric wires, and so forth, it may not be worthwhile to rote-learn labels for gross perceptual discriminations such as green/blue, despite the psychological salience of such contrasts. (*loc.* cit.)

They cite the case of the Damara, a herder people of South-West Africa (now Namibia) from Magnus (1880):

> Insofar as the color table coincides with the colors of livestock, i.e., of cattle, sheep and goats, there is no difficulty in naming colors. They cannot name colors which do not pertain to livestock, especially blue and green, although they can distinguish the colors from each other and can name them with foreign words if necessary ... (B&K, 1969:141)

Tent-dwelling Negev Bedouin seem to me to display a comparable bias in favor of natural colors and find irksome the effort of naming commercially produced colors, which they perceive as *iši jdīd* 'something new,' or *ṣanaᶜāt jdīdih* 'new products' (Informant: Swēlim Abu Blayyih 67).

A striking counter-example to the Damara and the Negev Bedouin in the matter of color-naming ability is the striking case of the aforementioned Mursi cattle herders whose entire color paradigm derives from terms for cattle colors, but who are, nonetheless, able to name conventional colors with ease:

> If their color terms did refer primarily, in a perceptual sense, to cattle colors, it would be reasonable to expect that they would find it more difficult to name colors the more these colors diverged, perceptually, from those found in cattle. But this is not so. Informants had no difficulty—less, indeed than one would expect the average English speaker to experience—in naming a wide range of commercially produced color stimuli, the great majority of which, furthermore, they had almost certainly never seen before. Equally striking is the fact that informants did not see cattle colors as 'focal.' (Turton, 1980:320)

Not all pastoralist communities model their color categories exclusively after their ecology. Thus the Tuareg color paradigm described by Prasse (1999) lexifies a wide range of hues, both natural and synthetic. It might be instructive to examine comparative data on the color paradigms of other pastoralists and *Naturvölker* from different cultures for insights into how the languages spoken by these groups come to terms with modern color stimuli.

7. A Note on Color Symbolism

In my remarks on NA color terms for 'black,' I mentioned a symbolic restriction on the use of *aswad* 'black' among the Negev Bedouin and other Arabic-speaking groups. In map 34 of their Egyptian Arabic dialect atlas, Behnstedt and Woidich (1985) make this comment on their informant's conscious avoidance of this color term:

> 'schwarz' als Farbe ist i.a. *asmar.* Eine ganze Reihe von Informanten lehnte es schlicht ab, das Wort *aswad/aswid* überhaupt auszusprechen ...

which closely replicates the situation I described above (§5) for the Negev Bedouin.

In effect, three color categories predominate in the color symbolism of the Negev Bedouin: white, black, and red. Willis (1985:218) drew attention to the centrality of this triad in the symbolism of non-literate cultures:

> It seems likely that physiological factors underlying visual perception in all human beings have produced the high incidence in non-literate cultures of symbol systems that exploit the chromatic differences of white, black and red. V.W. Turner has suggested that the white-black-red triad is 'a primordial classification of reality' that is common to all human beings because it is rooted in physiological experience (2004: 81). Since Turner's now classic paper, Berlin and Kay (1969) have produced evidence for the existence of universal 'focal colours' in human perception and suggested an evolutionary schema in which white/black, and then red, are the first colours to be nominally distinguished in all cultures. Subsequent experiments ... have pointed to a pre-linguistic structuration of colour perception in human cognitive development (Heider, 1972:20).

Morabia (1986:700) recognized the function of these three colors in the symbolic language of Classical Arabic but failed to indicate an appropriate cognitive framework. Taking as her point of departure the work of Claude Lévi-Strauss, Victor Turner, and other researchers of symbolic anthropology, Jacobson (1978) investigated cognitive aspects of this color triad in relation to a mode of thinking observed among certain peoples of Central Africa, for whom these colors implement a classification of phenomena and cultural values relating to social order. In this system, white signifies 'positive,' black, 'negative,' and red, 'ambiguous.' I find this classificatory framework very suggestive vis-à-vis symbolic values assigned to these colors by several Bedouin communities in the Middle East including the Negev Bedouin.

(a) Black vs *white*

Briefly, the semantic opposition 'white' : 'black' is firmly embedded in the metaphorical codes of several Arab nomads in honor-related contexts. Writing about Arabian Bedouin, Sowayan (1985:44) observed that

> To cope with the volatile and potentially explosive politics of the desert in the absence of central authority, the nomads devised various codes of honor which served to minimize danger and prevented the breakdown of order … This system includes the right of protection to companions, tent-neighbors, and fugitives.

Among Bedouin in the Negev and Sinai, the legal terms *tabyīḍ̣ al-wijih* 'whitening of the face' and *taswīd al-wijih* 'blackening of the face' designate an individual's worthiness or unworthiness, respectively, of being accorded honor as the Bedouin understand it (cf. Stewart 1994, *passim*). A Bedouin tribesman might decide to impugn the honor of another Bedouin by blackening him. This might take the following form:

> A will say, 'May God blacken B's face,' or words to that effect. A may set up a black flag, or a black stone, in some appropriate place, for example, near a well, where people will see it and ask who put it there and why (Stewart, 1994:82–83).

The symbolic association of 'white' and 'black' with positive and negative honor values, respectively, harks back to Pre-Islamic times and is explicitly reflected in Old Arabic literature. Interpreting the expression *aswadu l-wajhi* (lit., 'black of face') in texts from this period, Fischer (1965:275) writes:

> Bei Menschen bedeutet *aswad*, im Gegensatz stehend zu *abyaḍ, azhar, aġarr* 'hellsichtig,' 'von edlem, reinem Charakter, edler Herkunft,' den entsprechenden Gegensatz 'von gemeinem, niedrigem, feigem Charakter,' 'von niedriger Gesinnung oder Herkunft.' Die Charakterisierung eines solchen Menschen als *aswad* geht wie bei *abyaḍ* von der Vorstellung des 'dunklen, schwarzen Gesichtes' aus ...

Among present-day Arabian Bedouin, a suppliant expressing gratitude to a benefactor, would fly a white flag in his honor "showing that the benefactor has performed all his obligations and that his face is white" (Sowayan, 1985:48).

At a more mundane level of symbolism, the Negev Bedouin fly a white flag *(rāya bēḍ̣á)* above a tent on joyful occasions, for instance, during the festivities celebrating a circumcision *(ṭahār)*, a wedding, the beginning of a pregnancy, or the return of a pilgrim from the *ḥajj*. White also has a place in popular religious rituals: during a visit to a saint's tomb it is customary to burn incense beside the grave and to spread a white cloth on the tomb.

(b) Red

The color red among the Negev Bedouin and other Middle Eastern Arab nomads tends to be associated with liminality, and the semiotic function of this color in Negev Bedouin society finds its most explicit expression in clothing. Traditionally, red is never worn by men, but is a standard color in women's apparel. Among Palestinian Bedouin,

> The dominant colour of southern bedouin embroidery is red, and is explicitly associated with sexual maturity and marital status. Unmarried girls wore dresses embroidered in blue; and only after marriage or becoming pregnant were they permitted to adorn their dresses with red embroidery (Weir, 1989:139).

Red or saturated pink is also the color of the woollen girdle *(ṣūfiyyih)* worn by married Bedouin women in the Negev (Weir, 1989:141). The social symbolism of red conveyed by women's apparel and its association with gender among Middle Eastern Bedouin have been insightfully examined in Abu-Lughod (1986:17).

8. Synopsis and Conclusion

The present preliminary study, which forms part of a broader ethnography of color categorization among tent-dwelling Bedouin in the Negev, set out to accomplish two main objectives: (a) to describe the most archaic color paradigm in NA, and (b) t o discuss cultural aspects of color in relation to the Bedouin 'world view.'

The area of linguistic particularism discussed in this paper is evidently also valid for other nomadic vernaculars of Arabic and provides the linguist with an instrument of dialectal *and* cultural differentiation which, to the best of my knowledge, has not been utilized in the study of Bedouin Arabic.

The NA color data presented in the main body of this work have been classified in the following manner:

abyaḍ—*abyaδ guḥḥ, awḍaḥ, aš^cal, ašgaḥ, abraṣ, [baraṣa, raġamūn];*
azrag—*azrag, azrag ġaṭīs, asmar, aswad, adġam, [yaḥāmīma];*
aḥámar—*aḥámar gāṭi^c, aḥámar, amġar, adham, adkar, adra^c, zahriy, ^cinnābiy, gaháwiy;*
axáḍar—*axáδar ^cišbiy, axáḍar baṭṭīxiy, axáδar zētiy, axáḍar luksiy, dukrun;*
aṣfar—*aṣfar, δahabiy, aṣfar lamūniy;*
ašhab—*ašhab, adġaθ, adxan, ramādiy, sakaniy, raṣāṣiy, ṣīniy, nīliy. ašhab milḥiy, ašhab kuḥliy, ašhab ġrābiy.*

Basic colors are here given in larger print; these are followed by their hyponyms (including the basic color name itself when this also denotes a specific hue, e.g., of a camel), and then by covert color terms enclosed in square braces.

Assuming that the indirect manner of elicitation I adopted in my fieldwork has not occasioned serious lacunae in the corpus of color terms noted, a striking cultural feature of NA color categories is the distribution of lexified points within the color solid and within individual categories.

The following general trends merit attention in this regard:

(i) the areas of the color solid most densely represented in the NA paradigm of level-2 color words correspond typically to nonfocal, desaturated, natural colors in the areas of red and yellow, and along the achromatic continuum between white and black;

(ii) level-2 color terms for natural hues are extensively retained by the oldest generation of tent-dwelling tribesmen, who are often unable to name non-focal, especially synthetic, colors;

(iii) some expansion of the NA color paradigm has occurred in the domain of green and, among younger speakers, in that of blue, but hyponyms for conventional colors appear to be few and often loans from urban Arabic: *zahriy, ʿinnābiy, nīliy,* etc.

The restricted nature of the NA basic color paradigm supports the view that the Bedouin's referentially precise vocabulary for natural colors has traditionally been more serviceable to them than more general terms. There is a school of thought in research on lexical semantics that is sympathetic to such a viewpoint; thus Lyons (1968:432) has stated that:

> ... the language of a particular society is an integral part of its culture, and ... the lexical distinctions drawn by each language will tend to reflect the culturally important features of objects, institutions and activities in the society in which the language operates.

The prolix lexification of ecological hues and their stability over time in the usage of tent-dwelling Negev Bedouin and other Arab nomads suggests that, even with an established system of basic color categories, a speech community may, nevertheless, be culturally conditioned to regard perceptually non-focal colors as somehow more 'real' in everyday discourse, and to ascribe psychological salience to areas of the color solid away from conventional foci.

Much current work on color theory is wedded to what Donald (1991:254) has called 'the dictionary model of the lexicon,' which tends to assign basic color terms a higher salience over non-basic ones in an absolute fashion. Donald's alternative to this perception of the lexicon is the 'embedding model':

> Words are virtually never used outside of an embedding cognitive context. The notion that words are embedded in mental models is not new; Wittgenstein (1922) appreciated this aspect of language and perhaps expressed the complexities of word functions better than anyone else ...

Ideally, linguistic research on color categorization should distinguish between the intrinsic psychological salience of colors and their communicative prominence in actual discourse accounting for their distribution in every-day usage in terms of competing semantic hierarchies.[26]

From the evolutionary standpoint, the salience traditionally enjoyed by natural colors in the NA color paradigm may explain why the more focal areas of their basic color categories have remained largely uncharted and, possibly, also why the dialect never acquired the later categories of the B&K evolutionary sequence. This may justify the inference that when basic color systems stagnate over unusually long stretches of time, a contributory factor in some cases may be the parallel existence of an elaborate and functionally salient level-2 system.

Notes

1. The present research was undertaken at the Social Studies Center of the Jacob Blaustein Institute for Desert Research, Sede Boqer, Israel. I am deeply grateful to my ʿAzāzmih Bedouin neighbors for their patience and generous hospitality during my fieldwork and to Prof. Gideon M. Kressel, who introduced me to the field of Bedouin studies and encouraged me in pursuing the present line of research.
2. Though here, too, it is easy to over-generalize. Fieldwork undertaken in the 1920s on certain South Italian vernaculars revealed the absence of a 'blue' category that is well-established in standard Italian (Kristol, 1980).
3. On historical aspects of the Arabic color system, see Borg (to appear).
4. To date, with the exception of a few studies—Evans Pritchard (1946), Bailey and Danin (1981), Bailey (1984), Hobbs (1989, passim)—the Bedouin's linguistic categorization of their desert ecology has received only minimal attention.
5. In order not to prejudge color categories as basic or nonbasic, I shall adopt Conklin's 1955 terms 'level-1' and 'level-2.'
6. In effect, the aggregate of these color points corresponds to the area of the color solid exemplified in the *Munsell Soil Color Charts*.
7. There are approximately 150,000 Arabs of Bedouin ancestry in the Negev district.
8. In several varieties of colloquial Arabic, color terms also display special syntactic and semantic features; thus, their syntactic distribution in noun phrases of the form [noun + def. art. + adj.], particularly common in lexicalized phrases and descriptive placenames—e.g., NA *Wādiy al-abyaḍ* 'White Riverbed'—is isomorphic with that of antonyms (cf. Blanc, 1964:127, iii; Borg, 1989). This is suggestive in the light of semantic research undertaken in Katz (1964) and Lyons (1977:283), which motivates formal grouping of adjectives encoding antonymic and color contrasts in the same semantic class.
9. Lakoff (1975) makes a general claim that women tend to employ a more precise and more differentiated color lexicon than men.
10. In the following remarks on the basic categories of NA, color names at the head of each category include the masculine, feminine, plural, and diminutive

forms; this last can usually be rendered in English by color adjectives ending in *-ish*: reddish, etc.

11. Fischer (1965:36) derives OA *asmar* from *samur* 'Akazie.' For the etymology of *aswad*, see Fischer, 1965, p. 273ff. NA *azrag* continues OA *azraq*, which was not a color term.
12. The lexical distinction between the two terms perpetuates a virtual taboo among the Negev Bedouin on family alliances with black Bedouin (cf. Jaussen, 1948:60–61).
13. See also Marçais (1955) on Algeria, Stewart (1999:109ff.), Behnstedt (1982) and Behnstedt and Woidich (1985: Map 34) on Egypt, Reichmuth on the Sudan (1981:65), and Morabia (1986:710) on Morocco.
14. Different shades of red and pink are very salient in the traditional embroidery of Bedouin women's clothing.
15. Classical Syriac, however, extended the green category in the direction of yellow, yielding a typologically marked color category (cf. MacLaury, 1999: 21): *yarūqō* 'green and yellow' (Audo, 1897:440–1); cf. also *yarōqō* 'the yolk of an egg' (Manna, 1975:317). I am indebted to Mr. Assad Sawma for these references.
16. Solaymân and Charles record the lexeme *ṭāry* 'vert (bois)' (1972:133) in the jargon of Lebanese sailors; cf. Maltese [tāri] 'tender (e.g., meat)' (own language).
17. In the Arabic dialect of Upper Egypt, the 'greenness' metaphor extends to young offspring of certain fowl *wizz ʾaxḍar* 'Gänsejunges,' *baṭṭ ʾaxḍar* 'Küken (Ente)' (Solayman and Charles, 1972:292).
18. For this meaning, cf. also Hebrew *raʿnán* 'saftig grün' (Beyer, 1984:697).
19. A reference to milk in relation to the color of the sky occurs in at least one other Arabic dialect but, oddly, with a different meaning: Omdurman *axadar labani* 'Milchfarben, hellblau' (Reichmuth, 1981:56). The association of sky-color with whiteness in NA recalls Benno Landsberger's observation: "... Das in späteren Zeit 'Blau' bedeutende Wort, *glaukos* war ursprünglich 'hell schimmernd'; der Himmel ist für die Griechen und Römer ebensowenig 'blau' wie für Sumerer, Akkader und andere Semiten" (Landsberger, 1967:139).
20. My informant Abu Xalīl (from Šgēb) refers to it as *al-finjān aṣ-ṣīni* 'the Chinese coffee-cup'; cf. *ṣīn* 'porcelain cup' in the dialect of the Rwala bedouin (Musil, 1928:107).
21. Color terms for herd animals have been recorded for several Bedouin groups: the 'Utaybah of Central Arabia (Hess, 1920), the Āl Murrah of the Empty Quarter (Ingham, 1990), erstwhile Galilean Bedouin (Sonnen, 1952:42–48), North African Bedouin (Roth, 1986), and Mauritanian Bedouin (Monteil, 1952:107).
22. The theme of color terms in toponyms has been widely studied for the Germanic *Sprachraum* (cf. Maas, 1990a, 1990b); there is no comparable

treatment as yet for Arabic color toponyms. Writing about the Khushmān Bedouin of the Eastern Desert in Egypt, Hobbs (1989:81) draws attention to the way in which these nomads "develop roots in their landscape, fashioning subjective 'place' from anonymous 'space.'" Color terms conceivably impart to placenames a sensory immediacy reflecting 'the actual experience of space as natural and sensual phenomena' (Highwater, 1981:131; Durkheim, 1912:23).

23. Cf. also Jaussen (1948:148).
24. Observe a similar classification in a text by the 6th century Arab poet Ḥātim al-Ṭāʾī (Fischer, 1965:337): *ʿindī miʾatu nāqatin saudāʾa wa-miʾatu nāqatin ḥamrāʾa wa-miʾatu nāqatin admāʾa* 'ich habe 100 schwarze, 100 braune und 100 hellfarbige Kamelinnen.'
25. Ringel (1938:82) exemplifies for Old Arabic the use of a color term as a camel 'name': *Dahmāʾ* 'Schwärzliche.' NA camel colors as labels for specific types of this animal can also be used to generate camel names: *Uδayḥān* (f. *Uδayḥih*) 'Bright One' < *awδaḥ*; *Zrēgān* (f. *Zrēgih* 'the Dark One') < *azrag*, etc.
26. An indigenous Arab view on the issue of basicness or salience of a color term in specific contexts was adduced by the 14th century historian and philosopher, Ibn Khaldūn, who noted that context-restricted color terms cannot always be replaced by the respective superordinate designations. In choosing an example illustrating his point, the author focused precisely on animal colors:

> For instance, 'white' is used for anything that contains whiteness. However, the whiteness of horses is indicated by the special word *ashhab*, that of men by the word *azhar*, and that of sheep by the word *amlah*. (*Muqaddimah* III:330).

By way of contrast, certain semantic domains, like that of food and drink, rule out such lexical hierarchies in favour of basic terms, especially *white, black,* By way of contrast, certain semantic domains, like that of food and drink, rule out such lexical hierarchies in favour of basic terms, especially *white, black,* and *red*. In ancient Arabia, *bayāδ* 'whiteness' and *sawād* 'blackness' designated milk and dates, respectively (Lane, 1863:1461), while fresh ripe dates were called *δu ḥumra* 'having redness' (Lane, 1863:640). The same source also cites the following striking usage from the medieval Arab author Zamaxšarī (d. 1143): *naḥnu min ahli l-aswadayni lā l-aḥmarayni* 'We are of the people of the two black ones (dates and water), and not of the two red ones (flesh and wine).' Observe also the post-biblical Hebrew classification of wines into *lābān* 'white,' *kāḥōl* 'dark,' and *ādōm* 'red' (Demsky, 1972) with parallels in modern European languages: *Weisswein, Schwarzbrot,* etc.

PART IV

RESEARCH

Amos Richmond, the founder of the Desert Research Institute, records some of his activities during the first five years as he recruited scientists to come and live and work in the desert. Short accounts are given of the ways that living in the desert year around affected the scientific work of scientists involved with solar power, solar energy, fossil water, microalgae, runoff agriculture, fish, and architecture.

Chapter 11

Founding of the Institute for Desert Research

Amos Richmond

Over half a billion people, one sixth of the world's population, live in arid lands which comprise one third of the earth's surface. Arid lands are usually found inhabited by poor people whose rate of reproduction is high. As the stress on land usage intensifies and the shortage of food increases a vicious cycle of poverty occurs. Demographic pressure, occasional droughts, growing loss of land cover by poor tillage practices, over-grazing, and excessive removal of vegetation for firewood, shrink the arable plots. The productive capacity of the land plunges from bad to worse, resulting in desertification, malnutrition, and famine.

This grim situation is not beyond hope as it may be generally envisaged. Innovative technology may be used by which arid wastelands may be transformed and yield improved productivity. This is also true for the Negev desert in southern Israel, which accounts for nearly two thirds of the small country's land area.

Learning to cope with the desert should make it possible to populate the Negev, live more comfortably, and prosper.

David Ben-Gurion, Israel's first prime minister, thought that making the Negev flourish would provide the vision needed to up-lift society and urge it to go on. "In the Negev the pioneering willpower and creative talent of Israel will be put to test, a test that will be critical for its future." His view allocated the lead in the efforts to make the desert flourish to the country's scientific community. Believing, that for western scientists, desert research would not be of particular interest Ben-Gurion's thoughts assigned the duty of developing new methods for inhabiting deserts to Israel's scholars. He foresaw new technologies e.g., for finding sweet water, including practical methods for desalination of brackish water, harnessing of solar energy as electric power, designing reservoirs for runoff water, and sorting out useful desert-adapted plant species. Scientists who would chart the road by which to make the Negev desert flourish would, in effect, contribute to the most important problem facing an ever growing part of humanity, the natives in the arid lands.

Quoting Proverbs (29: 18), Ben-Gurion believed that "Where there is no revelation, the people cast off restraint ...," and asserted that flourishing the desert should be the "unifying vision" for the people of Israel. Once the elite move to live in the Negev, many would follow.

Ben-Gurion's call for a pioneering uplift, however, left no echo in Israeli society. Nevertheless, a move in support of a Negev project was made by a small group of Ben-Gurion admirers who in 1963 founded 'The Negev Fund,' that together with the Israeli Government, established a sort of youth-center named 'Midreshet Sde-Boqer Ba-Negev,' near to Kibbutz Sde-Boqer where Ben-Gurion lived.

Thinking of an educational center soliciting the graduates to establish themselves in the Negev, a High School for new immigrants' youth, a regional 'Ort' school of trades, a Teachers Seminar, and a Field School, were opened at the Midrasha.

With time however, 'The Negev Fund' accrued debts and the refunding conditions were succumbed under a public forum, run by the Ministry of Education and the Negev Fund, entitled the 'Midreshet Sde-Boqer Corporation,' which had the authority to lay down a municipal administration as well as develop the educational youth center. In the decade following the inauguration of all the educational projects at Sde-Boqer, all except the Field-School, were closed for lack of public interest.

A ray of hope arrived then (January 1st, 1971) as a draft of a project, worked out by A. D. Bergman, a Professor of Chemistry at the Hebrew University, proposing the foundation of an academic institute for desert studies in the Sde-Boqer area, in honor of David Ben-Gurion. Submitted to the National Council for Higher Education, Bergman's plan was drawn on the importance of mobilizing scientists to the nation's priority assignment, and was attentive to Ben-Gurion's claim that the challenge of settling the Negev, crucial for Israel's future, should be launched by scientists.

Professor Bergman predicted 6 to 7 billion people by the year 2,000, i.e., the spreading, in effect, of hunger conditions. His plan for the Institute included a desert agriculture unit, a department for flora, fauna, and human physiology in desert climates as well as a department of environmental studies, attentive to the ecosystem as well as weather modification.

The National Council for Higher Education appointed Professor J. Yortner to chair a 'Midreshet Sde-Boqer Committee,' commissioned to test Bergman's proposal. In its June 30th meeting 1972, the Council accepted the committee's recommendation to establish an Institute for desert research in Midreshet Sde-Boqer, in the framework of Ben-Gurion University of the Negev.

The objectives set for the Institute were:
1. Enhance the development of the Negev.
2. Increase the Negev's appeal to academicians of high standard, whose permanent settlement will serve as a lodestone for many others to come, and
3. Discover ways for inhabiting arid lands and thereby facilitate solutions of similar problems faced by many other arid-land countries.

At its meeting on 19th December 1972, The Council for Higher Education decided to submit its recommendation, in the spirit of Yortner's committee, to the Israeli Government. On January 21st, 1973 the Israeli Government endorsed this proposal and decided to establish at the Midrasha an Institute for Desert Research which would be open for researchers from all Institutes of higher learning and would form an integral part of the University of the Negev (later renamed Ben-Gurion University) in Be'er Sheva.

Ben-Gurion died on December 1st, 1973, and he was buried on the verge of the cliffs facing the Zin valley, in Midreshet Sde-Boqer which was renamed 'Midreshet Ben-Gurion.' His death underscored the obligation to act, put on Ben-Gurion University, founded a few years earlier, and on its president Professor M. Prives.

In March 1974, Professor Prives appointed me Director, commissioned to start building the Desert Research Institute. Actual work started in October of that year.

In addition, I was given overall responsibility for the new Ben-Gurion Memorial Institute, also to be built at the Midrasha, in which the archives with Ben-Gurion's notes, documents, and correspondence material of a lifetime were to be stored in the service of information as well as for education and research of historians to come.

Having nominated me 'Officer in Charge of the Midrasha Campus,' Ben-Gurion University in effect created overnight an additional, albeit virtual, campus alongside the main Be'er Sheva campus.[1]

For years, only goodwill arrangements existed without any official relationship, between the University and Midreshet Ben-Gurion, on which grounds the two University Institutes were being erected. In 1976, Midreshet Ben-Gurion Corporation nominated me as their Chair, with the authority to transfer to the University the property vacated by the closed Ort School as well as allocate apartments in the Midrasha for the arriving university scholars.

Within a short time and at a very small expense therefore, a University campus was in effect unfolding with the Desert Research Institute, taking over the Ort school, in which rather modest laboratories as well as office space were improvised.

This meager start was significantly augmented when, on January 21st 1980, the University signed an agreement with the Jacob[2] and Hilda Blaustein Fund, run by their successors. In accordance with this agreement, the Blaustein family established a renter fund that with a matching of the Israel Government, provided for the initial operation of the Institute, to be named after the late Jacob Blaustein (BIDR = The Blaustein Institute for Desert Research).

Upon being nominated director of the Institute (March 1974), I prepared an academic plan, in which the major targets for the Institute were laid down. The first goal concerned the challenge Israeli society faces in settling the Negev. To succeed in this mission, the Institute would have to address and research the various areas which together comprise the unique body of knowledge for the best mode of settlement in remote, arid lands such as the Negev desert.

This meant a framework that would integrate research of the ecological system, innovative agricultural and industrial development as well as relevant social aspects, forming an Interdisciplinary web. In general, the academic plan for the Institute called for a thorough study of the desert environment with particular reference to the ecological relationships which shape the desert land; research of plant, animal and human physiology which addressed mechanisms of adaptation to aridity; social research of the Negev population with special reference to the native Bedouins; research applications of solar energy; efficient use of local water resources including groundwater, runoff, water desalination, and waste-water management; develop unique architectural modes and urban design patterns addressing problems imposed by the extreme desert climate and finally, study of the economic interrelationships involved in resource development of deserts.

This straightforward, practical approach for building the Institute stemmed from the realization that pioneering spirit alone, though vital to call up and bring idealist scholars, would not be a sufficient driving force for mass settlement of the Negev. In reality, new settlers must come bound with the prospects to improve their quality of life and find satisfactory employment, to which practical targets our research should lead the way.

This academic plan was approved by the authorities of Ben-Gurion University and the Israel Council for Higher Education and served for many years as our ideological planning chart. At that time, the Planning and Grants Committee together with the Ben-Gurion University set up a guidance committee for the Institute, whose duties were to study our progress and evaluate our research efforts as well as recommend further developments of the Institute. The committee was first chaired by Professor Y. Yortner and somewhat later by Professor Y. Birk who served as chair for many years.

It had been originally suggested by A. D. Bergman and was indeed obvious to us that in order to excel in our mission of becoming a meaningful, influential research center, we must engage the international scientific community with our activities and facilitate the hosting of foreign scholars coming from all over the world as well as students interested in the fields of our specialization. From the very beginning, as indicated in my academic plan, it was clear that a major task of the Institute would be the establishment of a graduate school for desert studies through which the work carried out by Institute scientists as well as other scholars of deserts would be disseminated. The graduate school, open to the international student community should become a major instrument by which to achieve our sought after leadership in desert research, as well as providing incentives to our scientists in the pursuit of excellence. With this in mind, I wanted to recruit "joint appointments," open for leading, well recognized scientists involved in desert research among the established universities in Israel. These scientists would maintain regular appointments in their respective universities but would devote some of their professional efforts, compensated properly, to the Institute at the Midrasha. This approach went hand in hand with the original government decision regarding our Institute as a national center but did not come through, having been rejected by the entire university establishment in Israel who found little interest in sharing some of their best scientists with an Institute belonging to a rival university. I was thus forced to hire relevant scientists from other universities on an individual, non-permanent, part time basis. Some of the people thus recruited (e.g., E. Marx, J. Gale, A. Shkolnick, A. Yair, U. Safriel) and others from the Be'er Sheva campus (e.g., E. Hochman, U. Regev, Y. Grados, A. Weingrod) were helpful, particularly in the initial period, in augmenting our scientific caliber.

Indeed, the greatest challenge confronting me in establishing the Institute was attracting outstanding or promising scientists to the remote, desolate Midrasha, so deficient in infrastructure and basic research means. Evidently, setting up a center of scientific excellence under these demanding circumstances would be possible only with daring, imaginative people, appreciative of new, pioneering challenges. Adapting the observation made by Adam Smith that people are at their very best when catering for their own interests, I operated along an ideological framework which invoked freedom for scientists to develop their work in any directions they chose, as long as they adhered to the basic reasons of existence of their respective research units, as well as to the goals of the Institute dedicated to desert research.

The very limited budget available and the need to address many divergent research fields, favored the operation of small teams. In lack of conventional means and confronting a great many difficulties, improvisation was called for and the organization of small, harmonious, highly specialized research groups seemed to provide a workable solution. Heads of research units were given the Institute's permission to recruit within their allotted budget their choice of team members and seek any means of funding of their choice, including donations from their own families.

Some technical and administrative support was provided by the Institute, not including, as a rule, research money. Unit heads and senior personnel were expected to amass the means for research. The dozen small units established had to get along with a meager expansion in the number of positions and overcome interpersonal tensions, implying intensification of teamwork.

My perception of multiple small research teams, as was in effect brought forth in the Academic Plan, was challenged by many. Some argued that the Negev desert represented primarily a climatic phenomenon, thus our Institute must engage in studying meteorology, mainly that. Another claim had it that work should be confined to study water aspects, because it was the lack of water which created the desert. Accordingly, concentration of the limited means we had should better put to test but one or two of the crucial problems, rather than have fractions of teams, dealing with a myriad of subjects. These points of view caused us inter and intra debates but I remained firm, believing that tackling the issues posited by studying the desert and the modes of its settlement dictated an organization with multidisciplinary skills. Synergism amongst divergent though well defined object-minded small units, lead by senior scientists, each determined in effort to obtain his professional objectives within the general context of desert research was my version.

In retrospect, this organizational build up has gradually demised. The small unit concept was abandoned, the units having been forced to merge as big departments and the departments were recently re-organized into three grand Institutes. Has this been necessitated concerning the scientists and their mode of research or the administrative management and its competence? One way or the other, the advantages of small think-tanks tackling substantial scientific matters observed from divergent expert view-points, diminished.

Addressing our financial affairs and pattern of expenditure, I insisted on a 'closed system,' accentuating the Institute's independence in the use of budgets within the university framework. In a similar manner I allowed each research unit the freedom, within regulatory limits, to use the allotted annual budget as it found fit. It did well to enhance the spirit of independence and ingenuity but most important, assured that the small budget would be used optimally, spending only on real necessities as judged by those directly concerned. Decentralization provided an added incentive for creativity as well as encouraging the research units' webs of contacts with colleagues in Israel and abroad. Unit heads and members were granted full freedom to collaborate in search of research funds and invite scholars and students, organizing mutual projects, as long as these activities were fully covered by the unit budget and adhered to the unit's basic program. No initiatives coming from the units were permitted to burden the general Institute budget.

Having to ponder my duties as the Institute Director in all that, I could recall an anecdote told by the late H. B. Tuky, one of my professors in Michigan State University in 1962, re academic administration: A football team captain of a known American university was asked a pointed ad hominem question: How come such a tiny guy (like him) functions as a football team captain. He retorted: "I call the tricks and run out of the way." "This" said Tuky, who was the department chairman, "was the secret of a good administrator."

Thanks to this mode of decentralization, monitoring of scientific management and current affairs on the units' agenda were in the hands of unit heads, who, each in her/his fields of specialization knew far better than me. I saved my authority to matters of coordination, representation, recruitment of donations, and promotion of the Institute's development projects.

In retrospect, a drawback of the small research group organizational concept was that much of the unit's chances for success depended on the unit head. It took an open, self assured, trusting, and honest individual who took pleasure in good scientific work performed by researchers in the group, giving due credit and could yet express criticism if necessary. Not all unit heads passed this test of character and in some units there were junior researchers who felt choked and constrained. The trial of years confirmed however, that while very few of the units had to be abandoned and others only survived, many grew to become distinguished, internationally recognized centers of research and knowledge.

By 1978 most of the research units were founded. Then we called for the first international conference and issued the first scientific report. In what follows, the scientific ideology and reasons of existence of the research units unfold.

Establishing the Research Units

The first years of building the Institute, starting in 1974, represent the formative period, in which the general framework as well as the thematic organization of the Institute were set for years to come. By the end of 1978, some four years from the very beginning of operations, most major research units had been established and the first annual scientific report came out.

The research units formed represented, in effect, the practical interpretation of my academic plan although serendipity also played a role in that availability of gifted and dedicated persons involved in desert research who showed interest in the Institute affected the decision to establish the appropriate research units. In what follows, their pertinent stories unfold.

Building Climatology

Baruch Givoni, a professor for Building Climatology from the Technion in Haifa, represented one example of serendipity. His expertise, which assumed particular significance following the oil-price crisis of the 1973 war, had particular relevance to building in the desert, and we were fortunate he expressed interest in joining the Institute.

The research group he established in Building Climatology which first included Engineer Dan Benor, Architect Mati Cones joining the project later, aimed to study adaptation of building design and materials to the ambient climatic conditions, characterized in the Negev by extreme diurnal as well as annual variations in temperature. The challenge was to modulate temperatures in the building throughout the year drawing on useful resources in the unique desert climate. One obvious resource—solar energy—is plentiful the year round and may be utilized directly for heating the home and providing hot water supply the year round. Other natural energies prevalent in the desert may be used for cooling purposes. Night cooling, for example, may be obtained by circulating cool night air through a heat storage system. Night radiation cooling, using cooled night air (through radiation to the clear sky), is also an option. Finally, night evaporative cooling, based on water evaporation during the cool summer nights, facilitates storage of the coolness produced at night in the building, for daytime use.

Givoni's message concerning the advantages obtainable in proper utilization of environmental resources in the desert represented, in effect, the basis on which a significant part of the Institute's research rested.

Hydrogeology and Water Resources

Professor Arie S. Issar was one of the very first scientists to have joined the Institute. He was at that time already a well recognized authority in hydrogeology and was thus put in charge of research concerning water resources in the desert. Issar pointed out that at the last ice age, some 18 thousand years ago, glaciers covered Europe all the way to the Po valley and heavy rains were falling on a zone extending from the Atlantic Ocean through the Sahara desert, Libya, and Egypt all the way to the Sinai and Negev deserts. Lakes abundant with wild life spread over wide tracts of land in these areas, prehistoric man leaving his tools on their shores. A significant amount of this abundant water was not lost with the change in weather that took place since, the ancient rains' water having percolated into the subsurface, accumulating in various depths on impervious layers in the Nubian sand stone.

Professor Issar suggested that substantial underground water resources of this essentially non-renewable "fossil water" exist in the Negev, representing a potential resource of water for agriculture and industry worthy of attention. The main objectives for the Hydrogeological Research Laboratory, which he organized together with his students Ronit Nativ and Eilon Adar, (Dr. Y. Ben-Asher joining somewhat later), were to define the optimal methods by which to exploit the two major types of water resources found in the Negev, i.e., flood water, originating from the brief but heavy torrents of rainfall falling at times in winter and the underground reservoirs of fossil water originating in the last ice-age.

These objectives raised several questions concerning the potential of renewable water resources, e.g., the best methods by which to catch desert floods. Should water be dammed in the upper part of the collecting (so called catchment) areas, when it is of small volume, requiring relatively small structures for its storage? Water stored on the surface, however, is susceptible to extensive evaporative losses, casting doubt as to whether large reservoirs should best be built in the lower part of the river basins. Should water be stored by allowing it to infiltrate into the subsurface, adding to the shallow groundwater resources, or should flood water be directly utilized for irrigation of winter crops and orchards?

Exploiting the deep-lying aquifers containing the ancient waters raised many questions pertaining to the best places in which to try and locate these aquifers e.g., what is the mechanism of mineralization of these waters and what should be the policy of their management? A study of movement of bodies of brackish water from the northern part of the region to the southern part was also contemplated.

Runoff Farming

It was a fortunate coincidence that Professor Michael Evenari, a world acclaimed botanist had just retired from the Hebrew University in Jerusalem at the time the Desert Research Institute was being organized. Evenari joined the newly born, fledgling Institute with great enthusiasm. The background of his life long study in the Negev was exciting. In the Negev Highlands, around the ruins of six ancient cities (Avdat, Shivta, Ruhibe, Nizzana, Kurnub, Khaluza), extensive traces of ancient desert agriculture had been found in an area which at present is an overgrazed desert.

Evenari and his colleagues, L. Shanan and N. Tadmor, were attracted to these ancient Negev cities in search of an answer to a major question: How was it possible that ancient cultures dating back to the time of King Solomon (10th century B.C.), could carry out agriculture in an area which was a desert, no different than it is today? What was their source of water, without which no agriculture is possible in a region receiving only 3 to 4 inches of annual precipitation?

Answers to these questions were vital for our goal to renew desert farming.

Evenari's team, which included D. Mazigh who was managing the work on the Avdat farm, had been unfolding, in fact, the principles of ancient desert agriculture. The water source of the ancient farmers was runoff which produces floods after one of the short but heavy showers, typical of many deserts. The runoff in the Negev Highlands amounted on an average to 20-30% of the overall amount of rainfall. This is a high percentage, only possible because of the unique qualities of the loess soil in the Negev which compacts as soon as it is hit by rain, causing the rain to accumulate on the surface forming streams. The ancient farmers collected the runoff streaming down the slopes after a rain in channels, leading it into their terraced farms in the valleys. On an average the catchment area which belonged to each farm and from which it received the runoff was about 20-30 times as large as the farm itself, i.e., if the rainfall amounts to 4 inches per year and 25% of this amount (1 inch) runs off from an area which is 30 times larger than the farm itself, the farm receives 30 inches of water, an amount fully sufficient to sustain any crop without additional irrigation. By directing flood water into terraced lots, the ancient farmers could grow barley and wheat as well as other field crops including fruit trees, in a desert receiving only 4 inches of precipitation.

Having deciphered the ancient methods of runoff farming, Evenari's research was directed towards adapting modern agriculture to the concept of rain water harvesting. With time they won world leadership in this unique field. Upon Michael Evenari's death, Professor Pedro Berliner succeeded him as head of runoff research.

Desert Ecology

In addition to his botanical expertise, Professor Evenari was an authority on arid land ecology. He established the Desert Ecology group, first recruiting his students M. Shachak and Y. Steinberger, who were already working under his leadership in the young Midrasha, before the Institute was established. His student, Dr. I. Gutterman also joined this group, who established a few years later his own research unit of Eco-physiology and Desert Plant Introduction.

Desert ecosystems are notoriously labile because the main environmental factor limiting their production i.e., rainfall, is so variable particularly in the Negev desert. Precipitation for the 1962-63 rainy season, for example, amounted to 24 mm whereas in the following season it was 168 mm. The equilibrium between the biotic and a-biotic components of a desert ecosystem therefore is most delicate and even slight changes introduced by man interrupt this equilibrium. One such change is caused by over-grazing of nomads' herds which reduce productivity dramatically. In the semi-deserts around the fringes of the true deserts, misuse due to lack of understanding of the ecosystem, has resulted in converting large tracts of potentially productive land into unproductive super-deserts.

It is envisaged that population pressures will not permit man to leave the arid lands unpopulated, which would be no doubt the case in Israel, where population density is expected to increase for many years to come. Populating the deserts however, should be done rationally, based on an understanding of the desert ecosystem. It was the basic aim of the Desert Ecology research group to study the interrelationships between the various components of the desert ecosystem guiding the development of the Negev to environment-sensitive decision making. Finally, research of the Negev desert ecosystems and suitable practical applications may assist neighboring countries with similar problems.

"Our team," wrote Evenari, "has two basic research objectives: First, to study the desert ecosystems in their natural state and second, to investigate the ecological interactions between the effect of intensive human activities and the surrounding desert ecosystem." In this fashion, maximal protection of the environment may become possible.

A special project designed to support the quality of life in desolate places was the plan to develop concepts for creating verdant parks in the treeless, arid land of the Negev highlands. Such places would provide recreation facilities for the inhabitants of the towns to be built in the Negev, conceivably affecting the stability of new urban desert populations. One such plan involved the establishment of the Great Negev Park which would eventually spread over millions of dunams in the Negev highlands and Arava.

Creating sites of recreation for locals as well as tourists has been in effect tested and developed by Michael Evenari in the farms at Avdat and Shivta. Research involved the accumulation of runoff water and flood water in hollows and valleys in which trees and shrubs could be grown, as well as pumping of the shallow brackish water prevalent in many sites in the Negev, proposed by Professor Issar, to create spots of suitable vegetation that in time will also attract animals. The idea of damming wadis for the storage of winter flood water and for raising the local level of ground water to augment the water supply was also contemplated.

Arie Issar suggested using small brackish ground water resources, too small for agricultural use, by digging small wells from which water could be supplied by wind-pumps used in the pampas of South America to create garden spots.

The project also called for the establishment of a Botanical Garden on our Campus at the Midrasha, focusing on introduction and adaptation of new plants to the region. In retrospect, only a modest beginning of these ambitious plans had been carried out, and fulfillment of the attractive Negev Parks idea will hopefully be seen sometime in the future.

Animal Physiology and Husbandry

How do animals live in the harsh and arid desert environment? What are their mechanisms of adaptation to the extreme environment? These were some of the questions posed by Professor Daniel Cohen, a well recognized authority in veterinary medicine, who established the Unit of Animal Physiology to which Drs. B. Pinshow and A. Degen were joined. Professor Cohen believed that the study of animals living in the desert is of great importance from both a socio-economic and biomedical point of view. He observed that human populations which have successfully adapted to living in harsh ecologic conditions of the world's arid zones have only been able to do so by domestication of specifically selected animals which could share and survive in the unique and exacting conditions. Accordingly the camel, goat, sheep, llama, etc., were all selected and domesticated to provide a constant source of food and materials.

Professor Cohen suggested that one of the solutions to the problem of maintaining the ecosystem and at the same time expanding protein production is to develop appropriate wildlife populations, harvested for food. Indeed, certain wildlife species have the ability to withstand heat and water deprivation in excess of anything noted in domestic animals. e.g., the addax, which can go for years without water or animals conserving body energy by allowing their daily body temperatures to vary as much as 10°C.

Research was focused on determining the best wildlife species or combination of species which could be developed to maintain the ecosystem and to produce animal protein under our conditions of desert and marginal land. The mechanisms for survival of physiological adaptation possessed by wildlife species was also intended to be studied.

Finally, Cohen thought it would be important to map the Negev for its endemic animal diseases especially the zoonoxes, and to monitor these diseases from time to time to prevent their increase. This would be of particular importance, he stated, in new areas planed for human settlement.

In retrospect, not much of this research plan was carried out. Animal physiology research in this unit has gradually converged on domestic animals, particularly the camel, studying its unique physiology and economic potential. Since Professor Cohen terminated his services in the Institute, Professor Allen Degen has been serving as the Head of this group, which at present has became totally committed to veterinary medicine.

Desert Meteorology

Professor Lou Berkofsky, specialized during his service in the US Air Force in theoretical meteorology, and was the first scientist to be recruited to the Institute. He was appointed head of the Desert Meteorology Unit, Dr. A. Zangwil joining soon after, focusing his research on weather modification.

Berkofsky noted that ever since scientific weather modification (which had its beginning in 1946) started, a wide variety of cloud seeding experiments have been carried out around the world. In Israel, experimentation during the period of 1961-1967 indicated a 15% increase of rainfall on seeded days. Accordingly, the water potential of Israel could be augmented by some 300-400 million cubic meters per year at a low cost, representing the least expensive development of a new water resource.

A method which has been used with success in seeding tropical clouds was based on the so called "dynamic theory" of seeding, which worked particularly well with isolated cumulus clouds, such as had been observed in the Negev.

Professor Berkofsky believed that cloud seeding had a distinct possibility for rainfall augmentation in the Negev, a massive attack on seedable clouds possibly yielding good results. Berkofsky thought that extensive meteorological observations e.g., the amount and distribution of rainfall in the Negev, the frequency of rain occurrence, the types, characteristics and distribution of clouds, as well as the characteristics of the ambient atmosphere in the vicinity of the clouds, would provide valuable data for a wide variety of meteorological and climatological studies, in addition to the information needed for cloud seeding.

Applied Solar Calculation Unit (ASCU)

The tale concerning the birth of the unit of 'Solar Calculations' is unique, but nevertheless, seems to hold an important key to understanding how, against all odds, promising scientists were willing to risk their academic careers and tie their future in a resourceless, poor, and remote location, to which even a basic telephone connection was not available.

Professor David Faiman, a particle physicist at the Weizmann Institute approached me in 1975 stating his wish to join the Institute. His reason: he was seeking a "pioneering experience" in the desert, striving to contribute his talent and enthusiasm to the country to which he recently emigrated. He believed this would give direction and purpose to his life. Since there was obviously no need for a particle physicist in the Desert Research Institute, Faiman was more than willing to transfer his field of interest to a pertinent area, applications of solar energy. This is how the Solar Energy Calculation Unit came finally into being, the idea being for a group of engineers, physicists, and mathematicians which initially included Drs. J. Gordon and D. Govaer, (Professor Yair Zarmi joining sometime later), to avail themselves for advice and initiation of joint projects with industries involved in applications of solar energy.

The basic concept was straight forward. Intense radiation, available the year round, makes the desert an ideal place for utilizing solar energy. Industry in small countries like Israel, however, could not generally afford to devote sufficient scientific infrastructure to solar energy research.

This situation creates an opportunity for good intentioned and devoted academicians to become directly involved with industry. With this in mind, ASCU would represent a pattern (for other academic institutes to study and emulate), of an academic group which would see as its goals to provide basic scientific know-how in service to industry. This idea had been envisaged over 30 years ago. It could not have been even contemplated in today's Israel.

The long term purpose of ASCU would be to promote the use of solar energy by affecting an overall transformation in economic policy pertaining applications of solar energy. It was envisaged that this necessary change in policy may take place in five consecutive stages as follows: 1) Hot water for domestic applications; 2) Heating and cooling of buildings; 3) Application of heat in industrial processes; 4) Solar thermal transformation to electric power; and 5) Direct solar transformation to electrical energy.

With time, however and with many more physicists joining the group, ASCU was transformed into two groups, one continuing in research concerning use of solar energy, the other group expanded the scope to address environmental physics, i.e., identifying and researching physical processes and phenomena connected or related with the desert environment. This direction was initially headed by Professor Yair Zarmi.

Desert Architecture

The rationale for establishing the Desert Architecture group seems self-evident, i.e., to attract and accommodate a new generation of desert dwellers, suitable habitats will have to be developed. The purpose of the Desert Architecture Unit was to develop concepts based on scientific research with which to create architecture and urban planning responsive to the unique environment as well as catering to the needs of the new desert dwellers.

These concepts would encompass not only modern energy-efficient systems but also techniques and designs which have evolved over the centuries and have proven functional for life in the desert. A model desert community would conceivably incorporate shading of large and small spaces for cooling, integrate vegetation with housing, paying particular attention to the proper building orientation to maximize comfort and energy conservation.

By 1978, four years after work had started, the staff, some recruited by Architect Moshe Safdie who founded the unit and others coming with Architect A. Rachamimov, who took the helm as head of Desert Architecture following Safdie's short service, was concentrating on several projects.

The 'solar house,' first designed in 1976, was built, using adobe bricks made on the premise, Architect Levin Epstein being in charge of the work, know-how for adobe construction being supplied by Larry Ma'ayan.

Development of the urban fabric of the nearby desert town of Yeruham was addressed mainly by N. Borenstein. Another project saw the group investigating the ecological basis for locating new settlements in the Negev highlands. Particular attention was devoted to systems of public shading in a desert community, and various technologies and modes of shading have been investigated, seeking integration of a public shading technique within the structure of a desert settlement.

Desert architecture based on scientific research, however, has not enjoyed high popularity in Academia, and the recruitment of a proper leader for architectural research, who would devote his entire career to this purpose met with difficulties. Architect Moshe Safdie as well as Architect Arie Rachamimov served the Institute only on a part-time basis. Indeed the Desert Architecture program at the Institute was finally fully inaugurated only with the arrival of Architect Dr. Yair Etzion, who had re-established the group and brought it to its present recognized achievements in building and community planning in the desert.

Y. Etzion, together with the colleagues he recruited, Architects I. A. Meir, E. Erel, and D. Pearlmutter, expanded the philosophy first formulated in the Institute by Professor B. Givoni, accordingly the very same aspects of the desert environment which create difficulties for new desert dwellers, may hold the key for solutions to these difficulties. Thus the wide diurnal and seasonal temperature swings reflected in high midday heat also allow effective nocturnal cooling.

Intense daytime solar radiation, only rarely blocked by clouds in winter, may be harnessed to heat houses by direct gain, to heat water in special collectors or to create electricity using photovoltaic panels. In time this group won world recognition, assuming leadership in Desert Architecture.

Desert Biosystems, Algae-culture, and Closed-system Greenhouse Agriculture

Unique strategies, fundamentally different from those successful in the temperate regions, must be formulated for agriculture in deserts. Essentially, arid-land agriculture must be science-based rather than resource-based.

'Desert Bio-Systems' meant systems designed to exploit economically the unique features of desert climate for making a living. The basic climatic differences between a desert and temperate regions are the low levels of cloud cover and high irradiance as well as low precipitation. These are the basic characteristics which make deserts less hospitable for man, animals, and plants. An important factor is the intense solar radiation, which results in high daytime temperatures and dryness. In contrast, night temperatures tend to be low even in summer. The lack of fresh water and the infertile and saline soils is compensated by the availability of brackish groundwater or sea water coupled with large empty tracts of land. These factors create, paradoxically perhaps, unique economic potentials.

Micro-Algaculture

Among the very first research units to have been established at the very beginning of activity in the Institute was the group involved in algal biotechnology, which I started in early '75 with my two doctoral students at the time, Avigad Vonshak and Sammy Boussiba (both of whom are Professors today, Avigad Vonshak serving presently as director of the Institute). Somewhat later, Dr. A. Abeliovitch and Dr. E. Tel Or joined this group. This rather novel biotechnology represents a unique answer to challenges set by the desert environment. Algae are water plants comprising several thousands of species which range in size from the familiar multicellular seaweeds down to microscopic, unicellular micro-algae.

Unlike conventional agricultural crops however, many algal species grow well in salty or sea water thereby removing the limitation of available sweet water for plant production. They may be cultured in large reactors, utilizing the desert's high temperature and solar irradiance, as well as its abundance in brackish or sea water. The algal biomass thus produced represents a renewable resource for food, animal feed, raw materials, and energy.

The food potential of many algae has been studied. Our study began with Spirulina and Spirogyra, which have very high protein content and are being grown for human consumption in several countries. As an animal feed the quality of protein from Spirulina, as well as from other algal species, compares favorably with common animal feeds, most of which could not be readily grown under conditions which are suitable for algae.

Many algae contain chemicals of importance to industry, and bio-chemicals that are the basis of potent pharmaceuticals. Nitrogen gas is plentiful in the atmosphere but not in a form available to plants. Important nutrients which some species of algae provide are soluble nitrogen compounds which represent a natural fertilizer. Indeed, one of the most expensive inputs in village rice farming, for example, is the application of industrially prepared nitrogen salts and direct application of nitrogen-fixing algae in rice paddies is used to a great benefit. Fish-feed and food chain components for aquaculture are other important options for micro-algae.

Several types of fish, shrimps, and prawns depend for their growth on algae-feeders such as rotifers and arthemia.

Finally, a very wide range of natural products may be obtained from micro-algae. Some algal species are rich in lipids, including valuable fatty acids such as eicosapentaenoic acid.

Still other species accumulate a wide array of natural products such as polysaccharides, carotenoids and other pigments, e.g., astaxanthine, amino acids, and various food supplements as well as pharmaceuticals.

Closed Desert Greenhouses

Apart from only marginally successful attempts to increase rainfall by cloud seeding, there exists no technology for modifying weather for plant production in an acceptable economic manner. Even rainfall induction cannot be used in many deserts, where there are only few clouds suitable for such induction. Consequently, in order to live, work and practice agriculture in the desert, man must learn to modify the microenvironment.

Using modern engineering technology, almost any desired environment for plant production may be reproduced.

In order to profitably modify the desert environment, it is essential to take maximum advantage of the few, but substantial, favorable desert conditions, e.g., solar insulation, especially in winter. In fact, the annual integrated solar energy flux induced on the Negev desert in Israel is almost twice that in Western Europe. This is of great significance in plant production, the relatively high daytime winter temperature representing another characteristic of great economic potential.

The general goal of making maximum use of available natural resources, while at the same time causing very little perturbation of the natural habitat, is firmly achieved in the Controlled Environment Desert Agriculture research unit. This group was established by Professor Joe Gale, a plant-physiologist from the Hebrew University in Jerusalem, with the status of a joint appointment at our Institute.

Closed greenhouses, in contrast with conventional agriculture, require very little supply of fresh water or fertile soil, potentially providing sophisticated, profitable employment. Greenhouses in hot deserts however, face two main problems. The first concerns cooling during periods of high insulation and the second, heating during cold nights. The problem of overheating is solved either by ventilation or wet pad and fan cooling. Another possibility is limiting the use of the greenhouse to no more than six or seven months a year. On winter nights, expensive fossil fuel driven heating must be often used for cold sensitive crops. Daytime ventilation limits the very desirable possibility of carbon dioxide gas fertilization to only a few hours a day, when the greenhouse is closed (which is when solar radiation is low and the plants are least responsive to added CO_2).

The main practical problems to be overcome in closed system technology were conceived by Gale as the development of complete dynamic, simulation energy models, the basis of automatic control systems. Another goal was the development of a stable liquid filter circulating in the roof. This optical filter should transit the photosynthetic part of the solar spectrum and absorb the near infra red heat producing section. Several technological solutions were sought for a simple heat exchanger to cool the liquid optical filter; a low cost cooling tower as well as solutions concerning choice of materials and construction of a robust manifold for the roof panels.

These problems were addressed by Professor Joe Gale's group, initially including Dr. Aharon Kaplan, Reuben Kopel, and Dr. Moshe Zeroni. Preliminary experiments gave grounds to expect productivity could be some two times higher than that obtained in the best conventional greenhouses. The low energy costs and high yields were expected to defray the higher investment costs of the closed greenhouse, estimated to be about 25% more than conventional, hard covered, fossil-fuel heated greenhouses.

Social Studies of Desert Settlement

This project was first placed for a short time in the hands of Professor A. Weingrod from the Department of Behavioral Sciences in Be'er Sheva, whose prime concern was urban settlements in the Negev. A bird's-eye view of most Negev 'development towns' conveyed the feeling of isolation. Only a few towns (e.g., Arad) revealed success. The relevance of ethnic factors, family structure, and environmental conditions on an economic take-off were measured. The stress caused by the desert surrounding was checked in terms of past negligence and future requirements.

Second to chair this short-lived unit was Professor E. Marx of Tel-Aviv University, The Bergman academic plan included studies of the Bedouin, natives of the desert and E. Marx was invited on a part-time status to set up a study group for this purpose. The Nomad Settlement accent aimed to analyze and hence understand the Bedouin sensitivities so that, on the one hand, their cultural tradition will not be brought to an end, and on the other hand, the desert environment would be protected from their potential damage.

Third in this row was Professor G. M. Kressel who took over as full time head of this group. He brought to anthropological foci all patterns of social living, rural and urban, Jewish and Arab alike. The underlying philosophy was that in an era where new bounds confine the migratory patterns of pastoralists, nomad settlement is of significant social, if not political, consequence. Comparative studies of sedentary, once pastoral, nomads elsewhere taught the team important lessons.

Kressel thought that since the Bedouin's choice of their degree of urbanization is affected by the higher level of the civil services provided in town, an infrastructure on the rural side must provide equal services, not inferior to those provided in towns. Having the Bedouin live together in fortuitous encampments obliged the government to have a measure of organizational reshuffle and help modify the Bedouin traditional (nomadic) ways of life. The underlying philosophy of this research team was based on the premise that understanding the Bedouin's social networks and cultural pattern should identify the more durable elements in their culture, helping plot the desired course for a better integration of the Bedouin in Israeli society.

Desert Economics

The Desert Economics Unit, established in 1978 by Professor E. Hochman of Ben-Gurion University, was meant to operate jointly with the University's Economics Department. Dr. U. Regev and Dr. Y. Zur were recruited at about that time. The basic idea was for economists to assist in long term planning, designing analytical tools by which to guide economic growth in the Negev. Particular attention was to be given to the exploitation of natural resources, i.e., solar energy and water resources as well as to provide economic insight and analysis to pertinent projects carried out in the Institute. This group lacked momentum and was dissolved a few short years after being formed.

Environmental Education

Although the Institute was primarily devoted to scientific research, it also took responsibility in educating awareness and understanding of the desert environment and man's place in it. In the Midrasha a group of young scientists were working under the direction of Professor Evenari for some time before the Institute was founded on topics related to education.

Moshe Shachak was most active in this group and when the Desert Research Institute began operations, he was appointed as the leader of a Unit of Environmental Education. Professor Zeev Naveh, from the Technion in Haifa, provided important initiative and advice. The aim of Environmental Education was to develop and test programs for 'environmental education' in high schools. Through field trips and other outdoor activities, training courses for school teachers were given, preparing a program of studies and field workshops, as well as collecting information on environmental education. This project prepared the background for a new High School established in the Midrasha following these environmental philosophies that was recognized by the Ministry of Education as a specialized teaching program. The central concept upon which the school was organized concerned use of the desert as a medium for system-education in which teaching material is arranged in integrated themes, e.g., 'the desert' or 'Nabateen culture,' rather than in the conventional categories of Biology, History, or Geography. This approach had made a name for the unit and gave impetus to contacts with scientists from abroad, especially from the United States and Germany where there had been experiments with environmental schools.

After the environmental High School at the Midrasha was fully established, the Environmental Education Unit in the Institute was dissolved.

Following the completion of the 'Founding Period,' a few later units were established in the early eighties. Professor H. Lips established the Plant Adaptation Research Unit, Professor Y. Gutterman organized the Ecophysiology and Desert Plant Introduction Unit, Professor Abeliovich established Environmental Applied Microbiology, and Professor S. Appelbaum built the Fish Laboratory.

Epilogue

Over 30 years have now passed since work at the Desert Research Institute started at the Midrasha. These 3 decades saw a very modest beginning carried on in deprived conditions, turning into a flourishing University Campus which hosts over 70 scientists and 150 graduate students in the framework of three different Institutions, forming together The Jacob Blaustein Institutes for Desert Research.

Israel enjoys recognized leadership in the development of arid regions and its achievements in this field provide hope for unfolding a promising future to the under-settled Negev region, that comprises more than half of this small crowded country. The aims imbued in the Institute when founded were marked clearly: Generate information and know-how for support of mass settlement and improvement of life in the Negev desert, as well as in the poverty-stricken, arid regions of the world. Indeed, from Israel in general and the Blaustein Institutes in particular, should come the tidings concerning the potential for settlement in barren dry-lands the world over. This leadership should become an important value, engraved in the heart of our national character, a recognized contribution to humanity.

Development of the Negev desert into a flourishing region always represented a worthy target to which this country should aim for continuously, investing in this ideal much thought and national resources. During the years that have passed from the inception of the Institute, this goal has become even more important.

Notes

1. Some fifty Kms past Be'er Sheva near Sde-Boqer.
2. Jacob Blaustein, an engineer who made his wealth in the US oil industry, was a personal friend of the late Ben-Gurion.

Chapter 12

Desert Research

Solar Power Plants

David Faiman

In this interview I am going to tell you about a piece of ongoing research that I am very excited about. For many years I have been obsessed with the question of how to make solar generated electricity completely competitive on a dollar-to-dollar basis with fossil fuel generated electricity. Ultimately, if you cannot do that, then solar is not going to take over on a large scale. There will always be a niche market for it, but not a large-scale power market, and it is not going to save the world. The problem boils down to a fundamental weakness of solar, that it is a terribly dilute form of energy. It takes one square meter of Negev almost a year to receive from the sun the energy equivalent of one barrel of oil, and humanity consumes energy at the equivalent rate of about 200 million barrels of oil a day.

How can we overcome this problem? At face value, it looks as if the problem is insurmountable. But it is not insurmountable because there is a fundamental error in the thinking of how to harness solar energy on a large scale. You obviously need to have a very large solar collector, or a large area of collectors, in this case hundreds of thousands of square kilometers in order to provide the equivalent of 200 million barrels a day. The problem is that in the conventional photovoltaic panel paradigm you would spread out hundreds of thousands of square kilometers of photovoltaic panels. This is an expensive thing to do because photovoltaic material is very expensive. The reason that one is thinking along this incorrect paradigm is that intuitively one is using the same material to collect the radiation and to convert it to electricity. What one really ought to do is use a very large area of low cost material to collect the energy and then concentrate it on a very small unit that is actually going to do the conversion. That is why we built this giant dish a few years ago. The idea is to collect 400 square meters of incoming sunshine and then concentrate it onto a very small area of solar cells. This is referred to as concentrator photovoltaics.

What I am gunning for, ultimately, if I ever manage to raise the funds, is to put one square meter of photovoltaic panels at the focus. I have calculations that indicate it ought to be possible to obtain 100 kilowatts of electricity from a one square meter panel, compared to 100 watts of electricity if you put a one square meter photovoltaic panel out on a sunny day. So I would be basically increasing the power output of the expensive material by a factor of a thousand, or reducing its cost-per-watt by a factor of a thousand. Since the photovoltaic material is, at present, the stumbling block in terms of economics because it is the single most expensive part of the system, by reducing the cost by a factor of a thousand one is all but eliminating it from the economic equation.

So then the question is, how much does a big dish cost, like the one we have, and the cooling system (of course you have to keep the cells cool), and the computer sun-tracking system (because the dish must follow the sun). All of that is simply steel and glass and plastic and what have you. These are the same materials that automobiles are made of. Automobiles can be mass-produced for something on the order of 10,000 dollars per ton. So if you translate that into dollars per watt for our dishes, you end up with one dollar per watt, or less, for the whole system - under the conditions of mass-production comparable to the mass-production or automobiles. You can then expect to build solar power plants for a dollar a watt or less. By comparison, conventional power plants also cost a dollar per watt to build, but their electricity costs more because they have ongoing fuel costs. However, a solar power plant does not. This way, in principle, you can beat the fossil fuel people at their own game.

This realization caused me to be very excited about three years ago. I have lectured on it extensively and written papers. I even managed to pick up a European-funded research grant which includes additional partners from various parts of the continent. They will make the cells and the electronics and we will put it all together here. But the project we have funded will not produce one square meter of cells. It will only provide a 'mini module' of size 10 cm by 10cm that can produce a maximum of two kilowatts. But if we can demonstrate that the whole thing works, even though most of the mirrors on our big dish will need to be covered over, it may lead to funding for a full scale project.

So had you caught me approximately three years ago, that would have been the exciting thing that I wished to talk about. However, since that time, an interesting gentleman by the name of Dov Raviv became interested in the project. He is known in Israel as the 'father' of the Arrow Missile project. This is the only anti-missile missile system that actually works. He steered the whole project through from an initial design concept to a fully working system. He has also organized a number of earth satellite projects. About a year ago Raviv started to take an interest in solar. He did not have any experience with the subject so he was able to approach it from a different direction: Namely, "how can solar save the world?" He studied the literature and came to two conclusions, one was that you had to use concentrator photovoltaic cells, together with 'off the shelf' equipment, where possible, in order to keep costs down. The other conclusion was that we need to start right now because mankind cannot wait, and the technology has to be introduced on a massive scale. He performed calculations that indicated that if you work on a massive enough scale: (a) you can reach a situation where a country like Israel could employ solar for something like 80% of its electrical requirements within 30 years and (b) this could be done at a cost that is cheaper than fossil fuel. When I say electrical requirements I do not mean electrical requirements today but the electrical requirements 30 years from now. In Israel we should stop building fossil fuelled plants and start building solar plants: not today but five years from now. Within the coming four years Raviv would erect a manufacturing facility that could enable one giant solar plant to be turned out, connected, and go on line, every year from year 6 onwards. By giant, I mean much larger than any solar plant that has ever been made. The largest solar plants that have been built to date are those that were constructed by Luz Corporation in California. They produced one 15 megawatt plant, six 30 megawatt plants, and two 80 megawatt plants. However, large as those Luz plants were by today's solar energy standards, what Raviv is talking about are plants of 1,500 megawatts each. They would occupy a field of 20 square kilometers apiece. Within 30 years we should need about 500 square kilometers of Negev in order to house all of these plants.

This may sound like megalomania, but Raviv has worked out an investment algorithm which operates in such a way that for the first 5 years money is consumed in order to build the manufacturing facility, and then the first solar electricity-generating plant. But starting from year 6 the scheme starts to earn money because of the electricity that is generated by this first plant. By year 7 the earnings are twice as much, because there are now two plants on line. By year 8 it makes three times as much. By something like year 20, the entire loan, plus all of the accrued interest, has been paid off. Now the plants become truly profitable because the only costs are for operation and maintenance.

So the credit line to cover all of the costs has to be started right now and it reaches its maximum value of about 10 billion dollars around year 12. This is the cost of 10 conventional power plants. This is the maximum credit that the government would need to put up. But it will get it all back. It is a grant rather than a gift. Then two amazing things happen. After the loan has been paid off in something like 20 years, which corresponds to less that the expected lifetime of the solar plants, they are now generating so much revenue that not only have they paid off the loan completely, but you can continue to install new power plants purely from the profit that you are making by selling solar electricity at say 5 cents a kilowatthour, which is far below today's price of 9 or 10 cents a kilowatthour.

For the first 20 years or so, i.e. however long it will take to pay off the loan, you will probably be selling electricity at the same tariff that it costs today. However, after paying off the loan you can drop the price radically and you have a situation where the process of plant building is sustainable because electricity revenues enable you to continue building solar plants ad infinitum. However, if you make the more realistic assumption that the lifetime of a plant may be something like 30 years, then from year 30 onward you need to start de-commissioning the oldest plants and replacing them. It turns out that by year 30 you are making so much electricity that you have enough earnings both to be able to sell the electricity super-cheaply and to build two new power plants annually: One is a replacement for an old plant, and the other is a new one which continues to increase your revenue. What is so exciting is that this is triply sustainable: The energy is renewable; revenues suffice to 'breed' new plants; and also to replace older plants.

I am a member of an International Energy Agency specialist working group who are studying the technical and economic feasibility of setting up very large solar photovoltaic power plants in desert regions. I have been allocated the Middle East. Other members of our team are studying Africa, Australia, the Gobi Desert, etc. The paper that Raviv and I are preparing is most revolutionary, as everyone else is speaking in terms of the standard, expensive, paradigm of conventional photovoltaic panels. We have a solution based on concentrator photovoltaics, economies of scale, and using large mass-production rates. Our solution shows that you do not need subsidies, you need an initial grant to get it going. The grant is not astronomical in size. It is merely comparable in cost to a dozen conventional, polluting, power plants. Moreover, it is suitable for the entire Middle East. We have statistics for populations and land areas. The only things that we do not know accurately are: (1) the amount of solar radiation in the other countries. So we are making a guess that it is similar to the Negev. (2) We also do not know what their true electricity costs are. Not all of these countries publish the kind of data that the Israel Electric Corporation publishes. Again we are using Israeli figures. These two simplifications could be easily corrected should any of the other countries want to institute a plan like this.

Raviv also goes into detail about the number of jobs this is going to create. There is very much left to do. One example: There are two radically different approaches to developing a light concentrator for photovoltaic cells. One is to use a single giant collector for an entire panel of cells. The other approach is to treat the cells independently and have each cell illuminated by its own mini-mirror, or small lens. You would make a large array of such units. The former is known as the dense array approach, the latter, as the individual cell approach. Both types of approach have been demonstrated to work on a small scale.

There are advantages and disadvantages to each of these approaches. My big dish—dense array—approach appears to be much cheaper than the use of an equivalent area of lenses. But it has a number of technicalities which need to be overcome. One is that I have to cool my cells artificially because they are too close together to be able to cool themselves. In the individual cell approach, each little cell is bonded to a heat sink which is the same size as the lens that illuminates it. It can therefore dissipate the heat without needing to be cooled. This is the approach that Raviv believes should be employed at the start of his program. It makes the system much simpler as there are fewer things to go wrong.

I would like to be able to solve the problems involved in using my large dish approach. If I can, there will be a large amount of waste heat, in addition to the electricity. This heat has a value and can be used for other purpose.

Solar Surgery

Daniel Feuermann

***Introductory note:** Feuermann is a mechanical engineer. He works in a small group of scientists developing optics for special applications. One of the applications the group worked on was related to shaping a laser beam to be used in laser surgery. He and his colleagues work with MDs and other specialists with the emphasis on creating design tools for shaping optics for a variety of applications. On some theoretical problem he may work only with physicists, although they may test their ideas with computer models or simulations. Sometimes he works on individual projects. More recently all work is done in teams.*

The project I am going to tell about involves using solar energy in place of laser surgery. We needed to design optics that would take radiation from one place to another with minimal loss of radiation. As part of our search for this newly developed theory we went to Soroka hospital to see the surgeon who uses lasers to operate on people. Jeff Gordon, a Professor of at the Jacob Blaustein Institutes for Desert Research, Ben-Gurion University, made the contact. The surgeon invited us to see what he was doing so that we could judge whether there was anything we could do to help improve the efficiency of the system. At that time we were not thinking of solar applications. We attended two operations in the operating theater. We discussed with the surgeon his needs and how his equipment could be improved. He explained all the benefits of laser surgery, such as less bleeding, less infection, and reduced time for recovery. There are many benefits when lasers are used for surgery as opposed to using a knife. You can cut people with a knife. You can take out tumors. With lasers you can get into the body through fibers. It is minimally invasive, because you just need to cut a small hole. Of course you have to have some imaging system to locate and observe the surgery. Then you can kill tumor cells by heating them up. Then they die off.

The main reason why this is not being done very frequently in Israeli hospitals is because there are only a limited number of lasers. They were so incredibly expensive that the hospitals would not buy these instruments. They cost about 100 to 150 thousand dollars including special infrastructure. You also need a technician. The lasers pull a lot of power. The regular 220 volt outlet is not sufficient. You need a cooling system. So the main reason for not using lasers is because they are too expensive.

That was the initial visit. Then, coming back home, Gordon noted that we had been working with solar energy at high concentrations. The power level that the surgeon needs is several watts coupled into a small diameter fiber. This could be done with the sun. But maybe the sun is impractical, because there are clouds during the day, and there is night. Why not use a light source. So we investigated the properties of existing light sources. At the time, the brightness or power density that one could achieve was not sufficient for the power level required for laser surgery. In principle, lamps can go to a very high power level but not to sufficiently high power density. The power density of the light sources was an order of magnitude below what the surgeons wanted, at least at that time. But the sun could do ten times better. That was about 1997. Light sources were not strong enough. Not in the sense of enough watts but they did not have the intensity, the power density at the surface of the light. So this brought us to the idea of using the sun. A quick calculation showed that we could do it very cheaply. We could concentrate sunlight into optical fibers. Then the question was, is it worth it, given that there are clouds and nighttime. When this was discussed with the surgeons in the hospital, they said that if we could produce a replacement for lasers so much cheaper it would be worthwhile. If a solar system would only operate 180 days a year, since this is surgery that is not emergency surgery but is scheduled surgery, then you could schedule surgery on those days when the sun is shining. You have a window of about 6 to 8 hours a day when you can perform solar surgery. You could tell the patients that you would call them on the next day when it is sunny. The nice thing about it is that this type of surgery is like an out-patient procedure. You can send the patients home the same day. You do not have to keep them in the hospital. However, when you cut them open, then the patients must be kept for several days. This is how the story developed.

We first did a theoretical paper on the subject and published it. CNN and Nature gave a report on our publication. Once it appeared in the high-exposure media others thought it was a great idea. Someone representing a fund said that they would provide the money and suggested that we should produce a prototype. We did. That is how we became involved in doing solar surgery on rats. The rats were sacrificed at the end of each procedure in order to investigate the tissue to determine if the procedure was effective. This involved pathology. There had been surgery on the livers of the animals. The animals lived after the operation, but only for a few days before it was necessary to see what had happened.

Our current project is on a side issue. When we began, electric lamps were not strong enough. However, with the development of the PC projector, there was an incentive for manufacturers to produce smaller and smaller and brighter and brighter lamps. The smaller and more compact the system, the more precise the picture. Ideally you would want to have a point source. You want to make it as small as possible and still have high power. In the last few years lamps have been developed that approach the power density we need to do the surgery. So now we have another project. We are now developing the optics to use light from such a light source and concentrate it into a fiber and then all this should fit into a little box that we can give to a surgeon. There will be a little fan in there for cooling (like a PC projector). This will have only a low cost, about the same as a PC projector, about $2,000. All the elements are in a PC projector. But now the light would be focused onto a fiber tip. So, although the solar surgery got so much attention, it will be a passing episode.

Suppose the electricity went out? When we were experimenting with solar, doing surgery on chicken livers, the electricity did go out on occasion. However we had photo-voltaic cells supplying power for the machinery that tracked the sun with the solar dish (collector), so the operation was not interrupted. With the hospital it is a different story. There are other things going on at the same time, such as monitors on the patient, that depend upon electricity, and for that reason the hospital has large emergency generators. So electricity outage should not be a problem.

Question: For the solar project, at what point did you bring in other people? We had a post-doc joining us who is a mechanical engineer. The initial discussions were held with one surgeon. Then a second surgeon joined us who was very enthusiastic and performed the surgery on the rats. We followed the protocols for treatment of animals, so that there was no unnecessary pain to the animals. They were treated properly with anesthesia. A pathologist, from Soroka hospital, joined us. We needed to know how much tissue had been destroyed with our procedure. How does it compare with something that would have been done with an ordinary laser? We did not have a laser available to do the comparison directly but we had information from the medical literature.

There were all kinds of side issues. We realized that there was delayed tissue death. Under high radiation a certain fraction of the tissue would die immediately. But if you let the animal live for a few days, you find that the volume of killed tissue becomes larger. This was something that not many people had observed. This has given rise to another publication that had nothing to do with solar energy.

Also we needed to decide which method to use in order to determine what is dead tissue. The usual way is for the pathologist to use stains. This does not detect the real tissue death. There was a discrepancy with what we actually saw because there is a change in the color of the tissue. It becomes white-ish. However, under the microscope, from the point of view of pathology, the tissue did not look dead. That had to do with the wrong method of checking the tissue.

In the beginning there was a tense situation because the pathologist said that she knew what she was doing. But we said that cannot be. It is as if we measured something with a ruler and we say it is ten millimeters and you say it is only six. If the tissue is changing color, something must be happening. She then found another method that was more suitable and which confirmed our observation.

The same people are still interested in the lamp surgery development. However, first we have to develop the lamp and the optics and have that measured to make sure the technology works. Once that is done, we will build a prototype as we did for solar surgery. Then the surgeons will come in and do experiments on tissue and on animals.

On Being Creative

The basic framework to be creative and come up with ideas is pressure. We have a problem and we cannot go on without finding a solution. Or we are trying to do something and it does not work. For example, we try to put light through a fiber and we find that there is much less coming out than we expected. So what is going on? You dig into that and you find new things that occur. One of the nice examples is measuring photovoltaic cells at extremely high flux. At flux levels for which there are no previous measurements. We find that there is absolutely something strange going on. We see when we make measurements that the curves look very wrong. It is not something wrong with our experiment, there is just something strange. We have our technician take the whole thing apart and put it together again and it still does the same thing. There were four people involved. We were all wondering what was going on to account for this strange behavior. I was already on my way to America so I did not even have time to join in the discussion. Gordon was about to leave for sabbatical. Eugene Katz insisted that this was not an experimental error. Two days later when Gordon was already in the States he sent an e-mail and said "I have got it." Gordon remembered something he had read several years ago and said that this must be the reason. Sure enough, that was the right guess. That was indeed the problem. His idea was readily accepted. Gordon understood solid state physics. There are papers that describe this particular part of physics that interfered with our experiment, but not in conjunction with photovoltaic cells. No one had ever tested photovoltaic cells at 10,000 suns (10,000 times the usual intensity of the sun at midday). It is not a new idea but a new piece of physics. A paper about this has been accepted for publication with a remark "excellent science." In the literature we found reports of measurements on photovoltaic cells which show that there is a contradiction in what the authors say. They did not understand the data and described it in a strange way. They did not understand what was going on. Now this discovery can explain what they saw.

Out of 100 ideas that come up, 99 are discarded. The criteria for making a decision are very simple. Either the physics does not allow it or it is an idea but it is not practical. Or it is an idea but the economics is going to kill it. We are not working in basic physics but applied research. So these are the questions: Can it be done and is it worth it?

Do you recall a time then you contributed an idea to this project? Sometimes you are having a discussion and a few weeks later people do not remember who said what. Some people think they said it and others think they said it. I have my own version of what I contributed. For example, when we discussed using a fiber; this is more of a technical nature, I am an engineer. We all knew what to do. You take a parabola. You get a focus. And then you have the fiber placed at the point of the focus. So you have to hold the fiber very accurately in place. So I added a little mirror. Now the fiber could come from below, from the back. With the mirror you lose about 4 or 5 percent. The extra loss is compensated by the ease in cleaning the glazing without having a fiber sticking out.

We discussed the possibility of using this parabola with fiber for power production. There could be panels with lots and lots of little (parabolic) dishes in them. Then fibers would come out from each individual dish. If you bundle these fibers together, you have a string of fibers. Again the problem was what does one do with the fibers that are sticking out. Now you can have a flat piece of glass without all the fibers sticking out.

Fossil Water

Arie S. Issar

I was born in Jerusalem, a city spread over the crests of the Judean mountains, on both sides of the water divide between the Mediterranean and Dead Sea. The mountains, reaching an average altitude of eight hundred meters, impede during the winter the trajectories of the rain bearing clouds coming over the Mediterranean. This causes the eastern escarpment of the Judean mountains to become arid. This is the Judean Desert. This desert rises above the Jordan and Dead Sea valley which is the deepest part, on land, of the colossal cleavage in the face of the earth called the Syrian African rift valley. The short time, geologically speaking, of a few million years which elapsed since the rifting took place was not enough to allow the forces of erosion to accomplish their leveling off activity. Thus the landscape remained immature, which is pronounced by deep gorges cutting down into the surface of the land, causing passage in this region to become extremely difficult, which made it an ideal place for outlaws and refugees to look for shelter. This brought David, the son of Issai, to choose the gorges around the oasis of Ein Gedi as a refuge when King Saul became suspicious that the young shepherd, who tricked Goliath the philistine warrior to approach within the range of his deadly sling, had also the pretension to seize the throne. When later the temple of Jehova was erected on mount Zion, by Solomon, the son of David, each year, on the Day of Atonement, the high priest of the Temple, would sent a he-goat to go tumbling down from one of the precipices, a sacrifice to the Azazel, probably the coequal of Ezuz-El or Adad-El the ancient Canaanite deity who was in charge of the lightning and thunder, and thus was also responsible for the rains which the lightning ushered in during the winter. Zion itself may have been a Canaanite or Jebusite deity of the desert, as the name Zia, which its meaning in Hebrew, a semitic language, is a desolate desert. The last heir to the throne of David, Zidkiau, tried to escape into the same desert, when the Babylonians conquered his city, and destroyed his temple. But he was caught, his sons killed before him, and he was blinded—a lesson to any other kings with a plan to rebel against the empire of Babel. A few centuries later, the Jewish rebels fighting the mighty Roman Empire had their last stand in this desert, in a fortress called Masada situated on a cliff overlooking the Dead Sea. They committed suicide when the walls of their fort were breached by the Roman siege machine, and they faced the fate of enslavement.

The whitish yellowish hills of this desert, during the long months of summer and autumn, and green during the short months of winter and spring, were a frequent sight for the boy growing up in the city of Jerusalem, watching its arid stretches from the heights of Mount Scopus, and even traveling through it, from time to time, down into the rift valley to the town of Jericho, or to the Dead Sea. The tortuous road went down from the altitude of about seven hundred meters, which is the altitude of the new quarters of Jerusalem, to the bottom of the Rift Valley, located about thirty kilometers to the east, at an altitude of four hundred metrs below sea level, which is the lowest point on earth. The passage was not only a sharp topographical one, but also into an entirely different country. In winter it was from the cold windy hills, where one had to wear an overcoat on top of a jersey, into a warm valley, where one could walk around in a short sleeve shirt, and bathe in the water and sun of the Dead Sea. In summer the difference was even harsher. The usually mild weather of Jerusalem, with its cooling winds during the evenings, was replaced by terribly hot weather during the day, with no relief during the night, in the pre-air-conditioning times.

In school and at the meetings of the youth movement, which the author joined, the desert was regarded as a place, which has to be changed and altered in order to accommodate people. This change was a promise made by the prophets of the Bible, who symbolized the return of the children of Israel to their land as the act of the greening of the arid desert. The symbol of this promise to become true was a communal settlement, kibbutz, by the name of Beit HaArava (The House of the desolate plain) which was situated in the midst of the salt rich lands north to Dead Sea, and the young members of this Kibbutz, have pumped water from the Jordan, flushed the salts out from the soil, and produced an oasis in the middle of the white blinding chalks of the desert. The sight of this man-made miracle helped, many years later, to convince the United Nations Commission, who came to investigate a solution to the Arab Jewish conflict, that the debated land can provide a solution to both people. Beit Harava was deserted and destroyed during the war of independence, which followed the United Nations resolution of the partition of Palestine between the Arabs and the Jews.

But before the promise of turning the desert into a garden could be materialized in a peaceful way, war was unavoidable. This the leaders of the Jews and the

Arabs knew, since the beginning of the settlements of Jews in this country. To prepare for this war, the desert became, for the Jewish illegal army the Hagana, an ideal place to exercise the use of arms, far away from the searching eyes of the British mandatory police. On one of the marches into the desert for this purpose, the author's underground army company nearly perished from thirst. They started their march in the Judean hills, from the Kibbutz Kefar Etzion, north of Hebron, where they were issued the illegal arms, from their underground hiding places. The pistols were given to the girls to carry below their skirts, while the hand grenades were carried by the boys in the lower part of their water bottles, which were converted into waterproof containers. The water supply thus being limited the additional supply had to come from cisterns, which were known to the scouts leading the march. This trip had also another purpose. It included the scaling up of the cliff of Masada, on the ruins of which the company had to pass through a ceremonial vow to defend the Jewish people. Unfortunately, the water holes in the desert were found to be empty of water, which forced the company to march two days, with a very limited supply of water, under the scorching sun of the Judean desert, until they reached the oasis of Ein Gedi. There they fell exhausted, and nearly entirely dehydrated, into the pools of water, without even caring to take off their sweat soaked clothes. This long day march, with the tongue swelling and filling up the dried up mouth, with the feeling that each hill is an impassable barrier, followed by the feeling of relief, and comfort lying later in the shade of willows and listening to the sounds of the flowing water, came back many times to the memory of the author during his many travels in desert countries.

Many years later, during one of the campaigns in the Sinai Peninsula, I spotted an Egyptian abandoned drilling machine and a pile of steel pipes. Wishing to investigate the reason for placing a well in this place, I steered my jeep towards the site. It was a machine abandoned by its crew, who most probably unloaded their equipment in order to flee faster from the approaching Israeli army. Between the pipes was lying the skeleton of an Egyptian soldier, who may have sighted the pipes, hoping to find there a drop of water to save his dried up body. Reaching the site his hopes vanquished he collapsed and died on the pipes, a symbol of vanquished hope for water in the desert.

The desert of Sinai is the ideal place to exemplify the futility of war. Three times it was crossed by the author, with the Israeli army. During all these campaigns I was appalled by the tremendous gap between the equipment made available to the Fellahs of Egypt for making war, and the tools which they used in their farms to produce food. While the latter did not differ much from that which their ancestors still used during Pharaonic Egypt, the machines of war were modern products, created by the workers of the communist countries to be destroyed and left to rust in the vast arid plains of the desert. Many times I thought to myself what could have been the state of this desert peninsula if the same funds, manpower, and technological ingenuity would have been invested in bringing life to this land, instead of destroying the life of the people on its border.

That such a positive endeavor was feasible was found out by the author and his team, while investigating the water resources of the deserts of Sinai and Negev. They discovered that below these deserts extend thick layers of sandstone containing thousands of billions of cubic meters of water. One can visualize it as a tremendous sponge made of sandstone, saturated with water. The water under many areas is fresh and good, under others brackish and even salty. Under some areas it is at a shallow depth, under some areas deep drilling is needed to tap the water bearing layers, and in some areas it comes up to the surface to flow as artesian wells or springs.

This water infiltrated and accumulated in the subsurface, tens of thousands of years ago, when the high latitude areas of the globe were covered by glaciers, and the low latitude deserts enjoyed more rains, turning the deserts into huge savannas, on which wildlife and pre-historical man prospered.

The personal gains of the author from this discovery, were in three realms. In the realm of my field of specialization, namely desert hydrogeology, I had to locate, evaluate and monitor this resource, which brought me to study the geology, prehistory as well as the history of the region. These I found most fascinating, but at the same time I had to comment on problems of the present and plans for the future for which the ground water resources found were needed. I thus became acquainted with the problems of the agricultural and industrial development of this region and involved in the conflicts between development and the protection of the natural environment.

The second realm was that of climate change, as the water which was found was a product of another climate, it intrigued me to investigate how these changes influenced the physical as well as bio-environment of the deserts. The findings of these investigations and especially their relation to the events of Exodus and the wandering of the Israelites in these deserts, I summarized in my book *Water Shall Flow from the Rock* (Issar, c. 1990). For the time being it is sufficient to say that it undermined my conventional attitude to the deserts as eternal sites of desolation. I found out that there were long periods in pre-historical and historical times that these deserts were greener.

The third realm of discovery was in the philosophical aspects of science. The stubborn opposition to my findings, although they were backed up by many observations and data, by many of my colleague scientists, taught me a basic lesson in the way scientific innovations are accepted. I used this when I summarized my ideas on the evolution of science, published in my book *From Primeval Chaos to Infinite Intelligence* (Issar, c. 1995).

It is worthwhile to lay out before the reader three general conclusions: First, the author has arrived at the conclusion that the desert conceals tremendous resources awaiting for development and if this will be done wisely, man can benefit and nature will not be harmed.

Secondly, it was found out that man's endeavors to settle the desert and try to extract a living out of the barren land to support him and his kin is as ancient as man himself at different periods. These endeavors however assumed different ways and methods which generalized into three categories:

(a) The raping method in which man came, took his needs from the land and its people by force, not caring whatsoever what will be the results in the longer future.

(b) The parasitic method, namely that man found a way to extract some kind of living from the harsh natural conditions of the desert. This way of living was precarious and perpetually on the margin of catastrophe.

(c) In the third category, man by using his ingenuity and inventiveness was able to find an harmonious way to benefit from the positive sides of nature and overcome its negative aspects, and thus promoting his material conditions and most probably also his spiritual ones.

Finally, nature and man cannot be regarded as two different and separate systems, but they form one system with subdivisions that interact in all directions. Thus climate, vegetation, animal world, man and even rock and soil layers are all subsystems in one large system we call nature. This system, however, is what it is as a function of the dynamics of the subsystems and vice versa. Thus the approach to nature and its subsystem should also be a dynamic one. There is no moment that the system is at a standstill. It is always under the influence of a variety of force fields, and it is in the mind and hands of man to interfere in this play of forces. His interference, however, should also be understood in its true dimension— not overestimated nor neglected, but, objectively, in relation with the other forces and systems interacting in the desert.

I hope also to transmit my belief that the desert may provide a new-old challenge to mankind to practice its ingenuity and inventiveness in a creative positive endeavor and to abandon the path of war and destruction, the prospects of which are to turn all our earth into an eternal desert. This time devoid of the subsystem called man.

Microalgae

Zvi Cohen

Living in the desert makes one constantly aware of its harsh environmental conditions. Drastic changes in ambient temperature, from almost freezing at night in the winter to scorching hot during summer days. Due to the lack of precipitation, skies are mostly clear and solar irradiation is very high. The miniscule amounts of rain limits conventional agriculture and in many cases renders it non-economical.

The author has been living in the Negev for almost 25 years. The daily exposure to the elements must have an effect on one's frame of mind, directing the train of thought, perhaps even unconsciously, to think how can one convert the desert's disadvantages to advantages. Clearly, the upside of the lack of precipitation is the high solar irradiance. Cultivation of algal biomass can succeed where traditional agriculture fails, since in contrary to intuitive thinking, the limiting factor for algal cultivation is light, rather than water. Under optimal conditions an algal culture can double its biomass daily.

The desert is thus an ideal place to grow algae on a large scale. While algal biomass can be used as a source of food and feed, the cost of production is still too high to be economical. However, algae produce various chemicals that may have nutritional or pharmaceutical use for human or animals.

The idea of growing microalgae in the desert seems at first ludicrous. How can an alga which is essentially a microscopic water plant, grow in the desert? However, the actual water consumption of algae, when grown in specially designed reactors, is much less than traditional agricultural crops. Furthermore, the limiting factor for growing algae is not water but light, and the desert is therefore the most suitable place for growing algae. Unfortunately, the cost of production of algal biomass is still too high for it to be used as a source of food or feed. However, certain algae contain various chemicals with unique nutraceutically and pharmaceutically important properties.

Arachidonic acid is a polyunsaturated fatty acid (PUFA) containing 20 carbon atoms with four double bonds. Arachidonic acid is one of the most abundant PUFAs in the human body and it is particularly prevalent in organ, muscle and blood tissues. Arachidonic acid is a precursor to various eicosanoids, which consists of several families of compounds, such as prostaglandins, leucotrienes and thromboxanes, all of which have various regulatory functions in the human body. Moreover, arachidonic acid is the major PUFA of breast milk, as well as an important building block of brain cell membranes. While breastfed babies can build these membranes using mother's milk, formula-fed babies need to convert shorter fatty acids to arachidonic acid. Apparently, underweight and premature newborns have difficulty in doing so and could suffer subsequently from slower and lower development and their IQ test scores could be lower by as much as 9 points. In an effort to have infant formula match the long chain fatty acid profile found in breast milk, scientific and food regulatory bodies (e.g., the American FDA, the international FAO) have recommended that arachidonic acid be added to infant formulae, especially in formulae utilized for premature infants. Indeed, studies showed lately that adding arachidonic acid to infant formulae significantly boosted the average intelligence scores of a group of 18-month old children.

The total market size for infant food is around 5 billion dollars in sales worldwide. The market for arachidonic acid, as an infant food ingredient, could be as high as 150-200 million USD. Other uses are likely to increase these figures significantly.

The complex structure of arachidonic acid makes its synthetic production economically prohibitive. Moreover, no higher plant is capable of producing this fatty acid. Currently, the major sources are fungi and other microorganisms.

However, some of these microorganisms, in particular *Pythium insidiosum*, were reported to be pathogenic to humans and/or animals.

Although a fungal source of arachidonic acid has been commercially developed, a major difficulty encountered stemmed from the failure to persuade the public to consume fungal derived food additives. These findings prompted the search for an alternative source of natural arachidonic acid that is safe, acceptable, economical, and commercially feasible.

Many freshwater and marine microalgae were studied as sources for various PUFAs. These PUFAs generally reside on polar lipids that serve as components of the algal cell membrane and are considered to have a accessory role in photosynthesis. However, the cell's content of these membranes are rather low and therefore its PUFAs content is inherently limited. Algae produce also another type of lipids, triglycerides, which are essentially not different than higher plants' oils. These oils are considered to be the cell's energy reserves and are mostly accumulated under conditions that prevent the algal cells from exponential growth, e.g., when light is available but nitrogen is deficient, photosynthesis can take place but the nitrogen-rich proteins cannot be synthesized. The energy produced is in many cases utilized for the production of triglycerides. In some cases the oil content accumulated is up to 70% of the cell's dry weight. Unfortunately, these triglycerides consist, with almost no exception, of simple saturated and monounsaturated fatty acids. Indeed, if the only role for the accumulated triglycerides is to be used for energy, accumulating PUFAs in these triglycerides would be the equivalent of heating a room by burning currency notes.

The red microalga *Porphyridium cruentum* was shown to be a rare exception to this rule. Under nitrogen starvation, arachidonic acid made up about 40% of the fatty acids in the triglycerides of this alga. However, red algae do not produce much triglycerides. Still, research conducted at the author's laboratory, have shown that under these conditions, arachidonic acid accumulated up to 2.5% of the cell's dry weight. We were intrigued by the reason for the occurrence of arachidonic acid in triglycerides and were looking for a possible role, other than a source of energy. In an attempt to elucidate this role we have studied the biosynthesis of arachidonic acid in this alga. The research followed several avenues, among which, we have utilized radiolabelling techniques and selection of mutants deficient in the biosynthesis of PUFAs. One of the mutants we have isolated was different in several aspects from the wild type cells. Analysis of these differences revealed that the accumulation of arachidonic acid-rich triglycerides was utilized as a depot of arachidonic acid that could be mobilized under conditions requiring rapid production of arachidonic acid, e.g., when cells were shifted from 25° C, the optimal growth temperature, to 15° C, arachidonic acid was transferred from triglycerides to polar lipids.

When temperature decreases, the membranes' fluidity decreases as well. Eventually the fatty acids will solidify, resulting in the cell's death. To prevent this, cells modify the fatty acid composition of their membranes and increase the proportion of PUFAs, which increases the fluidity of the membrane. Most algae grow in large bodies of water whose temperature changes rather slowly, allowing the algae to adapt to the changing environmental conditions. However, *P. cruentum* grows on the surface of moist soil, an environmental niche whose temperature can change rather rapidly. The biosynthesis of arachidonic acid from simple starting materials would take more than 10 hours, which is much too long. We have thus concluded that the alga must have developed a mechanism that would allow it to accommodate to rapidly changing environmental conditions, consisting of a reservoir of arachidonic acid-rich triglycerides into membranes.

Was this mechanism an isolated case? We preferred to think otherwise and hypothesized that among micro algae that are found in soils or very shallow bodies of water and whose environmental conditions, predominantly temperature, change rapidly, there would be several that would be able to adapt to the changing conditions by mobilizing PUFAs deposited in triglycerides.

A search for such algae began in the snowy slopes of Mt. Tateyama in Toyoma county, Japan. A team from the laboratory for microalgal biotechnology including Professors Sammy Boussiba, Amos Richmond and Avigad Vonshak isolated several algae-containing samples, from which several tens of strains were isolated and cultivated. Fatty acid analysis of these strains showed that several of them contained significant amounts of PUFAs. One of those strains, later identified as the green alga *Parietochloris incisa*, was shown to be extremely rich in arachidonic acid. Even under optimal growth conditions, the content of arachidonic acid was as high as 7% (of dry weight), increasing to 14% under stationary conditions. However, when maintained in nitrogen-free medium, the arachidonic acid soared to an unprecedented level of 21%. As expected, over 95% of the accumulated arachidonic acid was found in triglycerides. This finding had also an economic significance since this is the form requested by the infant food industry. Electron microscopy pictures have shown that under nitrogen starvation the cells produce large oil globules taking up most of the cell's volume.

Further studies have indeed shown that in similarity to *P. cruentum, P. incisa* is capable of mobilizing its arachidonic acid-rich triglycerides and deposit it in polar lipids of membranes. Current studies are aimed at further elucidation of the biosynthesis of arachidonic acid in P. *incisa* and the characteristics of the enzymes that are responsible for the preferential deposit of arachidonic acid in triglycerides. Other studies are aimed at developing the technology required for the large scale production of arachidonic acid utilizing this unique organism.

Runoff Agriculture

Pedro Berliner

My story is as follows. Most of Israel is arid. I had studied in Israel, so I was well aware of the problems related to arid zones. I spent some years in South Africa before coming to the Institute. Even though conditions were relatively dry there they are not as arid. All of my career has centered around the use of water, so I was aware of the role it plays, but I think that I did not realize until I was here what it actually means to have the rain concentrated into a few days followed by a long dry period. This makes this area very, very special.

I doubt very much that I would have understood this point if I had not been living here, on site. You have here extremely arid conditions with high temperatures which results in the evaporation of water from the surface. What this means in practical terms is that you need to irrigate differently than you would in a more humid area. In the middle of summer I walk from my home to my office and back. Here we irrigate with drip irrigation along the route. In the morning I saw the wet area around a tree and when I came back in the afternoon, most of the area was already dry. This made me realize how strong this effect is. Everyone knows that there is evaporation, but here it is extremely important. The only way to overcome it, insuring that plants live and produce, is to use only a small amount of water and be able to minimize this water loss.

If I had been sitting in Tel Aviv, my ideas would have been completely different. A large part of my research is devoted to understanding this evaporation. There is a second aspect, the collection of runoff water. In the Byzantine period agriculture was based on the collection of runoff water. In my view, the only way of making sure that you can use this water efficiently, is by storing it in such a way that only a small fraction of if is lost through evaporation. The emphasis in my research for the past number of years was on this specific effect. Some of my predecessors, who did not live in the area, never put the emphasis on this effect. So this makes our research different from that of other people, say from Hebrew University. Our emphasis on water loss is unique.

When we experimented with evaporation, we completed two projects. In one, we covered the soil with polyethylene. This decreases the amount of water loss. Not only did we save water but we increased the production since the polyethylene cover also changes the temperature of the soil. What we are evaluating now, within the framework of our global change project, is the economics of this process, comparing the cost of the polyethylene with the increase in yield and the decrease in the loss of water. It is not clear what the price of water will be. For example, can we use water that has been desalinized?

In the second project, thinking of applications to third-world countries, we collected the runoff water in a rather shallow pit. When you dig a deep pit, the water flows into the pit, but it also moves horizontally to the side. Because the pit is relatively deep (80 centimeters), you have a dry layer that does not allow water to evaporate directly to the atmosphere. By doing this we decrease the amount of water that we lose. We plant our crops in the pit. We can save about 40% of the water, which is good. However, having pits one meter square was not useful for the farmers. So we dug long trenches. A trench can be dug relatively easily by a tractor. In a photograph you can see that the water flows from the area into the trench and floods about 30% of the pit. You see olive trees which are planted directly in the trench. A student thesis is currently considering the optimum depth in terms of minimizing evaporation and the orientation of the trench—should it be East, West, North, or South?

We also cover part of this area with polyethylene because this would give us 100% use of runoff water. When it rains, a relatively small portion of the water is transformed into runoff water which flows into the trenches or pits. Because we are in an area of very low rainfall, it is important to catch as much of the water as you can. This we can do by making the surface completely impermeable.

If we manage to store water in the soil it will not be lost directly to the atmosphere. Trees can develop very deep rooting systems and can take up the water. What is nice about the system is that the trees limit the amount of water they use as a function of its availability. The mechanism by which this happens is not completely known, it may be hydraulic contact or hormones, but when there is less water the plants close their leaves which means that they use less water. This in turn means that they cannot absorb as much carbon dioxide and grow. A plant under water stress grows slowly. Even though they grow slowly, they have water to keep them going for the arid conditions of the Southern Negev—provided that there are not three years of drought, such as we have just had.

There is another variable. The larger your catchments area, the lower is the fraction of rainfall that is converted into runoff water. Which means that if I have a very large area, I may have one tenth of a percent of the rainfall over that area which is transformed into runoff water. It is a lot of water, but only a small fraction of what has fallen. So we need to see how to optimize the catchments area. What I am saying may sound clear and obvious to everyone, but I feel that it would not have been clear to me if I were living somewhere else. This daily contact with the harshness of the climate, by looking at the plants and seeing what happens, made me aware of the importance of this aspect.

I think I can identify with a Nabataean living in the area. When you are dealing with production, I can see how closely he must have been observing the natural phenomena. For him it was crucial. Even though it is claimed that if there was drought, then wheat or fodder was brought in by the government to the outlying areas. So a Nabataean would need to understand why did we have runoff water here and why there?

I think that I can say that rainfall in the Nabataean period was much higher than it is today because the farm in Avdat was built with a series of dykes along the whole catchments area. The farm which has now been rebuilt was at the end of this cascade of dykes. Even though the dykes have broken down and for the past three years we have gathered water from the whole area, there has been no runoff water. If the dykes were in place we would have had zero runoff water. It would have been impossible for the Nabataeans to survive under present conditions.

How the Nabataeans grew fodder is difficult to say, but I think that they grew trees and in between the trees they planted other crops. We are doing this as well to try to understand how they did it. Again the competition for water is critical. The system that we use is that we manage our trees in such a way that we plant our intercrop, be it weeds or whatever grain crop, immediately after a flood event while there is still water in the upper layer. The intercrop can develop rather quickly. Then the deeper water is used by the trees. I do not see any evidence that the Nabiteans were doing it this way, but if they were able to construct a set of the cisterns, which are very sophisticated intellectually, they would also have reached the same conclusions that we have about intercropping.

Fish

Samuel Appelbaum

So you were working with fish before?

Yes, first in Germany and then in Israel. While I was studying in Germany I came to Israel and worked in few kibbutz farms. In Germany I was doing research on sense organs of fish, focusing on the olfactory organs. This involves physiology. I figured that if I can smell fish, perhaps they can smell me too. This could be true, but it is still to be scientifically verified. In nature smell is very important for fish, especially migratory fish because it enables them to know where to migrate. For deciding upon the time of migration there are other factors, especially the season, not simply smell.

For example, there is a term called 'homing,' as in salmon migration. The fish use their sense organs to learn where they should migrate to for spawning purposes. A fish that is born in a certain place will return to that very spot for spawning, and it is fascinating to realize that this is due to some imprint in its memory. We do not really fully understand how it works. In the case of salmon, the hatchling would be born upstream in a river far away from the sea. About a year later it will migrate downstream to the open sea. When it is time to spawn the fish must swim back upstream. When they migrate to the open sea, sometimes thousands of miles away, the fish sense the direction of the water flow. A few years later, when the fish has fully grown, its brain provides a signal that it is time to go home. So how does a fish in the ocean know where it was born? Reaching the shoreline may not be that difficult. There are many factors involved, not simply smell because in the ocean it would be difficult for the fish to detect the smell of the river. The fish orients itself according to the sky and the stars, and also use the global magnetic poles to find its way. As the fish progresses on its journey, it notes the differences in salinity of the ocean. As it approaches the shoreline the salinity decreases. But once it is near the shore, the fish uses its olfactory sense to detect the smell of the river in which it was born and grew for one year.

This is only the case for salmon. For other fish the process may be totally different. The eel is born in the sea and spends most of its life in the river. So how does the eel know when to return to the sea and how to get there? Again a number of factors tell and direct the eel to migrate to the spawning place which is for the American and European eel, the same place, the Sargasso Sea.

While studying the sense organs of fish I realized what an important role they play in feeding habits, i.e. in finding food. This knowledge would be useful in the field of commercial fish nutrition. Therefore it was important to find a way to apply the knowledge I acquired about fish nutrition in nature, to the controlled conditions in the lab.

At one point of my career I was involved in the development of ornamental fish in Israel. This was some time ago when some kibbutzim decided to make a profit growing ornamental fish. These fish are members of the carp family. The main economic aspect of ornamental fish is their color rather than their taste.

We were engaged in research aimed at establishing the quantities of algae containing pigments which are required to achieve optimal coloring of these fish. Fish cannot synthesize color, but have the genetic pattern to show it in their skin by utilizing the color in the food they eat.

Ninety nine percent of Israel's edible fish market is consumed locally. Approximately 70 thousand tons of fish are consumed annually in Israel, and about one third of this is produced locally by kibbutzim. Almost all of the fish farmed in Israel are from north of Tel Aviv. There are more than 70 kibbutzim which produce about 17 thousand tons of fish annually, and each year we stock the sea of Galilee, creating an additional form of aquaculture. In Israel there are very few private fish farms growing edible fish.

When I first came to Israel, after my studies abroad, no one was growing fish commercially in Ramat Negev. Anyone who farms animals of any kind for a living can never rely on his own labor alone, since animals require almost constant personal monitoring. The farmer's absence, even for a few days due to reserve duty, illness, or other circumstances can have irreversible devastating consequences for the health and well-being of the animals. Hence, the necessity for responsible employees capable of dealing with the unexpected (failures in electricity or water supply for example) during the farmer's absence. When people ask me about my gray hair I tell them it's the result of having to deal with the various technical problems and diseases that arise when raising fish.

The more intensive the system, the more concerned you become about all the things that can go wrong. Israel produces large quantities of ornamental fish for export. In the North of the country fish are grown in dams and other water reservoirs;

In Norway where salmon are grown inside nets in the fiords, cultivation is not anywhere near as intensive. You only have to supply them with enough food and make sure that they do not break through the net.

You ask if my living in the desert somehow affects or motivates my professional work. I think that if you devote yourself to something and you try to make the best out of it, then you develop a strong connection to the place where you do it. This is true not only for fish. One cannot be physically somewhere and emotionally far away and still concentrate on their work. You could be an excellent scientist in a lab during the day, and travel far back to your home in the evening, there is nothing wrong with that. But if you do applied research, you will succeed best in my opinion, when you sense with all your body and mind the environment in which the research will eventually utilized.

So now the question is, what if anything does this environment do for your sense of growing fish?

I fell in love with the environment, which is beautiful desert, and I do not wish to see it turned into a forest. However I would like to benefit from the resources of the desert, the sunshine, and the water found underground. There is no shortage of water in the world, however one needs first to desalinate sea water it in order for it to be of use for human consumption or in agriculture. In the meantime we can use the brackish water found underground for the cultivation of aquatic organisms for commercial purposes. The water from the national carrier, brought from the Sea of Galilee, is more expensive than the water we have here.

Under the desert the brackish water body comes in contact with the fresh water from the North. If you consume too much of the brackish water there is a danger that the Northern fresh water will be lost by penetrating the Southern brackish water body. Or if you take too much of the fresh water, the saline water will penetrate into the fresh water. So there should be a balance at the national level. Brackish water should also be used for other farm crops.

The more I live in the desert the more I become aware of the fact that arid land aquaculture is essential for Israel and for other parts of the world. The common opinion that arid land is useless is absolutely mistaken, particularly in regions where there is subsurface water.

When I walk to and from work or when I travel across the desert to any of the fish farms, I can sense the presence of water deep below the surface. This gives me great pleasure because I feel that the water below has been waiting from ancient times to be of use to us.

Desert Architecture

David Pearlmutter

I am often asked what is meant by this term 'desert architecture.' Why in fact should a building be different just because it is in the desert? If our goal as architects is to provide people with decent places to live, or to work, or to learn—places that meet their practical needs, and are at the same time beautiful—then why should it matter if we are designing in the Negev or anywhere else?

In a sense, architecture in the desert is just like architecture anywhere else. In the sense, that is, that as an architect you should always be paying attention to where you are. A successful building, in my view, is never isolated from its context. The context of a building may include the man-made surroundings of a neighborhood or city, and it may include the natural surroundings of a hilly forest or a coastal plain. A building's physical context always includes the climate of the place where it is built.

It has often been said that we should work with the realities of climate and environment, rather than having a head-on confrontation with them. When it comes to designing a building, this idea has very tangible implications. Perhaps the most fundamental role of architecture is to provide shelter; a building must be structurally sound, it must protect us from the elements, and keep us comfortable. Nowadays we expect our buildings to provide a very high level of comfort, and we usually accomplish this by applying enormous amounts of material and energy. By now it is well known that buildings use close to half of all the primary energy consumed, and the largest part of this requirement is for heating, cooling, and otherwise making these buildings habitable. It is also clear that making a wholesale difference in the energy efficiency of our architecture is not possible without understanding and responding intelligently to the local climate.

So if the 'climatic context' consists of an arid desert, an architect will first need to know what the limitations of the desert are, and what opportunities it has to offer. These realities are in large part intuitive, though they can easily become obscured when the option of air conditioning is so convenient and accessible. What is special about our local climate in the Negev Highlands? There is an obvious contrast with a more temperate place like Tel Aviv, because there is so little rain and such rapid evaporation, and because radiation from the sun is so intense. But as stressful as this situation may be for vegetation, not to mention for farmers and gardeners, the dryness is an opportunity when designing for people's comfort, both indoors and out.

First of all, with low humidity and clear skies come unusually wide diurnal temperature swings—and it though it can be can surprising for newcomers, it becomes intuitive when living here that in spite of the intense heat of the daytime, the evening air rapidly becomes cool and pleasant. In designing a building we can take advantage of these fluctuations, if we ensure that it has a high thermal inertia—that is, we cool the structure by flushing it with chilly air at night, and we 'store' this coolness in the dense material of the walls, floor and ceiling, which absorb excess heat during the day. What we've come to know in Israel as 'conventional' construction, despite its many shortcomings, happens to serve this function well by providing generous doses of 'thermal mass' in the form of cement-based concrete and heavy blocks. Ancient practices using stone and mud brick, or alternative materials exploiting fly-ash in place of cement do so as well—and in addition, they require vastly smaller amounts of energy to produce.

Of course the details matter—a massive building must be protected from overheating in the daytime, and this firstly means thermally insulating it from the outside: modern lightweight insulation materials are, once again, energy-intensive in their production—but they 'pay their way' energetically over a few short years of reduced heating and air-conditioning. Secondly, it means scrupulously restricting the heat-producing sunlight that is allowed to pass through transparent openings—which can be accomplished most effectively by using adjustable shutters, but is accomplished most wisely by first considering the solar exposure of windows in their initial sizing and placement.

The orientation of these windows—the 'eyes' of the building—takes center-stage in winter, when a southern exposure is necessary for collecting the solar radiation that in deserts like the Negev is abundant most days of the year. Passive heating by direct gain is probably the oldest, and still the most cost-effective, utilization of solar energy – and the key to making it work is, once again, the same combination of internal mass and external insulation that serves so well in summer (with the same operable shutters preventing the escape of heat at night).

These principles are hardly new—they are so well known, in fact, that it can sometimes be alarming how infrequently they are applied. And the reasons they are not are far from simple: short-term interests and pre-conceived notions of cost play a major role, certainly more than any evidence that passive buildings are incapable of providing comfort and vast energy savings. Many of the houses built in the Neve-Zin 'solar neighborhood' at the Sede-Boqer campus are examples which prove the opposite is true, reducing energy expenditures by an order of magnitude. My personal experience of living in such a house has made the benefits, and perhaps also the challenges, more tangible for me than they would otherwise be.

One of the realities that is hard to appreciate in theory alone is the idea that 'a passive house requires an active user.' Periodically adjusting shutters, windows, or awnings becomes second-nature—but it means following the rhythms of the day and the seasons in a much more conscious way than adjusting a thermostat. Unlike most people transplanted to the Negev, I grew up in the desert and in a sense have always taken it for granted. But watching the sky and being regularly on the lookout—for approaching rain clouds or dust storms, for sources of warmth and sources of overheating—has heightened my awareness to the desert's stark contrasts, and to the power of its elements.

If climatically-informed building design in the desert has not yet lived up to its potential, climatically-informed urban design is nearly non-existent. A building is not an isolated object, it is also a piece in a mosaic—a piece that can contribute to a larger whole, or detract from it. At the same time, this overall urban fabric has an effect on the building itself, impeding or supporting its climatic functioning. One of the most significant innovations in the Neve-Zin neighborhood is the institution of a mechanism for ensuring "solar rights"—guaranteeing that no individual is denied access to passive heating from the sun because of overshadowing by a neighbor's house. This is an example of desert architecture at the level of urban design, but it is a rare one.

One of the most glaring symptoms of the inattention to climate in the Negev is the treatment (or non-treatment) of open spaces—streets, pathways, and other public places where pedestrians are routinely exposed to the most inhospitable conditions. As with the individual building, this lack of attention to the climatic design of outdoor spaces can be explained in any number of ways, but here an additional problem enters in: an insufficient understanding of the basic physical phenomena and their interactions in a complex urban environment. Fifty years ago, attempts were made at building 'Garden Cities' in the Negev—leading not so much to gardens but to a proliferation of wide-open spaces with little protection from the elements. Experience has suggested that a more 'compact' urban fabric is preferable for a hot-arid environment, but the consequences of a densely packed urban arrangement are not trivial: while deep, narrow streets enhance pedestrian shading, they can also increase the 'trapping' of radiation and obstruct the flow of air, leading to higher temperatures.

The aim of our research into 'urban microclimate' has been to clarify such basic relationships between urban design physical parameters affecting human comfort in a desert region like the Negev. Starting with a systematic field study in a densely built 'patio house' neighborhood, we found that air temperatures in summer were indeed higher, and wind speeds significantly lower, in 'compact' pedestrian streets than in more open areas—but that in terms of the overall balance of energy exchanged between a pedestrian and the urban environment, these narrow streets could be considered far more comfortable physiologically—and this was mainly due to the dominant role of solar shading.

A particular challenge was presented, though, when trying to broaden the conclusions of a very site-specific study. Existing models in urban climatology tend to either oversimplify the complex atmospheric phenomena that come into play, or to lack the resolution necessary for understanding the effects of individual buildings or streets. For this reason, physical scale models are used for simulating specific processes, but only in isolation—such as air flow over building arrays within a wind tunnel. Our novel approach, developed together with Prof. Pedro Berliner, began as an attempt to overcome some of these persistent limitations of modeling by making use of an 'open-air scaled urban surface'—that is, building an array of small-scale buildings and streets in a variety of configurations and subjecting them to the actual climatic conditions of the Negev.

By using this unconventional research tool, we have identified patterns in the design-climate relationship that are of practical use to urban designers. Stated in the form of a very general recommendation, it could be argued that neighborhood-scale planning should strive to create a 'selective' urban fabric—recognizing that the value of a 'compact' street geometry depends, for example, on the axis orientation of the street in question. When walking along a street that runs north-south, a pedestrian is likely to benefit from higher walls and closer spacing during most hours of a hot summer day, because the effect of deep shading is so dominant in the overall energy balance. As the direction of the street changes, though, the balance between the direct and indirect effects of the sun, along with effectiveness of ventilation due to changing wind patterns, is altered as well—so that for an east-west oriented street axis, the advantage of compactness becomes negligible. In fact, there is good reason to widen the spacing between buildings on the opposite sides of such a street, because—as in Neve-Zin—it can facilitate solar access to their south-facing windows, and thereby contribute to energy-efficiency on an urban scale.

Obviously there is much more to successful and humane urban design in the desert than these simple relationships. The influences of vegetation, building materials, and heat-generating activities in a dense urban setting, and peoples' subjective perceptions of comfort and their related patterns of behavior are but a few aspects of the larger question. But the use of systematic methods can, and is continuing to, contribute to our understanding the basic realities of the desert climate—knowledge which, when applied together with wisdom, can benefit future desert dwellers and builders.

Apology for Architecture, or the Planner's Craft

Isaac Meir

Instead of an introduction

'Architect' is a strange and misinterpreted term. Coming from the Greek '*arkhitekton*,' meaning master builder, it implies a broad background of knowledge in town and site planning, building design, structures and construction, materials and techniques, systems and details, and not least, the arts—sculpture and painting, frescos and stained glass. Such were the great masters that designed the buildings and monuments we all like to visit and study. Architecture may thus be defined not as a discipline but as an umbrella for, or a conglomerate of related disciplines. Architecture has been defined therefore as 'mother of all arts,' yet to Arnold Toynbee is often attributed the infamous quotation "but what can one say about the mother when the daughters work the streets?"

In past ages it was mostly religious, institutional, and monumental buildings that were designed by architects, whereas the vast majority of shelters, or homes of the average individual, were built by artisans and the end-users themselves. Since the 18th and 19th centuries, however, architecture has evolved into an academic profession, which eventually has led to an unfortunate disconnection between the architect and the other building related professionals, not least through an over-indulgence of architects in matters of 'higher order' philosophical questions, matters of style and aesthetics (Salingaros *et al*, 2004). It is quite often that students of architecture, and even qualified professionals, may have a broad knowledge of the most recent stylistic discourse between deconstruction and late post-modernism, yet may have little to say about energy in buildings, the urban heat island, or physical planning and how it affects public health.

This general academic, bourgeois discourse usually leaves out marginal populations and regions, among them deserts. In the latter resources are limited, constraints are extreme, indigenous populations usually are poor, and shelter has a very flexible yet basic meaning. It may well be that living in a desert—something I have done for the past 20-odd years—has sharpened my perception of and pointed my antennae to all of these problems. It may also be that city living blunts certain instincts, whereas life in the desert returns us to our right place in relation to nature, natural forces, and our ability to affect our environment (usually adversely) and suffer from the boomerang effect this has on our lives and those of our children.

The next few pages have no pretence of being an academic paper, but are rather a personal communiqué of what I perceive as the real priorities of my profession. This is what I have been asked by the editors to do.

Challenges

Design and construction in the near future will be challenged by the following three decisive processes: accelerated urbanization in developing countries; the progressive depletion of fossil fuels and other natural resources; and the impact of human activities on the environment.

These topics have not yet attracted the attention they deserve in the architectural discourse, though they are critical to our future. The lack of interest of architects in these issues is the origin of the title of this article; a sort of paraphrase of Marc Bloch's book, *"Apology for History or the Historian's Craft."* The demographic trends of the last decades predict that by the year 2030, about half of the world's population will live in the cities of the developing countries (INFO, 2006). These processes are not controlled and certainly are not planned. Their significance is in the addition of large numbers of people to cities whose existing services and infrastructure are already collapsing under current pressure. The residential zones springing up around the big cities are usually slums without infrastructure for water and electricity supply, and without orderly sewage systems. Surveys show that only about 40% of the urban population in Africa have access to running water (and sometimes even that is limited to a single water tap in the center of a neighborhood), and that less than 20% are hooked up to any type of sewage system. The percentages in Asia and South America are higher than in Africa, though not nearly as high as in the industrialized countries (UNESCO, 2003).

In addition to the health implications of these two topics, there exists the problem of construction from nonstandard materials (corrugated sheet metal, industrial waste, cardboard, polyethylene sheets, etc.) that cannot provide adequate living conditions or thermal comfort. The tenants of these substandard structures also suffer from fuel poverty. Weak populations in the industrialized countries also suffer from this phenomenon, though for different reasons: while fuel is widely available in developed countries, disadvantaged populations simply cannot afford to pay for it. When standard sources of fuel are unavailable, people tend to use whatever they can find for cooking and heating, including animal dung and waste materials (Sauerhaft, Berliner, & Thurow 1998). Combustion of these materials is a health hazard, especially when they are burned in a closed space (Smith, 2003).

Architecture of minimalism: cow dung as fuel, India (left); and as a building material in a Maasai manyata in Maasailand, Kenya (right).

People of the wealthy world are, ostensibly, spared these problems since they have access to available, relatively inexpensive forms of energy. Today, about half of the energy consumed in industrialized countries is invested in buildings primarily for heating, cooling, lighting, movement, but also in the production of the materials, and the construction and demolition of the buildings. Mechanical systems such as air-conditioning have enabled the development of unique building types that rely on high energy input for their normal operation, as opposed to the traditional, vernacular, and historic precedents.

On buildings and fossil fuels

An example of modern buildings are multi-story ones that are dependent on mechanical user transportation systems (i.e., elevators, escalators, etc.) and on pumps to raise water to high levels (including fire extinguishing systems). Other examples of modern building systems are deep-plan office buildings that require artificial lighting, ventilation, and air conditioning due to the distance of the main part

The vernacular as a paradigm: traditional mud house in the Atacama desert, Chile (left); and a contemporary bioclimatic experimental adobe house in the Negev desert, Israel (design by Desert Architecture & Urban Planning and Applied Solar Calculations, Blaustein Institutes for Desert Research, BGU).

of the space from the facade; and buildings with shells of glass and steel or lightweight materials that lack insulation and/or thermal mass to store energy and are thus unable to regulate their inner climates without air conditioning systems. It has become more and more apparent that the sustainability of such structures over time is doubtful, since the energy sources on which these buildings rely, are being depleted at a worrisome rate. Both researchers and petroleum companies estimate that the turning point will take place between 2010 and 2020 when the extraction of petroleum will reach its peak rate and go into decline, although demand may continue to increase (Bartsch & Mueler, 2000). These estimates are based on consumption trends and present development, but already energy demand is growing exponentially in relation to the potential supply. The economy of China (estimated to grow by over 9% in 2006) and other fast-developing countries is based on the growing exploitation of dwindling sources of energy. The present rate of energy consumption cannot continue indefinitely, and this threatens the future of the building types most common in our modern cities - or more correctly, the survival of their tenants.

The prevalent building and construction styles in the world's largest cities, especially in the city centers, create knotty environmental problems. One of the most tangible environmental problems is the urban heat island. This refers to the phenomenon of higher temperatures in a city, especially its core, compared to the surrounding countryside, caused by the combination of deep urban canyons with hard surfaces, lack of shade, trapping of incoming solar radiation, and heat retention of the buildings and structures. This contributes to the consumption of more energy to air-condition the buildings found in these heat islands; and this, in turn, probably exacerbates the heat island phenomenon as well.

The world discourse regarding global warming is also related to our discussion here. The summer of 2003, one of the hottest in European history, inflicted many casualties. France alone recorded about 15,000 deaths above average for the season, and these were directly connected to nights in which the temperature did not dip below 29 degrees centigrade. We can assume that the air temperatures in the crowded city centers were even higher than this, and reached even higher levels inside the buildings—and this gives us a formula that links physical planning and morbidity/mortality. True, the polemics regarding anthropogenic contribution to climatic changes has not yet been resolved, but more and more evidence attests to our non-negligible influence (Schär *et al*, 2004).

The individual building and the context in a desert case study

The author's bioclimatic house (design by I.A. Meir)

The solar neighborhood in which this house is built ensures solar and wind rights (masterplan by Desert Architecture & Urban Planning, Blaustein Institutes for Desert Research, BGU)

Summer monitoring showing four locations within the house fluctuating at around 24-26 deg.C (daily ambient average) without air conditioning

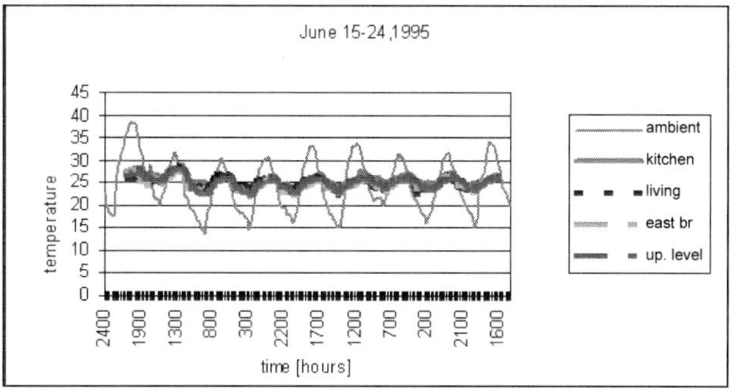

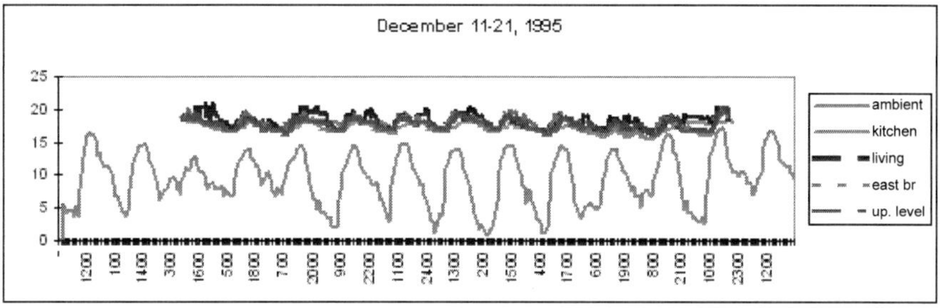

Winter monitoring showing four locations within the house fluctuating at 19-22 deg.C (well above the daily ambient maximum) without auxiliary heating

On buildings and health

A fascinating discussion is taking place between the public health people and physicians on the one hand, and atmospheric scientists and city planners on the other. These latter professionals deal with the problematic relations between the built-up space in which we live and the by-products of the use of natural resources (including fuel). They study the effects of these factors on air quality both outside and inside buildings, and on our health. New studies, for example, point to a direct link between proximity of neighborhoods and educational institutions to main roads, and an increase in asthma outbreaks in children, and between proximity of residential areas to power plants and acute respiratory system problems among children (Dubnov *et al,* 2007); between sealed buildings with expensive, energy intensive air-conditioning, and the 'sick building syndrome'; between unwise land allocation for building, and severe problems such as flooding, subsidence of buildings, penetration of contaminants, and more. The flooding of New Orleans may be an extreme example of such improper land allocation, though it is definitely not the only one. Recent studies show areas potentially flooded under specific climate change scenarios, among them parts of the Netherlands and the United Kingdom, Bangladesh and areas around the Mekong river, to mention but a few.

Some of the world's environmental and climatic changes are connected to the desertification processes. In the last twenty years, deserts have expanded by about 50%, and today, drylands make up around 45% of the world's continents. Yet our view of desertification remains ambivalent. Arid, sparsely populated zones are perceived as useless (beyond the exploitation of their limited natural resources), or as venues for problematic activities such as nuclear experiments and the disposal of hazardous waste. On the other hand, we must remember that deserts are home to and affect, directly or indirectly, some two billion people. The desert's expansion brings many people to the frontier and others to the heart of the desert, and this creates migrations of refugees and economically-motivated immigrants.

Though we often have a hard time relating to such macro-scale events and chains of events, the following example may prove a good illustration of the immediate and intimate relations between the lifestyle of an individual and the global changes and effects. In the 1980s and 1990s a prolonged and extreme drought in the Sahel caused the death of 100,000-250,000 people, affected 20 countries and 150 million people, 30 million of whom were in urgent need of food aid, and created 10 million refugees seeking food and water. Originally the Sahel Catastrophe was attributed to ignorant and primitive pastoralists of the Sahel and the way they overexploited their environment by overgrazing, thus causing desertification and drought. However, a few years down the line a strange connection was identified between cooling of the seas around Europe and a change in the monsoon regime, weakening the rain-bringing winds, thus causing aridization of the Sahel.

The seawater's temperature reduction was eventually attributed to global dimming, which is caused by aerosols in the atmosphere (Giannini, Saravanan,&

Chang, 2003). The source of such airborne particles is coal-fed power plants, vehicles running on combustibles, and industrial plants. Whereas none of these sources was significantly present in the Sahel, all of them were in massive presence in Europe. Thus, what was originally thought to be the 'crime and punishment' of ignorant people and the way they took advantage of their environment, proved to be the unintentional influence of the affluent world on the poor and hungry African desert. And here is the right place to remind the reader that some 50% of all energy used in the industrialized countries is invested in buildings!

This might have been the end of the story, coupled with some aid and development programs intended to somehow improve the situation of the refugees and the host countries in the region, had it not been for an additional detail and twist of destiny usually disregarded. Some 50% of the global dust in the air today originates in arid Africa. This has been the impact of drying, causing the planet's atmospheric dust loading to increase by 33% (Flannery, 2005). This in turn has been shown to have a direct influence on morbidity and mortality, as demonstrated by a study connecting dust storms in the north-western Provinces of the People's Republic of China with mortality in Taiwan (Chen *et al*, 2004). Can this then prove to be a new nemesis for the industrialized, non-desert world?

These three trends or processes—urbanization, depletion of natural resources, and human effect on the environment—should be a focus of interest for all planners and architects. The real challenge for professionals and decision makers lies in understanding the phenomena, and responding with appropriate policies, in the following fields:

- Adaptation of design and construction to environmental constraints, particularly desert conditions, through the utilization of alternative energy sources and materials.
- Development of passive heating and cooling systems for buildings and semi-open spaces.
- Post Occupancy Evaluation (POE) of projects aimed at the creation of benchmarks for future planning and design.
- Study of the urban micro-climate and adaptation of settlement forms and patterns to the desert conditions.
- Water policy and resources management.
- Proactive contingency planning.
- Study of refugee-related problems such as food and water security.
- Study of historic settlement and building patterns and construction technology, allowing better understanding of low-tech construction upgrade for the future.

Instead of an epilogue

The major challenge of the coming years is to adapt buildings and settlements in general, and those in arid zones in particular – both in developing as well as developed countries – to the needs of the future. An interdisciplinary approach needs to be promoted as the essential basis for sustainable planning (Roaf, Chrichton, & Nicol, 2004). The abuse of the environment, desert and non-desert, cannot go on without heavy repercussions, and it is up to the planners and the architects to take a more active role in the decision-making processes (Meir, 2005). It is not a question of choice, but rather one of necessity—I might even say sheer survival, but that would be too dramatic coming from an architect.

Is this relevant to desert architecture? After all, that was what the editors asked me to write about. I am confident it is of relevance. Deserts, after all, are more extreme than their neighboring non-desert regions. Deserts are characterized by a wide diurnal and seasonal temperature fluctuation, the former reaching some 30°C in the Atacama Desert, the latter reaching some 90°C on the Iranian Plateau and in Mongolia. They are also very erratic in terms of precipitation, with rainfall being concentrated spatially and temporally in a small number of events, usually causing floods. Indigenous building materials are limited and demand special structural systems, details and maintenance to provide appropriate and safe shelter. Water availability puts constraints on water use in general, and in particular on the viability of conventional landscaping, often used as a microclimate modifier. Deserts cover large parts of the planet, practically in all continents. Vast numbers of people are affected by the deserts themselves and their expansion—desertification. All of these make the deserts more than legitimate study areas, and desert architecture more than relevant.

So the answer is positive—all this discussion is relevant to desert architecture. But more than this, it is of relevance to architecture at large—as a discipline, as a profession, as a main player in a game that affects the present and future of all of us. And it is an apology for the wrong turn architecture has taken in the last few decades, misleading the public in buying products that won't last, will malfunction and put the user in danger—products within which we spend some 90% of our lives.

Let's put architecture back to where it belongs, shall we? Let's rediscover the "mother of all arts," and restore a bit of her old dignity—and future relevance!

Notes

1. Based on a shorter version published in A Voice from the Desert, A Bulletin of the Jacob Blaustein Institutes for Desert Research, October 2005, pp. 6-7.
2. The author is architect, town planner and archaeologist, and current chair of the Department of Man in the Desert, BIDR–BGU.

PART V

EDUCATION AND SCHOLARSHIP

Part V contains three chapters. In Chapter 13, Sol Brand describes the mission of the residential high school in the Midrasha, whose purpose is to introduce students to all aspects of desert life, with excursions to other locations in Israel. In Chapter 14, Eran Doron describes the activity of the Midrasha branch of the system of Field Schools that are all over Israel. In Chapter 15, Allon Gal describes and analyzes the scholarly work of the Ben-Gurion Research Institute, Ben-Gurion University, and features the Ben-Gurion Heritage Institute, which elaborates on and disseminates Ben-Gurion's vision in national and international contexts.

Chapter 13

Environmental High School

Sol Brand

The desert encompasses about two thirds of the area of the State of Israel, David Ben-Gurion, one of the founding fathers of the State, believed that Israel must learn to utilize the resources of the desert in order to develop into a successful modern state. Ben-Gurion succeeded in convincing the authorities that an educational complex at the Midrasha in the Negev Desert could fulfill the task of providing the facilities and atmosphere for desert studies at all levels from grade school projects to advanced scientific research.

In the mid 1970's Ben-Gurion University of the Negev established an institute at the Midrasha explicitly for promoting desert research in a variety of disciplines including hydrology, ecology, sociology, agrobiology physiology, architecture, and others. The concept was to understand the structure and function of the desert from all aspects.

At the time of the establishment of the Desert Research Institute, the campus of the Midrasha contained three educational facilities. There was a Teacher's college and two high school programs. One of the programs was for pupils from English speaking countries, where the curriculum was taught in English. The other program was for pupils from the area around the Midrasha and a boarding school for pupils who came to study away from their families. In the 1970's the Israel Board of Education decided to close the three educational facilities under the allegation that they were not meeting necessary standards.

After the closure of the educational programs, the Midrasha campus contained just the newly established Desert Research Institute and a Field School for guiding nature tours in the desert. A number of educators who had worked in the programs that had closed developed a new program that would promote the establishment of a high school adjacent to the Desert Research Institute. The idea being that the school would be selective where highly qualified students would be accepted. In addition to the national matriculation program they would work on projects sponsored by academic researchers of the Desert Research Institute.

This program was started but did not succeed in attaining its goals. The educators in the program then decided to adopt a new educational concept that had been advanced in the USA by two educators. The educators were Professor Schultz from the University of California and Professor Novak from Cornell University. Their premise was that many intelligent pupils find high school programs irrelevant because subjects are studied independently without consideration to those studied in other courses. History, chemistry, and mathematics were studied without any concern for the real world. The program suggested by Schultz and Novak was called environmental education. This program entailed studying the world holistically. A case study is chosen and then studied from all aspects. The case study may be building a bridge. In order to properly construct the project the pupils must understand the criteria involved. History of the area, mathematics, economics, ecology, English, and other disciplines are integrated into developing the blueprint for the project. A major tool in understanding how to analyze a case study is system analysis. The pupils must learn to construct models for simplification and abstraction of the case study in order to deal with the complex interdisciplinary tasks involved.

In order to carry out our goal of environmental education in a high school at the Midrasha, we developed a program that started from simple concepts in the ninth grade to gradually addressing complex decision making in the upper grades. The idea was to advance from knowledge to understanding to awareness to decision making or activism. The environmental education program was to be taught in the environment by going on five day workshops to learn about the environment in order to be able to protect the environment. Before going on the workshops there were preparations in the library and classroom and after the workshop there were projects and reports that had to be presented to summarize the workshops.

In the ninth grade the workshops are: The Negev Workshop – the pupils hike for five days and sleep in the field. They learn about the flora and fauna of the desert. They study geology, archaeology, topography, and other aspects. The aim is for the pupils to be able to recognize aspects of the desert and to understand relationships between them. The second workshop in the ninth grade is the Coastal Workshop. In this workshop the pupils study the same concepts as before but in a different environment.

In the tenth grade the workshops are: Ein Gedi Workshop – the pupils go from Lehavim, in the northern Negev, to Ein Gedi and learn to recognize that a rainfall gradient from 250 to 50 mm average annual rainfall coincides with changes in other climatic variables, flora, fauna, geology, and human habitation. They also deal with conflicts involved with living in a desert oasis such as Kibbutz Ein Gedi. The conflicts are for limited water resources that must be appropriated to Kibbutz Ein Gedi, agriculture, tourism, and a nature reserve. The second workshop is the Maquis Workshop which is a geobotanical study. The pupils learn to recognize vegetation from the Midrasha to the Carmel Mountains. They learn to associate average annual rainfall to vegetation cover and species diversity.

The workshops in the eleventh and twelfth grades integrate cultures, religions, and values into the environmental studies program.

The two workshops in the eleventh grade are: Desert Environmental Workshop—this workshop includes studying the Bedouin culture. The pupils relate the culture of the Bedouin to environmental factors. In addition, the pupils study different human settlements in remote areas of the Negev. The idea is to understand how the desert affects the individual's behavior. The second workshop is the Water Resource Workshop—water quantity and quality in Israel is investigated from hydrological, ecological, economic, health, and geopolitical aspects. In this workshop the pupils get to understand the diverse complex demands for the limited quantity of water available.

In the twelfth grade the workshops are: The Galilee Workshop—the pupils travel to the galilee and learn about the different religions; Druze, Moslem, Christian, and Ultra Orthodox Judaism. They try to understand how and if the different cultures are related to environmental factors. The final workshop is an urban workshop in Tel Aviv or Jerusalem where the pupils are exposed to cultural aspects they may not have been exposed to: foreign workers, deprived individuals, drug addicts, homosexual community, artistic community, stock exchange, and others. The basic idea is that our values are an integration of many factors that are not easy to quantify. The factors include genes, economics, surroundings, family, and other psychological, physiological, and environmental features. People are different and it is not appropriate to characterize different life styles in terms of good or bad.

The goal of the environmental education program at the Midrasha is to educate high school pupils to understand the complexity and vulnerability of the environment as well tolerance for all individuals. We want the pupils to appreciate the beauty and value of the desert to Israel and much of the world. We believe that with knowledge, understanding and awareness, the individual can then intelligently choose in which direction he desires to be active. This is accordance with the vision of Ben-Gurion, who foresaw that the Negev Desert could fulfill the task of providing the facilities and atmosphere for desert studies for the benefit of Israel and for mankind.

Chapter 14

Field School

Eran Doron

"Here it comes," someone screamed and the entire group, deep in the mud, looked through the pouring rain to see the new wave of flooding water coming down the river bed. Ecstatic, a few of the girl instructors began to move in circles, singing and yelling, wet to their bones, and the rain went on powerfully, and the entire group followed, thus welcoming the powers of nature. After two years of drought, all were waiting for a flood to come and redeem the Negev highland from its dryness; to germinate the annuals, to save the perennials from dehydration, to fill up the pits and thereby enable the renewing of animal life.

Here, on the spur of the moment the rains had arrived. Much that we had said on the greenhouse effect, casting doubts on the future of life on earth, was instantly gone. Teaching about hydraulic models of the deep storage of fossil water seem unnecessary once a waterfall 80 meters high rushes loudly into the darkened canyon.

The Field School at the Midrasha was founded by Mr. Yehoshua Cohen and Mr. Michael Gal in 1962 at the request of David Ben Gurion. The empty cliffs of the Zin gorge, they thought, would be the right place to locate a Field School. David Ben Gurion had left the government in 1953 and moved to live in Kibbutz Sde-Boqer. Gal, born in Kibbutz Yagur, was appointed to be the School's founding director. Among his first School instructors were students of archaeology and later on professors Y. Tzafrir, Y. Yom-Tov, Z Meshel, and A. Klonner.

The founding of the Midrasha Field School was second to the one in Ein Gedi. The emphasis of the founders for both schools was 'Bio-centric,' i.e., an accent put on nature to be the source of inspiration for humans. At the week-long school classes, the teaching placed nature as an object to be observed, to be kept from intervention of humans with their artificial touch.

At the Midrasha, however, the emphasis changed to see mankind as affected by and affecting its environment. This was not surprising since archaeologists who dealt with ancient cultures and their efforts to survive in the desert had also done a considerable amount of research here. This difference of approach left the Midrasha Field School alone vis-à-vis The Society for Protection of Nature, which had planned an additional 25 field schools. In the long run, however, the line of thought shaped at the Midrasha was accepted by all.

How to inculcate the values implied in deserts?

Beginning in 1999 and the peace agreement between Israel and Jordan placed our dealing with Negev highland as a miniscule part of the wide desert area, including the Sinai and Jordan's Eastern deserts, that were made available and inviting for our pupils to learn about. We had already begun to include sites in the neighboring deserts when the '*Intifada*' of September 2001 forced us to discontinue our ideas about collaboration and school exchanges.

Our former goals brought us to treat seriously the 'Agenda 21' of the 1991 Rio de Janiero conference. The objectives of sustainability and preservation of nature contrasted in part with the principles of development and the founding of permanent pioneer settlements in the Negev. Right at this time began the debate concerning the establishment of individual farms, an issue initiated by our Regional Council. Social and green organizations objected to the individual farms.

External debates such as this one committed us to reconsider, then readjust our pedagogical philosophy, to include the theme of social justice e.g., with thoughts of permanent settlements for the Negev Bedouin. We were obliged to address our pupils with new perceptions of center and periphery, and new developmental paradigms. We called our readjusted development scheme 'Environmental Zionism,' implying a world view that commits the citizen, State servant, as well as each young pupil in years to come, to contribute to maintain joint social, national and environmental assets intact. The present State organs must take care so that the future development will not come at the cost of coming generations.

This approach brought us from the classical 'Get to Know the Land' program we had, teaching related geology, history, biology, and botany, to include in our program socio-economic problems. We could not train our teachers to delve deep in their instructions the value judgments needed, as e.g., discussing the big crater and speaking of the values implied that are important for our progeny to know. Moreover, we could no longer focus on the Negev, leaving aside the global problem of deserts and their concerns. Desert conditions, to tell the truth, are tough ones. They can be merited only if they teach us a story of modesty, to put off extravagance and prevent the use of whatever is unnecessary. When there is no flora in arid lands, then we must search to replace the photosynthesis there, to substitute all lacuna, and foremost, endorse an attitude that spirit should replace any physical provision that does not exist.

In essence, deserts are contrary to capitalism with its made up images of happiness, of freedom to choose the best out of a plenty, of reaching out rather than in, to search for the meaningful, and in viewing oneself as the center to be offered and served, rather than as one in reciprocal relationships, one of a whole.

The Field School at the Midrasha provides more than 1,500 class days a year and more than 40,000 nights spent in its dormitory facilities. Special courses are provided at the Bedouin schools in the area, and for schools of the Jewish townships of the Negev. We also accept tourists from Israel and abroad. We have offered the myriads of our students and visitors a different view of affairs, and have tried to teach them to consider more ways of being by means of the desert experience.

Chapter 15

Ben-Gurion Research and Heritage Institutes

Allon Gal[1]

The Law of David Ben-Gurion, passed in the Knesset (the Israeli parliament) in November 1976 (three years after Ben-Gurion's death), was designed to manifestly pursue Ben-Gurion's name and ideological heritage for generations. Accordingly, an institute bearing his name was established in the Sde-Boqer area, in the Negev Heights. The settlement of the Negev has been a crucial element in this legacy. Those who initiated that law in 1976 believed that Zionism could best be realized in the desert environment. Like David Ben-Gurion, they envisioned Zionism as a noble endeavor, one whose democratic and pioneering qualities could be most effectively pursued in the Negev, where Jewish national renewal faces a vast, neglected, and sparsely populated area. (The Negev composes about 60 percent of Israel's territory.) Hence, the reality of the situation in the Negev subtly and persistently challenged Zionists—with minimal national conflict—to concentrate on building the Jewish national home from the sandy bottom up.[2]

As is well-known, Ben-Gurion suddenly left the government of Israel and joined a kibbutz in the Negev (Sde-Boqer) to do agricultural and historical-literary work. Far from being an egotist, purely spiritual act, and beyond possible political considerations, his mission to the Negev was an intentional attempt to blaze a course for the Jewish people, especially the youth. With this in mind, in his later years, Ben-Gurion envisioned a site near Kibbutz Sde-Boqer being developed into a special high-level, pioneering academic institute that would combine Jewish spiritual creativity with science, weaving the Jewish and Western civilizations together at their best ("Yavneh and Oxford together," as he loved to put it).

In 1976, it had been the Minister of Education, Aharon Yadlin, a member of Kibbutz Hatzerim in the Negev, who had zealously pushed for this law. This, of course, was not merely a case of regional lobbying politics. At that time, Yadlin was a prominent Labor Zionist and part of the decisive majority in the Knesset. His life in the Negev and his pursuit of that law were intimately linked with a broad, social-democratic conception of Zionism. Nor should the passage of this law be interpreted in terms of partisan politics, because the whole Zionist gamut backed it.

Crucially, the 1976 Ben-Gurion Law falls right in line with the democratic aspect of Zionism, as expressed in the Israeli Declaration of Independence (May 1948). Nothing is said, though, in the Declaration—the fountainhead of all Israel's Basic Laws and at the core of the Knesset's esprit—about the commitment of the State to pioneering ideals. Thus, the Ben-Gurion Law is, in a way, an extension and completion of the 1948 Declaration, eloquently suggesting that the desert is where ideal or utopian Zionism can be closely realized.

While the ideological message of the Ben-Gurion Law, innovative as it is, is clear enough, it is quite complicated once we consider its scholarly implications; actually it combines two different functions. On the one hand, it is designed to pursue the legacy of David Ben-Gurion, as witnessed in the name of the Institute established at the Midrasha: *ha-Makhon le-Moreshet Ben-Gurion*, namely, Ben-Gurion Heritage Institute. This fundamental Institute is "allowed" to transfer the functions of research and teaching to a University center, named: *ha-Merkaz le-Moreshet Ben-Gurion*, i.e., Ben-Gurion Heritage Center. The disturbing problem that results is that an ideologically commissioned center cannot be part of an academically unbiased university, committed to honest research and the pursuit of truth.

An important step toward solving this conflict took place in June 1982, when an *Amanah* (treaty) between the Institute and the Ben-Gurion University of the Negev (whose main campus is in Beersheba) was signed. Accordingly, a special Center was established at the University for the purpose of teaching and research. Yet, the conflict between 'research' and 'ideology' was not entirely resolved. The Ben-Gurion Heritage Center retained its original name, officially committing its work to ideological purposes.

It is to the credit of Israeli society, its academy and concerned activists in the Negev and the Midrasha Campus in particular, that they kept the cardinal issue of science versus ideology persistently and relentlessly on their agenda. Indeed, this was a genuine challenge for academicians and public figures who cherished Ben-Gurion's democratic-pioneering heritage and also hoped for a worthy scholarly, humanistic endeavor in the Negev.

It took about two decades (after the above-mentioned Treaty was signed in 1982) before this very real conflict could be resolved. During that period, the impact of the University on the Center gradually became decisive and eventually (June 2003) the official name of the Center was changed to: *Makhon Ben-Gurion le-Heker Yisra'el, ha-Tziyonut, ve-Moreshet Ben-Gurion,* that is, the Ben-Gurion

Institute for the Research of Israel, Zionism and the Heritage of Ben-Gurion. Thus the 'heritage' finally has become an object for research, rather than an ideological guideline.

In parallel, the original mother institute, Ben-Gurion Heritage Institute at the Midrasha has gradually channeled its activities to deeper, more sophisticated educational (*hinukh*-bound) goals.[3] This institute now rarely and very selectively serves University students; its general clientele is composed of members of youth movements, elementary and high-school classes, trade-union members and leaders, people from community centers, State and municipal officials, new immigrants, visiting Diaspora youth, social workers, and Israel Defense Force officers. The typical subjects discussed in the Heritage Institute's workshops, symposia and lectures are: the processes and struggles toward the establishment of Israel; the social aspects of the emergence of the State; the historical desire for an enlightened society; the development of the Israel Defense Forces as the people's army; *aliyah* (immigration to Israel) and the ingathering of exiles; Israel and the Diaspora; Israel as a democratic and Jewish state; the position of minorities in Israel; settlement in the Negev; and the question of Israel's frontiers. The Israeli Ministry of Education (not the University!) is financially responsible for this Institute.

Now, back to the University Institute—did the 1982 and 2003 alignments detach this research institute from the initial pioneering-democratic mission as conceived by the framers of the Ben-Gurion Law? In short—no, but this requires elaboration.

First, the director of the University Institute must still be approved by the Board of the original Ben-Gurion Heritage Institute and, traditionally, both these Institutes are still directed by the same person.

However, the deeper positive response to the ideological challenge originating in the desert environment lies not in the formalities, but in the scholars themselves. Are they somehow contributing to the cause of democratic-pioneering Zionism individually? The answer is not simple, since we are discussing an academic institute composed of self-reliant scholars, and the solution lays within the parameters of academic freedom. Actually, over the years, a set of 'rules of the game' has developed that—to my judgment—fully respects academic freedom on the one hand, while expecting a scholarly concern for the Negev and the Ben-Gurion heritage, on the other hand.

The first and basic criterion to test this new reality is the scholars' commitment to live and work in the Negev, preferably at the Midrasha. According to Israel's Basic Laws, an employer cannot force employees to live in a certain locality. Yet there are many subtle and overt ways, such as the personal example set by the Director and his/her associates, to achieve this precondition.

The scholars' residency in the Negev does not mean, of course, just a formal or a passive act, but rather participation in active existence of the Institute, cooperation with the educational institute, and making a positive contribution to Negev development.

The other criterion for pursuing the values associated with the Ben-Gurion Law is the commitment of these scholars to study and teach those topics specified in that Law. A chief responsibility of the Institute's Scientific Council (nominated by the University's Rector) is to thoughtfully and creatively elaborate on these topics and to oversee the scholars' work accordingly.

Again, these two criteria—an active residency in the Negev and the pursuit of legitimate topics—do not impinge on academic freedom; at the same time, though, they do direct the scholars to contribute to the ideals associated with the Ben-Gurion Law.

Now, the core of these topics—as defined in the Knesset's rationale for the Ben-Gurion Law and as reflected in the current (nuanced) name of the B.G.U. Institute—is the renaissance of the Jewish People in the Land of Israel (*'tekumat Yisra'el be-Eretz Yisra'el'*) and of the personality and historic endeavors (*'ishiyuto ve-po'alo'*) of David Ben-Gurion. In order to enable researchers to pursue these themes while living in the Negev, a huge effort was required to build up two basic facilities: a pertinent archives and a topical library.

The Ben-Gurion Archives at the Midrasha is the southern branch of Israel State Archives and is supervised by the State's Chief Archivist. Luckily enough, the Archives has two great advantages thanks to the Negev environment: a potentially large space available to them (an important factor in a tiny country) and the benefit of the dry desert climate (excellent for preserving manuscripts and papers).

In the heart of the Archives are Ben-Gurion's personal papers, diaries, and letters. This collection, important and huge as it is, is not enough to make the Archives generally attractive. Researchers hate, and rightly so, to be limited by the nature of the material at hand to one-dimensional inquiries. Thus, the leaders of the Institute, in true cooperation with the Midrasha archivists, have taken care to meaningfully expand and develop the Archives. Initially, some 750,000 documents had been deposited, but the Archives has grown over five-fold since then. More significant than the mere quantitative aspect is the diversified course of development, that is, the acquisition of collections of personalities and movements that varied from Ben-Gurion's milieu and influence.

The relatively new Archives uses new technologies and is highly computerized and easily accessible to interested scholars. In fact, the Ben-Gurion Archives Online is an enterprise designed to provide digitized documentation; it offers scholars, students, and the general public internet access to the wealth of archival material from a computerized database that uses full/free text and electronic imaging of actual documents. Last, but not least, helpful and mission-sensible archivists gladly serve scholars who are tired of older techniques or have suffered from indifferent archivists elsewhere.

Most of the above description is equally applicable to the Institute's Library at the Midrasha, as well. In the spirit of the Ben-Gurion Law, there are clear foci to this Library's purpose, purchasing policy, and collections: Zionism in general; the Zionist endeavor in Israel in particular; and the thought and historic work of Ben-

Gurion himself. At the same time, the Library flexibly and liberally offers books beyond the strict words of the Ben-Gurion Law. As in the case of the Archives, serious scholars are never satisfied with books confined to one particular historical narrative. The prevalent attitude is that the humanist scholar 'cloistered' in the relatively secluded Midrasha is entitled to access to a rich Library, to enhance his/her productive study and creative conceptualization of all possibilities. Thus the Library is not narrowly confined to Zionism, but significantly encompasses the larger field of Judaism. Similarly, it is not limited to the settlement of Israel, but includes parts of World Jewry. Moreover, it is not confined to David Ben-Gurion, but offers biographies and contributions by a long and colorful range of political leaders and thinkers pertinent to Jewish and non-Jewish national emancipation and state-building.

These two major responsibilities—the development of the pertinent and seminal Archives and Library—describe the unique circumstances surrounding the establishment of this scholarly, humanistic Institute in the desert environment. Furthermore, these goals required a certain collectivist effort; that is, an effort wherein all the scholars are involved, sharing and contributing their input to the general success.

The further scholarly development of this desert-located Institute also required other more academic collective efforts: the establishment of a publishing unit (a part of Ben-Gurion University of the Negev Press); the publication of a refereed yearbook (in Hebrew), *Studies in Zionism, the Yishuv, and the State of Israel,* that regularly hosts nationally acclaimed scholars and of an English periodical, *Israel Studies*, published three times a year by Indiana University Press; a weekly academic seminar with guest lecturers. All these projects are run by Institute fellows, who are also expected to organize frequent national and international conferences.

These shared efforts serve not just for the 'survival' of the desert-residential Institute, but also to dissolve the persistent danger of a 'provincial' kind of survival. Indeed, the Institute persistently reaches out to overcome provincialism, while liberally in line with its genuine, topical Zionist interest.

Characteristically, a Center for the Study of North American Jewry was established by the Institute's fellows. This new Center, affiliated with both the Institute and the B.G.U. Department of Jewish History, is dedicated to the study of those aspects of this Diaspora that are related to Israel or shared by the two largest Jewish communities in the world. The activities of this Center include international conferences, the publication of books and brochures and the enrichment of the Institute's Archives with the acquisition of more pertinent collections.

These and other collective efforts have come to shape the fellows' academic commitments in a unique manner—indeed, creatively responsive to the desert circumstances. In practice, roughly one third of their time is devoted to shared enterprises and responsibilities; another third is allocated to teaching at Ben-Gurion University of the Negev; and the remaining third is free for personal research.

The Ben-Gurion Research Institute is interdisciplinary and its fellows teach one yearly course in the department of their specialization. Another annual course is given in the State of Israel Studies Program (in the Department of Jewish History); since this program was devised by the Institute, naturally the Institute's fellows are responsible for running the Program.

The lecturers and researchers at the Institute hold University positions and are promoted professionally in accordance with B.G.U. standards of productivity and excellence. At the same time, as explained above, the Institute has its unique, partly communal orientation, esprit de corps, as dictated by its functions in the desert reality. Thus, the Institute is both an autonomous body in the Faculty of Humanities and Social Studies and directly under the University Rector's supervision.

In short, it lasted about a quarter of a century (1977-2003) for the scholarly-humanistic, pioneering Zionist vision of the framers of the Ben-Gurion Law to take shape and stabilize. As it often happens in real life and history, the 'right functional balance' has been a result of conflicts, struggles, personal ambitions and confusions.

However, the major conflict (a legitimate conflict in my opinion) was between the academic sphere and the political-ideological milieu. The world of scholarship, embodied by the University, inherently aspired for an open-ended, entirely free humanistic research institute, incidentally located in the desert. Contrary to this, the inner impulse of the Negev visionaries was to develop educational institutes specifically devoted to the advancement of Negev settlement and development, and to immortalize Ben-Gurion's example. Now, mainly due to the democratic-pluralistic quality of the State of Israel, the above polarization never took place. Actually, it could never have occurred. The framers of the Ben-Gurion Law, zealously adhering to pioneering ideals and the name of David Ben-Gurion, did esteem scholarship and respected academic freedom as well. The leading academicians at Ben-Gurion University of the Negev, on their part, also envisioned the University's progress in the context of the Negev's development; they were neither alienated nor merely instrumental regarding the namesake of the University. Thus, there were twenty-five years of continuing non-dogmatic though quite dramatic confrontations by aware and often self-tortured rival-participants. This was, I suggest, a quest of trial and error that took place in the context of a genuinely democratic country, committed to both free scholarly pursuit and national-social vision. I find the 'enlightened end' of that historical conflict an impressive accomplishment by all means (let alone in comparison with the democratically-failed almost all new countries established after World War II).

Therefore, in the end, there were three major winners of that quarter-of-a-century of protracted intellectual evolution. The primary winner is the Negev itself, since now it has two major, seminal institutes – educational and scholarly. The second winner is Science in Israel, as its proponents have effectively guarded the freedom and dignity vital for the pursuit of truth. Finally, and perhaps the greatest winner of all, is the Israeli society, whose solution to the problem brought two types of improvement: a) Israeli democracy has become more decent and refined, and b) Israeli society now embraces an exemplary formula responding to the challenge of the pursuit of humanistic scholarship in a difficult geo-cultural section of the State.

Yet, it would be somewhat misleading to conclude this essay on a simply happy note. It is doubtful if those accomplishments and the achieved 'functional equilibrium' are firm enough—surely they are not self-perpetuating from generation to generation. One may say, perhaps, that this is the fate of all arrangements in a democratic society, true all the more so then in the young 'soft' Israeli democracy. In our case—a humanistic, scholarly endeavor amidst the desert—even the 'conclusive' shape is rather tremulous. While in the first twenty-five years the dangers for a scholarly course were mainly provincialism and built-in ideological bias, the recently increasingly-felt mighty trends of globalization and super-modern technology, often work the other way—to erase the Institute's orientation on the Ben-Gurion Law and to reshape it to be merely 'another department' of the now 'closer' and more potent Ben-Gurion University. Thus, as in the past, so in the present, realistic visions, a tempered maintenance of the legacy, conscientious work and everlasting vigilance—are still crucially needed in order to sustain the project's original national commitments and pioneering qualities.

Notes

1. A few personal lines are a must in an article of this nature. I came with my family to the Midrasha in 1977 and we lived in the Negev until some years after my retirement in 2003. I served jointly as a Research Fellow and as a Lecturer, and later on as a Full Professor, at both the (presently named) Ben-Gurion Institute for the Research of Israel, Zionism and Ben-Gurion Heritage, and at the Department of Jewish History at Ben-Gurion University of the Negev [B.G.U.]. I have happily invested ever since in the academic development of the Research Institute and also have constantly worked to contribute to the educational efforts of the Ben-Gurion Heritage Institute since both their inceptions. As an Emeritus Professor, I now serve on the Scientific Council of the B.G.U. Research Institute and as an advisor to the educational institute at the Midrasha as well as on the Directorship of the Center for the Study of North American Jewry at B.G.U., which I founded in 1990.
2. Saying this does not imply, of course, that Zionism in other sections of Israel has been advanced by a significantly different course. It is the prevalent thesis (beyond memories of numerous past and living eye-witnesses), based on vast first-rate, scholarly work, that the main roads for Zionism's success have been via the processes of immigration, work, economic development, science, settlement, pursuit of an enlightened and effectively mobilizing democracy; and that the military endeavor generally came to defend and buttress the achievements in these and related areas.
3. The Hebrew term *hinukh* may be roughly translated as "education"; interestingly, there is no parallel English term that adequately reflects the full meaning of the modern Israeli Hebrew word *hinukh,* which stands for the instilling of positive (ethical, social and national) values and for the cultivation of a virtuous (an assertive, upright, and socially/communally-responsible) personality.

Archival Sources

[Discussions of the] Law to Immortalize the Name of David Ben-Gurion, First Call, June 9, 1976, Knesset Protocols, vol. 77, Jerusalem 1976, pp. 2962-2975.

David Ben-Gurion Law, 1976, Second and Third Calls, October 25, 1976, Knesset Protocols, vol.78, Jerusalem 1977, pp. 449-452.

David Ben-Gurion Law, 1976, in Israel's Book of Laws, no. 831, Dec.2, 1976, Jerusalem 1977, pp. 10-12.

David Ben-Gurion, A Lecture given at the Cornerstone Laying Ceremony for Sde-Boqer College, Oct.6, 1963 [a summary], Ben-Gurion Archives.

Published Sources

For Published Sources and Reports see Ben-Gurion 1997, Ben-Gurion 1962, Givon 1970, and Kabalo 2005 – in the general References, infra, pp. 189-201.

For Books and Articles see Adar 1998-2006, Armoni-Feiman 1999, Friling 1999, Friling 2001, Gal 1998, Gal 2006, Gorny 2002, Richnond 1998, Sheleg 1998, Shiff 1999, Shilony 1999, and Zerubabel 2004 – in the general References, infra, pp. 189-201.

References

Abu-Lughod, L. *Veiled Sentiments.* Berkeley: University of California Press, 1986.

Abu-Rabia, A. *The Negev Bedouin and Livestock Rearing: Social, Economic, and Political Aspects.* Oxford: Berg, 1994.

Adar, L. "Introduction." *David Ben-Gurion, A Bibliography*, vols. 1, 2, 3 (1998, 2003, 2006), Sde-Boqer Campus, pp. v-vi.

Al-Aref, A. *Tarîx bi'r al-sab' wa qabâ'ilhâ. Silsilat man hum al-badw?* (n.p.), 1934.

Al-Aref, A., with H. W. Tilley *Bedouin Love, Law, and Legend.* New York: AMS, 1944.

Al-Muzaini, H. Q. *Vowel Alternations in a Bedouin Hijazi Arabic Dialect: Abstractness and Stress.* Diss. University of Texas, Austin: Ann Arbor, 1982.

Allen, V. L., and K. E. Scheibe, eds. *The Social Context of Conduct: Psychological Writings of Theodore Sarbin.* New York: Praeger, 1982.

Amar, Y. *Desert Poetry.* (Photos by A. Bar Lev.) Be'er Sheva: Who and Whose, no date.

Ariel, Z., M. Blich, and N. Persky. "The Conquest of the Desert." In *Mikra'ot Yisrael Textbook for the Fourth Grade,* edited by Z. Ariel, M. Blich, and N. Persky. Jerusalem: Masada, 1958 [Hebrew].

Armoni-Faiman, O. "Making the Desert Eden." *`Al ha-Rosh*, no. 2 (January 1999): 9-10.

Audo, T. *Dictionnaire de la Langue Chaldéenne.* Mosul: Glane (Holland), (1897) 1985.

Badawi, El-S, and M. Hinds. *A Dictionary of Egyptian Arabic.* Arabic–English. Beirut: Librairie du Liban, 1986.

Bailey, C. "Bedouin Place-names in Sinai." *Palestine Exploration Quarterly* 116, no. 1/2 (1984): 42–57.

———. *Bedouin Poetry from Sinai and the Negev*. Oxford: Clarendon Press, 1990.

Bailey, C., and A. Danin. "Bedouin Plant Utilization in Sinai and the Negev." *Economic Botany* 35, no. 2 (1981):145–62.

Baines, J. "Color Terminology and Color Classification: Egyptian Color Terminology and Polychromy." *American Anthropology* 87 (1985): 282–97.

Bargal, Y. *Moledet and Geography in Hundred Years of Zionist Education.* Tel Aviv: Am Oved, 1993 [Hebrew].

Bar Lev, A. *Desert Illusions.* Tel Aviv, Israel: Aloha Communicarow, C. 1998.

Barthélemy, A. *Dictionnaire arabe-français (dialectes de Syrie, Alep, Damas, Liban, Jerusalem).* Paris: Paul Geuthner, 1935-54.

Bartsch, U., and B. Mueler. *Fossil Fuels in a Changing Climate. Impacts of the Kyoto Protocol and Developing Country Participation.* Oxford: Oxford University Press, 2000.

Bar-Yosef, O., and A. Khazanov, eds. *Pastoralism in the Levant: Archaeological Materials in Anthropological Perspectives.* Madison Wisconsin: Prehistory Press, 1992.

Bar-Zvi, S., A. Abu-Rabia, and G. M. Kressel. *The Charm of Graves; Mourning Rituals and Tomb Worshipping Among the Negev Bedouin.* Tel Aviv: Ministry of Defense, 1998.

Bauer, L. *Deutsch-arabisches Wörterbuch der Umgangssprache in Palästina und im Libanon,* 2. Auflage. Wiesbaden: Otto Harrassowitz, 1957.

Behnstedt, P. "Iz-zarga." *Zeitschrift für Arabische Linguistik* 7 (1982): 74–75.

Behnstedt, P., and M. Woidich. *Die ägyptisch-arabischen Dialekte,* Band 2: Dialektatlas von Ä. Wiesbaden: Dr. Ludwig Reichert, 1985.

———. *Die ägyptisch-arabischen Dialekte,* vols 3 and 4. Glossar: Arabisch-Deutsch. Wiesbaden: Dr. Ludwig Reichert. 1994.

———. *Die agyptisch-arabischen Dialekte,* Band 5: Glossar Deutsch-Arabisch. Wiesbaden: Dr. Ludwig Reichert, 1999.

Beilinson, M. "The Rebels Against Reality" published in *Davar* in 1929, reprinted as pp. 71-73 in M. Naor (ed.), *The Second Aliya, 1903-1914.* Jerusalem: Yad Yitzhak Ben-Zvi, 1984 [Hebrew].

Ben-Ari, E., and Y. Bilu, eds. *Grasping Land.* New York: State University of New York Press, 1997.

Benayahu, R., and M. Benayahu. *We Perform: Plays for Children and Youth.* Tel Aviv: Niv, 1955 [Hebrew].

Ben-Gurion, D. "The Conquest of the Land," reprinted in pp. 6-7 JNF: *The Conquest of the Mountain,* Jerusalem: Jewish National Fund, 1955a.

———. "A National Youth Educational Center will be Established in Sde-Boqer." *Davar,* 18.10.1962: 1-2.

———. *Like Stars and Dust: Essays from Israel's Government Year Book,* Sde-Boqer Campus 1997; translated from the Hebrew [all 10 essays, 1951-1962, wholly or partly discuss the Negev].

———. "Southwards" [1956], reprinted in English translation pp. 174-187 in *Like Stars and Dust: Essays from Israel's Government Book.* Sde Boker: The Ben-Gurion Research Center, Ben-Gurion University, 1997.

Benvenisti, D. *Teaching about the Conquest of the Mountain.* Jerusalem: Jewish National Fund, 1959 [Hebrew].

Berlin, B., and P. Kay. *Basic Color Terms: Their Universality and Evolution.* Berkeley: University of California Press, 1969.

Berlovitz, Y., ed. *Wandering in the Land: Travels by Members of the First Aliyah.* Tel Aviv: Defense Ministry, 1992 [Hebrew].

———. ed. *Inventing a Land, Inventing a People.* Tel Aviv: Hakibbutz Hameuchad, 1996 [Hebrew].

Betser, Y. "The Shack in the Transjordan." Pp.128-131-in *The Guard Anthology.* Tel Aviv: Labor Archives, 1937 [Hebrew].

Betteridge, H. T. *Cassell's German Dictionary, German-English, English-German.* London: Macmillian Publishing Co., 1978.

Beyer, K. *Die aramäischen Texte vom Toten Meer.* Göttingen: Vandenhoeck/Ruprecht, 1984.

Biasio, E. *Beduinen im Negev.* Zürich: Neue Zürcher Zeitung, 1998.

Blanc, H. *Communal Dialects in Baghdad.* Cambridge, Mass.: Harvard University Press, 1964.

———. *The Arabic Dialect of the Negev Bedouins.* Jerusalem: *Proceedings of the Israel Academy of Sciences and Humanities*, vol. IV, no 7, 1970.

Borg, A. "Some Maltese Toponyms in Historical and Comparative Perspective." Pp. 62-85 in *Studia Linguistica et Orientalia Memoriae Haim Blanc Dedicata*, edited by A. Borg, P. Wexler, and S. Somekh. Wiesbaden: O. Harrasowitz, 1989.

———. ed. *The language of Color in the Mediterranean: An Anthology of Linguistic and Ethnographic Aspects of Color Terms.* Stockholm: Almqvist & Wiksell International, 1999.

———. *Towards an Ethnography of Color Among the Negev Bedouin* (in press).

———. "Towards a History and Typology of Color Categorization in Colloquial Arabic." In *Anthropology of Color: Interdisciplinary Multilevel Modeling*, edited by R. E. MacLaury, V. Galina, V. Paramei, and D. Dedrick. Amsterdam/Philadelphia: John Benjamins (in press).

Boris, G. *Lexique du Parler Arabe des Marazig.* Paris: Imprimerie, Nationale: Klincksuek, 1958.

Brissett, D., and C. E. Edgley, eds. *Life as theater: A Dramaturgical Sourcebook.* 2nd ed. New York, NY: Aldine de Gruyter, 1990.

Burckhardt, J. L. *Die Kultur der Renaissance in Italien (The Culture of the Renaissance in Italy).* Berlin: Th. Knar, Vol. II, 1928.

———. *Travels in Araba, Comprehending an Account of those Territories in the Hedjaz which the Mohammedans Regard as Sacred.* London: Frankcass, (1829) 1968.

Burke, K. "Dramatism." Pp. 445-52 in *International Encyclopedia of the Social Sciences.* Vol. 7, edited by D. L. Sills. New York: Macmillan & Free Press, 1968.

Casson, R. W. "Color Shift: Evolution of English Color Terms from Brightness to Hue." Pp. 224-39 in *Color Categories in Thought and Language*, edited by C. L. Hardin and L. Maffi. Cambridge: Cambridge University Press, 1997.

Chen, Y. S., P. C. Sheen, E. R. Chen, Y. K. Liu, T. N. Wu, and C. Y. Yang. "Effects of Asian Dust Storm Events on Daily Mortality in Taipei, Taiwan." *Environmental Research* 95, no. 2 (2004): 151-155.

Chen, Z. The song "Watch, Look, and See" [Shuru, Habitu U-re'u], reprinted in T. Elyagon and R. Pesahzon, eds., *A Thousand Songs: The Israeli Sing-Along.* Tel Aviv: Kinneret, 1983.

Conklin, H. C. "Hanunóo Color Categories." *Southwestern Journal of Anthropology* 11 (1955): 339-44.

Dalman, G. *Arbeit und Sitte in Palästina*, Band VI. Hildesheim: G. Olms, (1939) 1987.

Dayan, S., "Here We'll Settle," Pp. 161-163 in *Mikra'ot Yisrael Textbook for the fourth Grade*, edited by Z. Ariel, M. Blich, and N. Persky. Jerusalem: Masada, 1958 [Hebrew].

De Haas, W. P. *The Spectrum of Moisture in Arabic.* 'S-Gravenhage: H. H. L. Smits, 1954.

Demsky, A. "'Dark Wine' from Judah." *Israel Exploration Journal* 22 (1972): 233–234.

Donald, M. *Origins of the Modern Mind: Three Stages in the Evolution of Culture and Cognition.* Cambridge, Mass.: Harvard University Press, 1991.

Drouin, J. "Occurrences Colorées: 'Noir' et 'Blanc' dans la Poésie Touarègue." *Littérature Orale Arabo-Berbère* 19–20 (1989): 1–27.

Dubnov, J., M. Barchana, S. Rishpon, A. Leventhal, I. Segal, R. Carel, and B. A. Portnov. "Estimating the Effect of Air Pollution from a Coal-fired Power Station on the Development of Children's Pulmonary function." *Environmental Research* 103, no. 1 (2007): 87-98.

Ducatez, G., and J. Ducatez. "Formation des Dénominations de Couleur et de Luminosité en Arabe Classique et Pre-classique: Essai de Périodisation selon une Approche Linguistique et Anthropologique." *Peuples Méditerranéens* 10 (1980): 139–172.

Duquesne, T. *Black and Gold God.* London: Darengo Publications, (1912) 1996.

Durkheim, E. *Elementary Forms of Religious Life,* trans. by Karen E. Fields. New York: Free Press, (1912)1995.

Eliad, M. *Myth and Reality.* New York: Harper Torchbooks, 1963.

Eph'al, I. *The Ancient Arabs: Nomads on the Borders of the Fertile Crescent 9th-5th Centuries B.C.* Jerusalem: The Magness Press, 1982.

Evans-Pritchard, E. E. "Topographical Terms in Common Use among the Bedouin of Cyrenaica." *Journal of the Royal Anthropological Institute* 76 (1946): 177–188.

Evenari, M. *Ökologisch-landwirtschaftliche Forschungen im Negev. Analyse eines Wüsten-Ökosystems.* Darmstadt, 1982.

———. *Und die Wüste trage Frucht.* Gerlingen: Bleicher Verlag, 1987.

Ever-Hadani, A. *An Enterprise in the Desert* [Hamifal Ba-arava]. Tel Aviv: Mitzpe, 1931 [Hebrew].

Eytan, B. "A Flourishing Oasis in the Heart of the Arava (Be'er Orah)," Pp. 185-187 in *Mikra'ot Yisrael Textbook for the fourth Grade*, edited by Z. Ariel, M. Blich, and N. Persky. Jerusalem: Masada, 1958 [Hebrew].

Fischer, W. *Farb- und Formbezeichnungen in der Sprache der altarabischen Dichtung.* Wiesbaden: Otto Harrassowitz, 1965.

Flannery, T. *The Weather Makers: The History and Future of Climate Change.* London: Allen Lane – Penguin Books, 2005.

Frazer, J. *The Golden Bough.* London: Macmillan, 1890.

Friedlaender, L. *Darstellungen aus der Sittengeschichte Roms in der Zeit von Augustus bis zu Ausgang der Antonine (History of Roman Life and Customs)*, Vol. IV, Aalen:1979 (reprinted in 1922 by Scientia Verlag), p.142 ff. Leipzig: S. Hirzel, 1910.

Friling, T. "Computerizing Ben-Gurion Archives." *`Al ha-Rosh*, no.2 (January 1999): 17-19.

———. "The Negev Motif." *`Al ha-Rosh*, no. 4 (November 2000): 28.

Fück, J. "Arabiyya." *Recherches sur l'histoire de la langue et du style arabe*, trad. par Claude Denizeau. Paris: Marcel Didier, 1955.

Gabrieli, N. *Knowledge of the Land: Textbook.* Tel Aviv: Omanut, 1934 [Hebrew].

Gabrieli, N., and B. Avivi. "Pangs of Conquest." Pp. 220-243 in *My New Textbook for the Fifth Grade.* Tel Aviv: Yavneh, 1950 [Hebrew].

Gal, A. *David Ben-Gurion and the American Alignment for a Jewish State*, Bloomington and Jerusalem: Indiana University Press and the Magnes Press, The Hebrew University, 1991

———. "Inherent Problems in the Research-work in the Ben-Gurion Heritage Center," *`Al ha-Rosh*, no.1 (July 1998):12.

———. "Israel Today: Nationalism and Ethnosymbolism. Pp. 221-230 in *Nationalism and Ethnosymbolism: History, Culture and Ethnicity in the Formation of Nations.* edited by A. Leoussi and S. Grosby. Edinburgh: Edinburgh University Press, 2006.

Gerlber, Y. "The Status of Zionist and Israeli History in Israeli Universities." Pp. 141-141 in *Israeli Historical Revisionism From Left to Right*, edited by A. Shapira and D. J. Penslar. London: Frank Cass, 2003.

Giannini, A., R. Saravanan, and P. Chang. "Oceanic Forcing of Sahel Rainfall on Interannual to Interdecadal Timescales." *Science* 302 (2003): 1027-1030

Givon, S. "Students Ask, Ben-Gurion Answers." *Maariv*, 21.10.1970: 1-2.

Goffman, E. *The Presentation of Self in Everyday Life.* Garden City, NY: Doubleday, 1959.

Goldstein, Y. *The Shepherd Association: The Idea of 'Conquering' Cattle Raising in the Second Aliyah and Its Realization*, 1907-1917. Tel Aviv: Defense Ministry, 1993 [Hebrew].

Gorny, Y. "On the Center…the Negev, the State of Israel and Ben-Gurion." *`Al ha-Rosh*, no. 5 (May 2002): 6-8.

Gradus, Y., ed. *Desert Development: Man and Technology in Sparselands.* Dordrecht: D. Reidel Publishing Company, 1985.

Hacohen, D. *The Grain and the Millstone: The Settlement of Immigrants in the Negev in the First Decade of the State.* Tel Aviv: Am Oved, 1998 [Hebrew].

Hardin, C. L., and L. Maffi, eds. *Color Categories in Thought and Language.* Cambridge: Cambridge University Press, 1997.

Hare, A. P. *Social Interaction as Drama: Applications from Conflict Resolution.* Beverly Hills, CA: Sage Publications, 1985.

———. "Dramaturgical Analysis: Sociological." Pp. 3834-3836 in *International Encyclopedia of the Social and Behavioral Sciences.* Amsterdam: Elsevier Sciences Ltd, 2001.

Hare, A. P., and H. H. Blumberg. *Dramaturgical Analysis of Social Interaction.* New York, NY: Praeger, 1988.

Hare, A. P., P. Golan, and Y. Osher, eds. *The Stage is Our World: An English-speaking Amateur Musical Theater Group in Israel.* Acco, Israel: Biblio Books Israel, 2006.

Hare, A. P., and G. M. Kressel. *Israel as Center Stage: A Setting for Social and Religious Enactments.* Westport, Conn.: Bergin & Garvey, 2001.

Hartmann, M. *Lieder der libyschen Wüste.* Leipzig: F. A. Brockhaus, 1899.

Hazan, B. *Man Subdues the Desert* [Adam Madbir et Hashemama]. Tel Aviv: Sifriyat Poalim, 1953 [Hebrew]; a section reprinted in *The Negev: A Reader,* 248. Novel reprinted: Tel Aviv: Hakibbutz Hameuchad, 1977.

Heider, E. R. "Probabilities, Sampling and Ethnographic Method: the Case of the Dani Colour Names." *Man* 7, no. 3 (1972): 448–66.

Hertz, R. *Death and the Right Hand.* Glencoe, IL. Free Press, (1909) 1960.

Hess, J. J. "Die Farbenbezeichnungen bei innerarabischen Beduinenstämmen." *Der Islam* 10 (1920): 74–86.

Hillel, D. I. *Negev, Land, Water, and Life in a Desert Environment.* New York: Praeger, 1982.

Highwater, J. *The Primal Mind: Vision and Reality in Indian America.* New York: Harper and Row, 1981.

Hobbs, J. J. *Bedouin Life in the Egyptian Wilderness.* Austin: University of Texas Press, 1989.

Ibn Khaldun, 'Abd al-Rahman Ibn Muhammad. *The Muqaddimah, An Introduction to History.* Translated by F. Rosenthal. Princeton, N. J., 1967.

INFO. *Population Reports.* Information & Knowledge for Optimal Health (INFO) Project. Baltimore: Johns Hopkins Bloomberg School of Public Health & USAID, 2006. http://www.infoforhealth.org/pr

Ingham, B. "Camel Terminology among the Âl Murrah Bedouins." *Zeitschrift für arabische Linguistik* 22 (1990): 67–78.

Israel, Y., and D. Nahleili. "Sride Henionium u-Mivnei Pulhan Bedarkhei Ha-Midbar." Pp. 145-154 in S. Ahituv *Megarim Be-Archaeologia Shel Navadim Ba-Negev u-Sinai.* Be'er Sheva, Israel: Ben-Gurion University, 1998.

Issar, A. *Water Shall Flow from this Rock: Hydrogeology and Climate in the Lands of the Bible.* Berlin: Springer, c. 1990.

———. *From Primeval Chaos to Infinite Intelligence: On Information as a Dimension and on Entropy as a Field of Force.* Aldershot, UK: Avebury, C. 1995.

Jacobson, A. "Symbolisme des Couleurs et Ordre Social." Pp. 525-51 in *Voir et Nommer les Couleurs*, edited by S. Tornay. Nanterre: Laboratoire d'ethnologie et de sociologie comparative. Paris: Universite de Paris X, 1978.

Jarvis, C. S. *Desert and Delta*. London: John Murray, 1938.

———. *Three Deserts*. London: John Murray, (1936) 1951.

Jaussen, P. A. *Coutumes des Arabes au Pays de Moab*. Paris: Adrien Maisonneuve, (1908) 1948.

JNF. *The Conquest of the Desert: An International Exhibition*. Jerusalem: Jewish National Fund [English Section], 1953.

———. *The Conquest of the Mountain*. Jerusalem: Jewish National Fund, 1955a [Hebrew].

———. *The Negev: A Reader*. Jerusalem: The Jewish National Fund, 1955b.

Justice, D. *The Semantics of Form in Arabic in the Mirror of European Languages*. Amsterdam: John Benjamins, 1987.

Kabalo, P., ed. *Ben-Gurion Institutes in Sde-Boqer. Reports*, nos. 1 & 2 (May 2005, October 2006).

Kark, R. *Pioneering Jewish Settlement in the Negev, 1880-1948*. [1974] reprinted Jerusalem: Ariel, 2002 [Hebrew];

Katz, J. J. "Analyticity and Contradiction in Natural Language." In *The Structure of Language: Readings in the Philosophy of Language*, edited by J. A. Fodor and J. J. Katz. Englewood Cliffs, N. J.: Prentice-Hall, 1964.

Kay, P., B. Berlin, L. Maffi, and W. Merrifield. "Color Naming Across Languages." Pp. 21-58 in *Color Categories in Thought and Language*, edited by C. L. Hardin and L. Maffi. Cambridge: Cambridge University Press, 1997.

Klincksieck, P., and Th. Valette. *Code des Couleurs à l'usage des Naturalistes, Commerçants et Iindustriels*. Paris, 1908.

Kodesh, S. *The Founders' Legend: The War against the Desert*. Jerusalem: The Jewish National Fund, 1972 [Hebrew].

Kristol, A. M. "Color Systems in Southern Italy: A Case of Regression." *Language* 56, no.1 (1980): 137–45.

Krivine, J. *Lives in the Desert*. Ben-Gurion University of the Negev, Sede Boker Campus: The Jacob Blaustein Institute for Desert Research, 1991.

Krutch, J. W. *The Voice of the Desert: A Naturalist's Interpretation*. New York: William Sloane Associates, 1954.

Kurpershoek, P. M. *Oral Poetry from Central Arabia*, Vol. 1. Leiden: Brill, 1994.

Lakoff, R. T. *Language and Woman's Place*. New York: Harper & Row, 1975.

Lamdan,Y. Masada. Tel Aviv: Hedim, reprint: Tel Aviv: Dvir, 56-58. English translation by L. I. Yudkin, (1971) in *Isaac Lamdan: A Study in Twentieth-Century Hebrew Poetry*. Ithaca: Cornell University Press, 1972.

Landsberger, B. "Über Farben im Sumerisch-Akkadischen." *Journal of Cuneiform Studies* 21 (Special volume honoring Prof. Albrecht Goetze), (1967): 130–73.

Lane, E. W. *An Arabic-English Lexicon*. London: Williams & Norgate, 1863-93.

Lawrence, T. E. *Seven Pillars of Wisdom: A Triumph*. Harmondsworth, Midd.: Penguin Books, (1926) 1935.

———. *Revolt in the Desert*. London: J. Cape, 1927.

Levi, S. *The Bedouin in the Sinai Desert: Patterns of Desert Society*. Tel Aviv: Schocken, 1987.

Liddell, H. G., and R. Scott. *A Greek-English Lexicon*. Oxford: Clarendon Press, 1996.

Loubignac, V. *Textes arabes des Zaer*. (Transcription, traduction, notes et lexique). Paris: Librairie Orientaliste et Américaine, 1952.

Lucy, J. A. "The Linguistics of 'Color'." Pp. 321-46 in *Color Categories in Thought and Language*, edited by C. L. Hardin and L. Maffi. Cambridge: Cambridge University Press, 1997.

Lucy, J. A., and R. A. Shweder. "Whorf and his Critics: Linguistic and Nonlinguistic Influences on Color Memory." Pp. 133-63 in *Language, Culture, and Cognition: Anthropological Perspectives*, edited by R. W. Casson. New York: Macmillan, 1981.

Lyons, J. *Introduction to Theoretical Linguistics*. London, New York: Cambridge University Press, 1968.

———. *Semantics*, 2 vols. Cambridge: Cambridge University Press, 1977.

Maas, L. H. "Colours as Place-name Elements, with Special Reference to Instances of Analogy." Pages 134-40 in *Proceedings of the XVIIth International Congress of Onomastic Sciences*, edited by E. M. Nãrhi. Helsinki 13-18, vol. 2, 1990a.

———. "De Toponymische Elementen Zwart, wit en Grijs." *Naamkunde*, 22ste Jaargang, Afl. 1–4, (1990b): 5–86.

MacLaury, R. E. "From Brightness to Hue." *Current Anthropology* 33, (1992): 137–86.

———. "Basic Color Terms: Twenty-five Years After." Pp. 1-37 in *Language and Color in the Mediterranean*, edited by A. Borg. Stockholm: Almqvist & Wiksell International, 1999.

Magnus, H. *Untersuchungen über den Farbensinn der Naturvölker*. Jena. 1880.

Manna, J. E. *Vocabulaire Chaldéen-arabe*, 2nd ed. Beirut: Babel Center Publications, (1900) 1975.

Marçais, W. "Le Dialecte Arabe des Ulâd Brâhîm de Saïda (département d'Oran)." In *Memoires de la Société Linguistique* (1906-08) XIV:97-164; 416-472; 481-500; and XV (1908-09):40–72; 104–129. Paris.

———. *Textes arabes de Tanger*. Paris: Imprimerie nationale, 1911.

———. "Nouvelles observations sur l'euphémisme dans les parlers arabes maghrébins." *Mélanges Isidore Lévy*. Bruxelles: Ed. de l'Institut, (1955): 331–91.

Marks, A. E., ed., *Prehistory and Paleoenvironment in the Central Negev, Israel*. 2 vols., Dallas: Southern Methodist University, 1976, 1977.

Meir, I. "Apology for Architecture, or: The Planner's craft." *A Voice in the Desert: Bulletin of the Blaustein Institutes For Desert research*, (October 2005): 6-7.

———. "Deserts: Ultimate dumps or last frontiers?" Pp. V. 3908-3912 in *Indoor Air 2005*, edited by Xudong Yang, Bin Zhao, and Rongyi Zhao. Beijing: Proc. 10th Int. Conf. on Indoor Air Quality & Climate, 2005.

Meirovitch, M. "The First Seeds." Pp. 115-117 in N. Gavrieli and B. Avivi (eds.) *Textbook for the Child for the Fourth Grade*. Tel Aviv: Yavneh, 1957 [Hebrew].

Meiri, D. *Dalia Meiri: Self–Surroundings*. Haifa: Ran Offset, 1998.

Mohar, Y. "The Sprinkler Hora." P. 110 in T. Elyagon and R. Pesahzon (eds.), *A Thousand Songs: The Israeli Sing-Along*. Tel Aviv: Kinneret, 1983, II [Hebrew].

Monteil, V. "Essai sur le chameau au Sahara occidental." *Études Mauritaniennes. Saint-Louis-du-Sénégal*, 1952.

———. *L'Arabe Moderne*. Paris: C. Klincksieck, 1960.

Morabia, A. Lawn. *Encyclopedia of Islam*, (1986): 698–707.

Morris, Y. *Masters of the Desert: 6000 Years in the Negev*. (Introduction by David Ben-Gurion). New York: G. P. Putnam's & Sons, 1961.

Mountfort, G. *Portrait of a Desert: The Story of an Expedition to Jordon*. London: Collins, 1965.

Munsell Soil Color Charts. Evanston, Ill.: Soiltest Inc (no date).

Musil, A. *The Manners and Customs of the Rwala Bedouin*. New York: American Geographical Society. Oriental Explorations and Studies, 1928.

Naor, M., ed. *The Settlement of the Negev, 1900-1960*. Jerusalem: Yad Yitzhak Ben-Zvi, 1985 [Hebrew].

Negev, A. *Nabatean Archaeology Today*. New York: New York University Press, 1986.

Nevo, Y. D. *Pagans and Herders: A Re-Examination of the Negev Runoff Cultivation Systems in the Byzantine and Early Arab Periods*. Jerusalem: Achva Press, 1991.

Nevo, Y. D., and J. Koren. *Crossroads to Islam*. New York: Prometheus Books, 2003.

Nishri, Y. "The Conquerors of the Desert: On Two Attempts to Make the Arava Bloom in the 1950s." Pp. 194-201 in M. Naor, ed. *The Settlement of the Negev 1900-1960*, Jerusalem: Yad Yitzak Ben-Zvi, 1985 [Hebrew].

Noll, C. "Beyond the Catastrophe." *Mut, Forum für Kultur, Politik und Geschichte*, Asendorf, Heft 461 (Januar 2006): 74-87.

Ofek, U. "A Small Village in the Mountains," Pp. 11-12 in *A Voice from the Mountains*, edited by Y. Tehar-Lev. Jerusalem: Sifriyat Adama, 1959 [Hebrew].

Orion, E. *Sculptures: 1962-1979*. Tel Aviv: Mabat. 1987.

———. *Sculpturing: A Bundle of Processes*. Tel Aviv: Modan, 1995 [Hebrew].

Orren, E. "The Security-Settlement Assault, 1936-1939." Pp. 13-34 in M. Naor (ed.), *The Days of the Wall and the Stockade*, 1936-39. Jerusalem: Yad Yitzhak Ben-Zvi, 1987 [Hebrew].

Palva, H. *Studies in the Arabic Dialect of the Semi-nomadic l-Ajârma Tribe (Al-Balqa District, Jordan)*. Göteborg: Acta Universitatis Gothoburgensis, 1976.

Parkin, D., ed. *The Anthropology of Evil*. Oxford: Basil Blackwell, 1985.

Patrich, J. *The Formation of Nabatean Art: Prohibition of a Graven Image Among the Nabateans*. Jerusalem: Magness Press, 2002.

Piamenta, M. *Dictionary of Post-Classical Yemeni Arabic*, vol. I. Leiden: Brill, 1990.
Powels, S. "The Historical and Cultural Background of Two Non-basic Terms for 'Blue' in the Arabic Dialect of the Negev Bedouin. Pp. 1-37 in *The Language of Color in the Mediterranean*, edited by A. Borg. Stockholm: Almqvist & Wiksell International, 1999.
Prasse, K-G. "Berber Color Terms." Pp. 167-174 in *The Language of Color in the Mediterranean*, edited by A. Borg. Stockholm: Almqvist & Wiksell International, 1999.
Reichmuth, S. "Die Farbbezeichnungen in Sudanesisch-arabischen Dialekten. *Zeitschrift für Arabische Linguistik*, Heft 6, (1981): 57–66.
Reifenberg, A. *The Struggle of the Desert and the Cultivated Land. 1950 [Hebrew].*
RHD. *Random House Dictionary of the English Language*. New York: Gramercy, 1976.
Richmond, A. "On Pioneering and the Development of the Negev." *`Al ha-Rosh*, no.1 (July 1998): 4-6.
Rieber, G. "Engel in der Wuste: Ein Besuch bei der Malerin Binah Kahana." *Mut: Forum fur Kultur Politik und Geschichte* 447 (2004): 78-87.
Ringel, H. *Die Frauennamen in der Arabisch-islamischen Liebesdichtung*. Leipzig: G. Kreysing, 1938.
Rivers, W. H. R. "The Colour Vision of the Natives of Upper Egypt." *Journal of the Anthropological Institute of Great Britain and Ireland* 31, no. (July-December 1901): 229–247.
Roaf, S., D. Crichton, and F. Nicol. *Adapting Buildings and Cities for Climate Change. A 21st Century Survival Guide*. Amsterdam: The Architectural Press, 2004.
Robertson-Smith, W. *The Religion of the Semites: The Fundamental Institutions*. New York: Schocken, 1972 [1889].
Rotbard, S. *White City, Black City*. Tel-Aviv: Babel, 2005.
Roth, A. "Introduction à l'étude des systèmes de désignation de la couleur dans les parlers Arabes du Maghreb." *Littérature Orale Arabo-berbère* 16–17, (1986): 21–65.
Salingaros, N. A., with C. Alexander, B. Hanson, M. Mehaffy, and T. M. Mikiten. *Anti-Architecture and Deconstruction*. Solingen: Umbau-Verlag, 2004.
Sauerhaft, B., P. R. Berliner, and T. L. Thurow. "The Fuelwood Crisis in Arid Zones: Runoff Agriculture for Renewable Energy Production." Pp. 351-363 in *The Arid Frontier: Interactive Management of Environment and Development*, edited by H. J. Bruins and H. Lithwick. The Netherlands: Kluwer Academic Publishers, 1998.
Schär, C., P. L. Vidale, D. Luethi, C. Frei, C. Häberli, M. A. Liniger, and C. Appenzeller. "The Role of Increasing Temperature Variability in European Summer Heatwaves." *Nature* 427 (2004): 332-336.
Scharf-Kluger, R. *The Archetypal Significance of Gilgamesh, A Modern Ancient Hero*. Einsiedeln (Switzerland): Daimon, 1991.
Schmiele, W., ed. *Poesie der Welt*. Frankfurt/M., Berlin, Wein: Verlag Berlin, 1985.

Sened, Y., and A. Sened. *Earth Without Shadow*. Jerusalem: Ariel, 1951; reprinted: Tel Aviv: Hakibbutz Hameuchad, 1977 [Hebrew].

Shafir, G. *Land, Labor and Origins of the Israeli Palestinian Conflict, 1882-1914*. Berkeley: University of California Press, 1996 (updated version).

Sharet, M. Introduction "Milhemet ha-yeshimon veha-midbar" in JNF *The Conquest of the Desert: An International Exhibition*. Jerusalem, Jewish National Fund, 1953 [Hebrew].

Sheleg,Y. *Desert Wind: the Story of Yehoshu`a Cohen*, Tel Aviv: Ministry of Defense, 1998.

Shiff, O. "Zionism, Judaism, and the Israeli Society." *`Al ha-Rosh* , no. 2 (January 1999): 33-34.

Shilony, Z. "The Academician Social Commitment." *`Al ha-Rosh*, no. 2 (January 1999): 29-30.

Shinar, P. "Quelques Observations sur le Rôle de la Couleur Bleue dans le Maghreb Traditionnel." Pp. 1-37 in *The Language of Color in the Mediterranean*, edited by A. Borg. Stockholm: Almqvist & Wiksell International, 1999.

Shlonsky, A. "We All," reprinted in *Mikra'ot Yisrael Textbook for the fourth Grade*, edited by Z. Ariel, M. Blich, and N. Persky. Jerusalem: Masada, 1958 [Hebrew].

———. "Against the Desert," in *Collected Poems*, I. Tel Aviv: Sifriyat Poalim, 1965 [Hebrew].

Shohat, E. *Israeli Cinema: East/West and the Politics of Representation*. Austin: University of Texas Press, 1989.

Smith, K. R. "The Global Burden of Disease from Unhealthy Buildings: Preliminary Results from Comparative Risk Assessment." Pp.118-126 in *Proc. HB2003. NUS: Int. Conf.*, Singapore, 2003.

Smolly, E. *The Frontiermen [Anshei Bereshit]*, Shtibl 1933; reprinted Tel Aviv: Am Oved, 1973. English translation by Murray Roston *Frontiersmen of Israel*. Tel Aviv: Masada, 1964.

Solayman, 'A., and H. Charles. *Le parler arabe de la voile et la vie maritime sur la côte Syro-libanaise*. Beyrouth, 1972.

Sonnen, P. J. *Die Beduinen am See Genesareth*. Cologne: Palaestinahefte des Deutschen Vereins vom Heiligen Lande, Heft 43–45: J. P. Bachem, 1952.

Sowayan, S. A. *Nabati Poetry: The Oral Poetry of Arabia*. Berkeley: University of California Press, 1985.

Steward, J. H. "The Concept and Method of Cultural Ecology." In *Evolution and Ecology: Essays in Social Transformation*, edited by J. H. Steward and R. F. Murphy. Urbana: University of Illinois, 1968.

Stewart, D. J. "Color Terms in Egyptian Arabic." Pp. 105-120 in *The Language of Color in the Mediterranean*, edited by A. Borg. Stockholm: Almqvist & Wiksell International, 1999.

Stewart, F. H. *Bedouin Boundaries in Central Sinai and the Southern Negev*. Wiesbaden: Otto Harrassowitz, 1986.

———. *Texts in Sinai Bedouin Law*, Part 2. Wiesbaden: Otto Harrassowitz, 1988.
———. *Texts in Sinai Bedouin Law*, Part 1. Wiesbaden: Otto Harrassowitz, 1990.
———. *Honor*. Chicago: The University of Chicago Press, 1994.
Stowasser, K., and M. Ani. *A Dictionary of Syrian Arabic*. Washington D.C.: Georgetown University Press, 1964.
Tartakover, D. "The Soldier Model in the Visual Communication, 1917-1950." *Studio* 27 (1991): 8-11 [Hebrew].
Tehar-Lev, Y., ed. *A Voice from the Mountains*. Jerusalem: Sifriyat Adama, 1959 [Hebrew].
Tehar-Lev, Y., and M. Naor. *Shiru, Habitu U-re'u: The Stories Behind the Songs*. Tel Aviv: Ministry of Defense, 1992 [Hebrew].
Thass-Thienemann, T. *Symbolic Behavior*. New York: Washington Square Press, 1968.
Tornay, S., ed. *Voir et Nommer les Couleurs*. Nanterre: Laboratoire d'ethnologie et de sociologie comparative, Université de Paris X. Paris, 1978.
Tryester, H. "'The Land of Promise': A Case Study in Zionist Film Propaganda." *Historical Journal of Film, Radio and Television*, 15, no. 2 (1935): 187-217.
Turner, V. W. *The Ritual Process: Structure and Anti-Structure*. Chicago, IL; Aldine, 1969.
———. *Dramas, Fields, and Metaphors: Symbolic Action in Human Society*. Ithaca, NY: Cornell University Press, 1974.
———. *Revelation and Divination in Ndembu Ritual*. Ithaca, NY: Cornell University Press, 1975.
———. *Process, Performance and Pilgrimage: A Study in Comparative Symbology*. New Delhi: Concept, 1979.
———. "Color Classification in Ndembu Ritual. A Problem in Primitive Classification." Pp. 47-84 in *The Social Anthropology of Complex Societies* (A.S.A. Monographs), edited by M. Banton. London: Routledge Library Editions: Anthropology and Ethnography, (1966) 2004.
Turton, D. "There's No Such Beast: Cattle and Colour Naming among the Mursi." *Man* 15 (1980): 320–32.
UNESCO. 2003. www.unesco.org/water/wwap. See also UNESCO-wwap 2006.
Unger, M. "The Water Festival." In *Holidays: A Cycle of Stories and Plays for the Annual Holidays*. Tel Aviv: Shlomo, no year [Hebrew].
Warburton, D. "Sini 'Blue' and Burtuqali 'Orange': An Historical Note on Early Chinese Coffee Cups." Pp, 148-51 in *Language of Color in the Mediterranean*, edited by A. Borg. Stockholm: Almqvist & Wiksell International, 1999.
Webster's Dictionary Third International Edition. 1971.
Weir, S. *Palestinian Costume*. London: British Museum Press, 1989.
Weitz, Y. "To the Fantasy and Back: Why Did Ben-Gurion Decide to Go to Sde Boker?" *Iyunim Bitekumat Yisrael* 8 (1988): 298-319 [Hebrew];
Wenning, R. "The Betyls of Petra." *Bull. Amer. Sch. Orien. Res.* 324 (2001): 79-95.

Whorf, B. L. "The Relation of Habitual Thought and Behavior to Language." Pp. 197-215 in *Language, Culture and Personality. Essays in Memory of Edward Sapir*, edited by L. Spier. Menasha, Wisconsin: Sapir Memorial Fund, 1941.

Willis, R. "Do the Fipa have a Word for It?" Pp. 209-23 in *The Anthropology of Evil*, edited by D. Parkin. Oxford: Basil Blackwell, 1985.

Witkowski, S. R. "Color Terminology." Pp. 218-222 in *Encyclopedia of Cultural Anthropology*, Vol. 1, edited by D. Levinson and M. Ember. New York: Henry Holt, 1996.

Wittgenstein, L. *Tractatus Logico-Philosophicus* (with a new trans. by D. F. Pears and B. F. McGuinness and with an introduction by Bertrand Russell). London: Routledge and Kegan Paul, 1922.

Yaacobi, Y. "Be'er Sheva: The City Rose from a Scorched Earth." *The Histadrut in the Local Governance* 1, no. 1 (May 15, 1955) [Hebrew].

Yizhar, S. *On the Edge of the Negev* [Befa'atei Hanegev], 1945. Reprinted Tel Aviv: Hakibbutz Hameuchad, 1978

Zahor, Z. *Vision and Reckoning: Ben Gurion—Ideology and Politics.* Tel Aviv: Sifriyat Poalim, 1994 [Hebrew].

Zakim, E. *Reading the Land: Zionism and the Construction of a Modernist Landscape.* Philadelphia, PA: University of Pennsylvania Press, 2006.

Zalmona, Y., ed. *To the East: Orientalism in the Arts in Israel.* Jerusalem: The Israel Museum, 1998 [Hebrew].

Zerubavel, E. *Time Maps: Collective Memory and the Social Shape of the Past.* Chicago: University of Chicago Press, 2003.

Zerubavel, Y. *Recovered Roots: Collective Memory and the Making of Israeli National Tradition.* Chicago, IL: University of Chicago Press, 1995.

———. "Revisiting the Pioneer Past: Continuity and Change in Hebrew Settlement Narratives." *Hebrew Studies* 41 (2000): 209-24.

———. "The Wilderness as a Mythical Space and as a Memorial Site in Hebrew Culture." Pp. 223-236 in I. Gruenwald and M. Idel (eds.), *Myths in Judaism.* Jerusalem: Zalman Shazar Center for the History of Israel, 2004 [Hebrew].

Name Index

Abeliovitch, A. 133, 137
Abu-Lughod, L. 112
Abu-Rabia, A. 3, 58
Adar, E. 126
Al-Aref, A. 92
Allen, V. L. 2
Al-Muzaini, H. Q. 91
Alterman, N. 39, 44
Amar, Y. 59
Ani, M. 99
Appelbaum, S. 6, 137, 157
Ariel, Z. 39
Auden, W. H. 71, 75
Audo, T. 115
Avivi, B. 44
Avriel, H. 21, 44
Bachrach, R. 19
Badawi, E. 99, 101
Bailey, C. 91, 98, 99, 102, 114
Baines, J. 100
Bambi, 21
Bargal, Y. 43, 44
Bar-Lev, A. 59
Barthelemy, A. 101
Bartsch, U. 166
Bar-Ziv, S. 58
Bauer, I. 99, 101
Behnstedt, P. 100, 101, 109, 115
Ben-Ari, E. 32
Ben-Asher, Y. 126
Benayahu, R. 44
Benayahu, M. 44
Ben-Gurion, D. 1, 4, 9, 27, 29, 43, 44, 119, 120, 121, 137, 177, 181
Benor, D. 125
Benvenisti, D. 43
Ben-Zvi, Y. 33, 34
Bergman, A. D. 120, 122
Berkofsky, L. 130
Berlin, B. 96, 99, 103, 108, 109, 110, 114
Berliner, P. 5, 127, 155, 165
Berlovitz, Y. 43
Bernadotte, F.22
Betlinson, M. 35
Betser, Y. 43
Betteridge, H. T. 101
Beyer, K. 115
Biasio, E. 97
Bilu, Y. 32
Black, A. G. 41
Blake, W. 74
Blanc, H. 91, 114
Blaustein, J. 121, 137
Blich, M. 39, 44
Bloch, M. 164
Blumberg, H. H. 2
Borenstein, N. 132
Borg, A. 5, 52, 86, 89, 114
Boris, G. 91
Boussiba, S. 154

Brand, S. 6, 173
Brissett, D. 2
Burckhardt, J. L. 76, 91
Burke, K. 2
Casson, R. W. 104
Chang, P. 169
Charles, H. 115
Chen, Z. 44, 169
Crichton, D. 170
Cohen, D. 129, 130
Cohen, Y. 22, 177
Cohen, Z. 5, 151
Cones, M. 125
Conklin, H. C. 95, 102, 114
Dalman, G. 106
Danin, A. 99, 102, 114
Dayan, S. 44
De Baceac, H. 74
Degen, A. 129, 130
Demsky, A. 116
Donald, M. 113
Doron, E. 6, 177
Drouin, J. 104
Dubnov, J. 168
Ducatez, G. 98
Ducatez, J. 98
DuQuesne, T. 107
Durkheim, E. 116
Edgley, C. E. 2
Eliad, M. 55
Eliot, T. S. 74
Epstein, L. 132
Erel, E. 132
Etzion, Y. 132
Evenari, M. 75, 127, 128, 136
Evans Prichard, E. E. 114
Ever-Hadini, A. 39
Eytan, B. 44
Faiman, D. 5, 130, 139
Faiman, O. 5, 67
Feige, M. 4, 27
Feuermann, D. 5, 143
Fischer, W. 92, 93, 98, 99, 100, 101, 102, 104, 107, 111, 115, 116
Flannery, T. 169
Frazer, J. 45
Friedlaender, L. 76
Fuck, J. 98
Gabrieli, N. 44
Gal, A. v, 171, 181, 187, 188, 193
Gal, M. 177
Gale, J. 123, 134, 135
Gavrieli, N. 43
Gerlber, Y. 43
Giannini, A. 168
Givoni, B. 125, 132
Goffman, E. 2
Golan, P. 2
Goldberg, L. 43
Goldstein, Y. 43
Gordon, J. 131, 143, 144
Govaer, D.131
Gradus, Y. 3, 123
Granot, Y. 5, 55
Granott, A. 41
Guri, H. 30
Guterman, I. 128
Gutterman, Y. 137
Hacohen, D. 44
Hare, A. P. 1, 2
Hartmann, M. 98
Hauff, W. 74
Hazan, B. 44
Hefer, H. 30
Heider, E. R. 110
Henkin, R. 114
Hertz, R. 52
Hess, J. J. 94, 115
Highwater, J. 116
Hillel, D. I. 3
Hinds, M. 99, 101
Hobbs, J. J. 114, 116
Hochman, E. 123, 136
Humboldt, v, 76
Ibn Khaldun 50, 52, 116
INFO 164
Ingham, B. 108, 115
Israel, Y. 56

Issar, A. 5, 84, 126, 129, 147, 150
Jacobson, A. 110
Jarvis, C. S. 103
Jaussen, P. A. 115, 116
Jarvis, C. S. 3
JNF 35, 36, 38, 39, 40, 41, 43, 44
Justice, D. 95
Kahana, B. 5, 64, 66
Kaplan, A. 135
Kark, R. 44
Katz, E. 114, 146
Kay, P. 96, 99, 103, 108, 109, 110, 114
Klincksieck, P. 94
Klonner, A. 177
Kodesh, S. 43
Kopel, R. 135
Kressel, G. M. 1, 2, 4, 45, 58, 114, 135
Kristol, A. M. 114
Krivine, J. 4, 19
Krutch, J. W. 3
Kurpershoek, P. M. 91
Lakoff, R. T. 114
Lamdan, Y. 35, 43
Landberg, von, C. 101
Landsberger, B. 115
Lane, E. W. 98, 102, 103, 107, 116
Lawrence, T. E. 3, 49, 50, 52
Lerski, H. 43
Lethellieux 94
Levi-Strauss, C. 110
Liddell, H. G. 101, 102
Lips, H. 137
Loubignac, V. 94
Lucanus 72
Lucy, J. A. 92, 108
Lyons, J. 102, 112, 113
Maas, L. H. 115
Ma'ayan, L. 132
MacLaury, R. E. 103, 104, 115
Mangus, H. 108
Mann, T. 74
Manna, J. E. 115
Marcais, W. 91, 100, 115
Marks, A. E. 52
Marx, E. 123, 135
Mazigh, D. 127
Meir, I. A. 132, 163
Meiri, D. 5, 77, 80
Meirowitch, M. 43
Meshel, Z. 177
Mier, I. 6
Milton, J. 74
Mohar, Y. 39
Monteil, V. 92, 115
Morabia, A. 110, 115
Morris, Y. 3, 4, 9
Mountfort, G. 3
Mueler, B. 166
Musil, A. 115
Nahlieli, D. 56
Naor, M. 43, 44
Nativ, R. 126
Naveh, Z. 136
Negev, A. 55
Nevo, Y. D. 55
Nicol, F. 170
Nishri, Y. 44
Noll, C. 5, 65, 71, 75
Novak 174
Ofek, U. 44
Orion, E. 5, 76, 77
Orren, E. 43
Osher, Y. 2
Palva, H. 91
Patrich, J. 57
Pearlmutter, D. 6, 132, 160
Persky, 44, 39
Piamenta, M. 101
Pinshow, B. 129
Powels, S.103
Prasse, K-G. 109
Prives, M. 121
Propper, B. 21
Rachamimov, A. 132
Raviv, D. 140, 141. 142
Regev, U. 123, 136
Reichmuth, S. 100, 115
Reifenberg, A. 43

Richmond. A. 5, 43, 119, 154
Rieber, G. 5, 64
Ringel, H. 116
Rivers, W. H. R. 100
Roaf, S. D. 170
Rosenhouse, J. 91
Rotbard, S. 32
Roth, A. 94, 115
Safdie, M. 132
Safriel, U. 123
Salingaros, N. A. 164
Saravanan, R. 168
Sauerhaft, B. 165
Schar, C. 167
Scharf-Kluber, R. 52
Scheibe, K. E. 2
Schmiele, W. 75
Schultz 174
Schwartz, M. 114
Scott, R. 101, 102
Sened, A. 4, 13, 44
Sened, Y. 4, 13, 44
Shachak, M. 128, 136
Shafir, G. 43
Shanan, L. 127
Sharett, M. 33, 41, 43
Shinar, P. 104
Shkolnick, A. 123
Shlonsky, A. 35, 39
Shohat, E. 43, 44
Shweder, R. A. 92
Smith, A. 123, 165
Smolly, E. 36, 43, 44
Solayman, A. 115
Solowey, E. 5, 81
Sonnen, P. J. 115
Sowayan, S. A. 91, 110, 111
Steinberger, Y. 128
Steward, J. H. 91
Stewart, D. J. 115
Stewart, F. H. 91, 111
Stowasser, K. 99
Tadmor, N. 127
Tartakover, D. 44
Tehar-Lev, H. 43, 44
Tehar-Zev, Y. 44
Tel Or, E. 133
Thass-Thienemann, T. 105
Thurow, T. L. 165
Trumpeldor, Y. 37, 44
Tryester, H. 43
Tuky, H. B. 124
Turner, V. W. 2, 52, 110
Turton, D. 108, 109
Tzafrir, Y. 177
UNESCO 165
Unger, M. 44
Valette, Th. 94
Vonshak, A. 133, 154
Warburton, D. 103
Weingrod, A. 123
Weir, S. 104, 111, 112
Weitz, Y. 44
Wenning, R. 57
Whorf, B. L. 95
Willis, R. 110
Witkowski, S. R. 93
Wittgenstein, L. 113
Woidich, M. 100, 101, 109, 115
Yaacobi, Y. 38
Yadlin, A. 182
Yair, A. 123
Yeats, W. B. 75
Yizhar, S. 44
Yom-Tov, Y. 177
Zahor, Z. 44
Zakim, E. 43
Zalmona, Y. 43
Zangwil, A. 130
Zarmi, Y. 131
Zeroni, M. 135
Zerubavel, E. 43
Zerubavel, Y. 4, 33, 43, 44
Zur, Y. 136

Subject Index

Architecture 160
Architecture, apology 163
Arts 59
Bedouin poetry 86
Bedouin, color symbolism 109
Bedouin, natural colors 104
Ben-Gurion Heritage Institute 183
Ben-Gurion Research Institute 181
Center for the Study of North American Jewry 187
Color categories, Bedouin 91
Desert 3, 4
Desert Institute for Desert Research, Founding 119
Dramaturgical analysis 2
Education 6
Field school 177
Fish 157
Fossil water 147
Four winds 45
Garbage can 27
High school, environmental 173
Holocene 45
Inspiration 3, 5
Literature 71
Microalgae 151
Midbar 27
Negev desert 9-12
Painting 64
Pioneer 19
Poetry 81, 84
Religion 55
Research 5, and see specific institutes and projects
Revivim, Kibbutz 4, 13
Runoff agriculture 155
Science 9
Sculpture 76, 77
Sde Boqer, Kibbutz 4, 19
Settlement 9
Settlement ethos 33
Settlements 4
Shmama 27
Solar power plants 139
Solar surgery 143
Theater 67

About the Contributors

Samuel Appelbaum is a Professor of Fish Biology and Physiology at The Bemgis Center for Desert Aquaculture, BIDR.

Arieh Bar Lev is a photographer who lives at the Midreshet Ben-Gurion.

David Ben-Gurion was the first Prime Minster of Israel.

Pedro Berliner is an Associate Professor of the Wyler Department of Dryland Agriculture, BIDR.

Alexander Borg is Professor of Linguistics at the Department of Hebrew and the Department of Middle Eastern Studies of Ben Gurion University of the Negev; he specializes in Semitic linguistics with a focus on Arabic, linguistic anthropology, and Mediterranean studies.

Sol Brand is a teacher in the High School for Environmental Studies.

Zvi Cohen is a Professor of Algal Biotechnology at The Albert Katz Department of Dryland Biotechnology, BIDR.

Eran Doron served as head of the Field School at the Midreshet Ben-Gurion.

David Faiman is a Professor of Physics, Chair of the Department of Solar Energy and Environmental Physics, and Director of The Ben-Gurion National Solar Energy Center, BIDR

Ofra Faiman is a Director at the Theater of the Negev, a group conductor, and was a drama teacher in the High School for Environmental Studies.

Michael Feige is a Lecturer at the Ben-Gurion Research Institute, Ben-Gurion University, at the Midreshet Ben-Gurion. His main field of interest is in collective memory in Israel.

Daniel Feuermann is an Associate Professor in the Department of Solar Energy and Environmental Physics, BIDR.

Allon Gal is a Professor (Emeritus) of the Department of Jewish History at Ben-Gurion University and a Senior Fellow of the Ben-Gurion Research Institute, Ben-Gurion University, at the Midreshet Ben-Gurion.

Yigal Granot is on the staff of the Library in Education Center at the Midreshet Ben-Gurion.

A. Paul Hare is a Professor of Sociology (Emeritus), BIDR.

Arie S. Issar is a Professor (Emeritus) of Hydro-Geology, BIDR.

Sabine Kahane (Binah Kahana) is an Artist-in-Residence at the Center for International Student Programs of Ben-Gurion University Be'er Sheva.

Gideon M. Kressel is a Professor of Anthropology (Emeritus), BIDR.

John Krivine is writer living at the Midreshet Ben-Gurion.

Isaac Meir is an Associate Professor of Architecture, BIDR.

Dalia Meiri, a sculptress, who creates images in stone, wood, and iron.

Chaim Noll is a Lecturer at the Center for International Student Programs of Ben-Gurion University Be'er Sheva, Co-Founder of the German Program, Secretary of the PEN Centre of German-speaking Writers Abroad, and Member of PEN Israel.

Ezra Orion, a sculptor, who lived and worked at the Midreshet Ben-Gurion.

David Pearlmutter is an architect specializing in energy-efficient urban design, BIDR.

Amos Richmond is Professor (Emeritus) for Biotechnology and first Director of BIDR.

Alexander Sened and **Yonat Sened**, husband and wife, are founders and members of Kibbutz Revivim, who wrote their novels together.

Elaine Solowey is the manager of the Experimental Orchards of the Arava Institute for Environmental Studies at Kibbutz Ketura.

Yael Zerubavel is a Professor of Jewish Studies and History at Rutgers University in New Brunswick and Director of the Allen and Joan Bilder Center for the Study of Jewish Life.

Note:
Contributors from Departments that are part of the Blaustein Institute for Desert Research, of Ben-Gurion University, are often indicated by "BIDR." Persons who work at other institutions in the community are indicated as belonging to the "Midreshet Ben-Gurion," which is the short version of the name of the original Teacher's College, established by Ben-Gurion, that gave its name to the Community.